BAD FRIEND

Also by Michelle Elman

How to Say No
The Selfish Romantic
The Joy of Being Selfish
Am I Ugly?

BAD FRIEND

Why Friendship Breakups Hurt and How to Heal

MICHELLE ELMAN

RENEGADE

RENEGADE BOOKS

First published in Great Britain in 2025 by Renegade Books

1 3 5 7 9 10 8 6 4 2

Copyright © Michelle Elman 2025

The moral right of the author has been asserted.

All rights reserved.
No part of this publication may be reproduced, stored in a
retrieval system, or transmitted, in any form or by any means, without
the prior permission in writing of the publisher, nor be otherwise circulated
in any form of binding or cover other than that in which it is published
and without a similar condition including this condition being
imposed on the subsequent purchaser.

A CIP catalogue record for this book
is available from the British Library.

Hardback ISBN 978-1-4087-4945-6
C-format ISBN 978-1-4087-4946-3

Typeset in Berling by M Rules
Printed and bound in Great Britain by
Clays Ltd, Elcograf S.p.A

Papers used by Renegade Books are from well-managed forests
and other responsible sources.

Renegade Books
An imprint of
Dialogue
Carmelite House
50 Victoria Embankment
London EC4Y 0DZ

The authorised representative
in the EEA is
Hachette Ireland
8 Castlecourt Centre
Dublin 15, D15 XTP3, Ireland
(email: info@hbgi.ie)

www.dialoguebooks.co.uk

Dialogue, part of Little, Brown Book Group Limited,
an Hachette UK company.

For everyone who has been heartbroken by a friendship and blamed themselves – you aren't alone.

AUTHOR'S NOTE

Some of the names and identifying details in this book have been changed to protect the privacy of the people in the examples used. All stories involving clients have been included with their permission. I am both informed and limited by my lived experience and therefore I accept that there are areas where I will not do justice. As an author, my intention is always to be as inclusive as possible, so I hope the examples within these pages can serve as a broad template to guide you through the friendships in your own life.

CONTENTS

A Note From a Friend   xiii

Introduction   1

Understanding Friendships

Why Are Friendships Important?   19

The Myths About Friendship   26

In Defence of Friendship Breakups   35

Am I the Problem?   46

Are Male and Female Friendships Different?   55

What Are You Looking for in Friendship?   63

Insecurities in Friendship

Does Everyone Have a Best Friend Except Me?   73

Why Do I Have So Few Friends?   86

Does Everyone Have a Friendship Group Apart from Me?   99

What Does It Mean if My Friend Doesn't Like My Instagram Posts?   108

Friendship When Life Changes

Why Does My Friend Disappear When
They Get into a Relationship?   123

What Do I Do If I Hate Who They Are
Dating?   129

Are We Really Friends or Just Colleagues?   140

Why Do Weddings Complicate Friendships?   154

Can Our Friendship Adjust Through
Families, Children and Fertility Issues?   163

Fractures in Friendship

How Do I Support My Friend Through
Mental Health Difficulties?   175

Is Living Together Going to End the
Friendship?   186

Why Are Female Friendships Full of
Competition, Jealousy and Gossip?   194

Why Does Personal Growth Make Your
Friendships Grow Apart?   209

How to Break Up with Your Friend

Can I Still Fix the Friendship?   221

Is It Ever Acceptable to Ghost a Friend?   234

How Do I Tell Them It Is Over?   244

The Aftermath of Friendship Breakups

Why Do I Feel So Guilty?   257

How Do I Stop Regretting We Ever Met?	266
Will I Ever Stop Missing Them?	276
Can You Ever Go Back to Being Friends Again?	285
What If Our Mutual Friends Take Sides?	296

Rules For Better Friendship

Why you Should Be Fighting for Your Friendships	305
Say What You Mean and Mean What You Say	320
Give Friendships the Effort They Deserve	327
Be Selective About Your Inner Circle	337
Build Trust Slowly	346

How To Make New Friends

Meeting New People	359
Facing the Fear of Rejection	372
Initiating Conversations with Strangers	380
Following Up and Maintaining Friendships	390

Epilogue	401
Acknowledgements	407
Endnotes	413
Further Reading	425

A NOTE FROM A FRIEND

'So, how do you two know each other?' we're often asked at work events, having been each other's faithful plus ones for nearly a decade.

We give an answer about meeting on the internet, about bonding over a shared belief in body positivity, about navigating the early years of being content creators together. Michelle tells the story of how she fell backwards down the stairs when we first met. We might mention how we grew closer when one of us inexplicably started dating someone the other went to primary school with. How we've witnessed the best and worst of each other's twenties: the single years, the career lows, the bad relationships, the hard self-growth. We tell a short story of two women who met, fell in platonic love and have been friends ever since.

What we don't get into, in those moments of light-hearted small talk, are all the things that could have got in the way of our friendship being what it is. We could have immediately seen each other as competition, letting jealousy and internalised misogyny turn the other into an enemy before we'd even met. We could have lost sight of each other completely once we were in relationships, as so often happens within our culture that places romantic love above all else. We could have thrown in the towel at the first misunderstanding, decided it was easier to end the friendship than to work through what was said. We could have broken up – drifted apart, outgrown one another, argued, called it off.

Any one of those options would be heartbreaking. You lose so much when you lose a friend.

You lose moments of giggling together and holding each other when relationships end. You lose a co-conspirator who encourages you to get another tattoo and hypes you up to flirt with strangers. You lose a safe space where you go to have meltdowns about life, and rebuild, together. You lose a companion to adventure with, to make memories and be excited for the future with. You lose the comfort of knowing that someone will show up for you, or at least try their best to. You lose community and support, and a kind of love that helps us get through life – the kind we all need at some stage.

No one prepares you for how hard it can be to hold on to friendships, or how hard it is when they end. It's time for a new narrative around platonic love and to heal from the wounds those heartbreaks have left. I can think of no better person than Michelle – who loves deeply, heals phenomenally and is truly a great friend – to show us the way.

Megan Jayne Crabbe – author, creator, Michelle's friend

INTRODUCTION

**'What's a ship that never sinks?
A friendship.'**

An idiot who was very very wrong

I am not sure I am healed enough to write this book. And yet I am writing it anyway because it needs to be said: friendship breakups suck.

Whenever I think about one of my ex-friends and the memory of them walking out of my life, it evokes a feeling that can only be compared to someone ripping out my heart and wringing it like a towel. Except instead of water coming out, every negative emotion falls to the floor: regret, shame, guilt, fear, anger, resentment, sadness, grief, loneliness, abandonment and heartbreak, along with all my energy too. When people speak of heartbreak, I never knew the feeling could extend beyond the emotional into a very physical sensation. I had no idea that the ache in my heart was literal, almost what I imagine the beginning of a heart attack would feel like. I also never thought that heartbreak could apply to friendship, but to go from knowing someone so intimately to seeing them and pretending you don't is a feeling unlike anything I've felt before.

I have always said that a friendship breakup can be as painful as a romantic one but I finally have the proof. The day after I publicly announced the ending of my engagement online, one of my friends that I have known since we were eleven ended our friendship, and it hurt more than what I was going through romantically. It felt crueller. Despite how awful infidelity is, I don't think his intention was to hurt me – I don't think he was thinking about me at all – but for a friend to send me that text the night before I was going on national TV to address my breakup to the world, without so much as asking if I was OK first, felt intentional – and it hurt in a way that my breakup didn't. Experiencing the grief of that friendship loss amid the grief of my romantic future makes me the perfect person to say that the pain of the friendship breakup is just as excruciating. The only difference is that the romantic heartbreak was understood in a way that the friendship breakup wasn't. When it comes to the ending of a friendship, it is often so much lonelier because societally, it's still shrouded in shame.

When a romantic relationship ends, it's the norm to be surrounded with love, empathy and kindness. Your friends gather around you and your family tell you that person didn't deserve you anyway. When a friendship ends, you're often met with silence. Imagine if you were to walk into your workplace crying. If someone asked you what was wrong and you said your partner of eight years had just broken up with you, you'd be met with compassion, sympathy and understanding. You'd be handed a box of tissues and asked if you would like

INTRODUCTION

some time off, or at the very least, would be granted some leeway if your performance wasn't up to its usual standard. Walk into the same workplace and say your best friend of eight years broke up with you, and you suddenly sound like a thirteen-year-old having a squabble in the playground. Never mind the fact that you and your bestie lived together for almost a decade, or that when you pictured your wedding, you couldn't picture the groom but you could picture her as the maid of honour.

My frustration with how friendship is treated by society isn't just about when it goes wrong, it's how friendship is treated in its entirety: from how it's only ever viewed as a second-tier relationship in respect to romantic connections, to how the conversation about friendship itself is so absent. For example, whenever I research a new book idea, I buy *a lot* of books on the topic. With my last one, *The Selfish Romantic*, I read nearly forty books on love, and there were hundreds more to choose from. For this one, I ordered fourteen books. Two were published this year and the rest I had to search high and low for. Even in academia, the conversation is lacking. In a 2005 article in the *Los Angeles Times*, Shelley E. Taylor, a social neuroscientist, is quoted as saying, 'Rigorous study of women's friendships remains in its infancy, but scientists are beginning to respond to the "wake-up" call'.[1] The message is loud and clear; we value romantic relationships over friendships. A person will have on average seven to ten romantic relationships in their lifetime and twenty-nine platonic relationships so why is it that the conversation on love is far greater than our conversation on friendship?

In a world that encourages us to be coupled, it makes sense

that romantic relationships have dictated more space among the topics we discuss daily. We all have a friend who disappears as soon as they get into a romantic relationship and, if we are being honest, we have probably all been that friend too. I will never forget a conversation with my housemates in the final year of university where they sat me down in our kitchen and told me that since getting into my first relationship, I constantly texted under the table while talking to them. They were right and from that moment, I vowed never to do that again. To this day, I keep my phone in my bag if I am out for lunch with a friend.

Get married, have kids and your friends are expected to adapt – to maintain the same quality of friendship with less time, energy and commitment. Even when it comes to the demise of friendship, there is a disparity. Now that mental health is relatively destigmatised, it would not be unusual to hear that a couple are going to therapy. If you said that you were going to therapy with your best friend though, you would receive strange looks. Why? Because romantic relationships are deemed worth saving but friendships are seen as replaceable.

When it comes to romantic relationships, we have language for every stage: from seeing each other to dating, from being exclusive to committing to one another, from getting engaged to eventually getting married. We even have multiple phrases with the same meaning, such as fuck buddies, non-exclusive, no strings attached, friends with benefits or a casual relationship. When it comes to friendship though, the language is absent. There is no differentiator between the friend who you're so close to that she may as well be your sister and the

INTRODUCTION

colleague who is vital to you getting through the workday but who you never see out of hours. Even to write this book, I've had to borrow the language of dating to make sense of what I mean. When the language we use to describe platonic relationships stems from romantic ones, it is evidence that our romantic relationships are perceived to be superior to our platonic ones. We only use the word 'ghosting' in friendships now because it was a word created in the context of romantic relationships. If we said the word 'breakup', we would assume a romantic ending and so we must distinguish it by prefacing it with the word 'friendship'. We borrow the word 'heartbreak' from our romantic conversations to evoke the same feelings around friendship loss but the truth is that while the grief might be similar, it is not the same. The devastation that comes with a friendship ending deserves a word to describe it in its accuracy, and our friendships deserve a conversation without comparison.

I have been guilty of comparing friendship to romantic love too. In my first book, I thank my best friend at the time for being my 'surrogate boyfriend'. In fact, she wasn't a surrogate for anything: she was the blueprint for love and she wasn't the only one. All my friends taught me love long before I knew what romantic love or even self-love was, and when the right men turned up in my life, I only knew they were right because my friends had shown me what to look for. I learned how to receive love because of my friends. I knew that love showed up in both actions and words because of my friends. Whether it was voice notes when I felt lost in the middle of writing a book or crying FaceTimes because another guy had let me down, my friends loved me before I knew how to love myself.

ALL MY FRIENDS TAUGHT ME LOVE LONG BEFORE I KNEW WHAT ROMANTIC LOVE OR EVEN SELF-LOVE WAS, AND WHEN THE RIGHT MEN TURNED UP IN MY LIFE, I ONLY KNEW THEY WERE RIGHT BECAUSE MY FRIENDS HAD SHOWN ME WHAT TO LOOK FOR.

INTRODUCTION

Friendship breakups can make you sceptical, or even just a little cautious, but for me, they have simply made me more resolute that we deserve friends who are the best people we know. As sad as a friendship breakup can be, sometimes it is necessary in order to meet the people you deserve. At thirty-one years old, I can say that I am surrounded by the best people and my friendships are now reciprocated in love, trust and respect in a way that they weren't always – and that is partly down to some friendship breakups along the way.

Being a good friend was my identity for many years. Growing up, I suffered from a myriad of health conditions, so a lot of my childhood was spent in hospital. This made keeping friends in primary school difficult. My friends never knew when I would be gone or when I would come back, and as childhood friendships are often based on physical proximity, they moved on quickly. I took this as proof that I was 'forgettable' or worse, not worth remembering. Those feelings of rejection stayed with me. In my young mind, how many friends I had equated to how lovable I was. The feeling of being forgotten after each hospital visit and then having to start the process of making new friends again was so painful that throughout school, I would do anything to avoid another loss. I promised myself I would do everything in my power to make my friends stay, which often meant settling for second best, lowering my standards and removing my boundaries. As a result, I always had more friendships than was sustainable, because with each new friend who liked me and wanted me in their life, I felt needed and wanted, which boosted my self-esteem. My mantra was 'the more the merrier', and even though I might not have liked myself, I told myself that at least I was a good friend. Since I didn't believe anyone would actually choose me for me, I made myself the 'reliable' friend. I would be the filler at the party when you had a spare seat, the person to accompany you to the club when no one else would and the one who sat and listened to you cry about your ex for the millionth time because everyone else was bored of listening. I often reassured myself by thinking I was their 'go-to' but the eye-opening truth I've only now realised in editing this book is that I was the 'last choice' friend. At the time, those friends might have only been keeping me in their lives for what I could do for them, but it didn't matter. What mattered was that I had friends. What mattered was that I was a *good friend*.

If you dig a little deeper into what stereotypically makes a 'good friend', especially in female friendships, it is not too dissimilar to what makes a 'good wife', 'good woman', 'good daughter' or even 'good girl'. In order to be a good friend, you must always be there for your friends, no matter what else is going on in your life. In many ways, being a good friend means prioritising your friends'. needs above your own, or at least that's what I believed friendship was when I was described as 'the best friend anyone could ask for' during a speech a friend made at my twenty-first birthday. On that night, five people gave a speech and each echoed that sentiment. One told the room about how I had travelled to see her in Cambridge because she was sad about a guy she was dating, despite the fact that I had moved from Bristol to London that very same day and only arrived in London twenty minutes before. Another friend spoke of how she called me at 2 a.m. while I was sound asleep, and the next thing I knew I was welcoming her into

IF YOU DIG A LITTLE DEEPER INTO WHAT STEREOTYPICALLY MAKES A 'GOOD FRIEND', ESPECIALLY IN FEMALE FRIENDSHIPS, IT IS NOT TOO DISSIMILAR TO WHAT MAKES A 'GOOD WIFE', 'GOOD WOMAN', 'GOOD DAUGHTER' OR EVEN 'GOOD GIRL'.

my bed with no questions asked. And another proudly declared how the best thing about our friendship was that we had no boundaries.

The person described in those stories sounds like a great friend, but the difference between me in my twenties and me in my thirties is that I can now recognise that a huge part of the story was omitted. These stories miss out how exhausted I was travelling from Bristol to London to Cambridge and back again in a day just for an hour's dinner. They miss out that the reason she called me at 2 a.m. wasn't because I was special but probably because I was the only person she knew who lived in Bristol and her train home was cancelled. These stories miss out on the fact that if a friendship has no boundaries, it's usually because one person is too scared to speak their mind, be honest and ultimately say no.

A lack of boundaries always leads to friendships that lack reciprocity. Not once did I ask if these people were a good friend to me, nor did I stop to question if they would do the same thing for me. It turns out having no needs and never asking for anything in return would be an integral part of keeping a lot of those friendships. If you walk through the world being worried about being called a bad friend, you never stop to think about whether they are a good friend to you. Much like how if you are desperate to be in love, you will settle for the first person who likes you without even asking yourself whether you like them back (and yes, I've done that too!). The moment I started questioning whether a friend had ever been there for me was the moment in which my friendships started crumbling. Each friendship breakup felt different but I was grief-stricken and heartbroken over every

A LACK OF BOUNDARIES
ALWAYS LEADS TO
FRIENDSHIPS THAT
LACK RECIPROCITY.

single one. With some, I was left with the feeling of wishing we had never met and with others, it was a mixture of frustration and a longing for understanding. Whatever unique combination of emotions each breakup elicited, one thing was for sure: I felt pain. Pain that I believe deserved a space but that was often pushed down because when society doesn't make room for a conversation about friendship breakups, you learn not to either.

With an absence of conversation on the topic, we assume we are the only one but that is far from the truth. A study conducted by Sky Atlantic shows that only six of our friendships stand the test of time.[2] Therefore if research says that, on average, we have twenty-nine friendships in a lifetime, that means people are going through roughly twenty-three friendship breakups in silence thinking they are alone in the problem.

When friendships end back-to-back, you can't help but wonder if you are at fault. Whenever I sought comfort in another friend, comments were made that confirmed the stigma of friendship loss. Whether it was being accused of being unforgiving by a mutual friend who wanted a reconciliation, or a quip made by a family member about how I couldn't keep any friends, immediately I understood why people don't talk about the end of friendships. I felt hurt and embarrassed, but predominantly I wondered why we shame those who end friendships when the alternative is to keep someone in your life just for the sake of it. Too many people keep others around when the relationship is long expired and often the result is gossiping and bitching, which leads to us becoming a person we are not proud of and behaving in a way

IF RESEARCH SAYS THAT, ON AVERAGE, WE HAVE TWENTY-NINE FRIENDSHIPS IN A LIFETIME, THAT MEANS PEOPLE ARE GOING THROUGH ROUGHLY TWENTY-THREE FRIENDSHIP BREAKUPS IN SILENCE.

we wouldn't like to be treated. We paint a friendship breakup as the worst outcome but surely it's better than pretending to be friends to their face and being inauthentic behind their back? Yet just like a romantic breakup, have one too many and society starts identifying reasons why your relationships keep ending. They might not say it, but they are most certainly thinking, *Well, maybe you are a bad friend.* But what if you aren't the problem? What if the problem is the way we think about friendship breakups?

This is not a book that will teach you how to be a good friend, but it will make you question everything you have been taught about friendship. You will not agree with me every step of the way, but more than anything, I want this book to make you pause long enough to think about something you might not have considered. In life coaching, we have a principle that says, 'take what you need and leave the rest', and that's how I would like you to use this book. Take the titbits that will benefit your friendships and accept that not every sentence will be useful to your own situation. There are text messages dotted throughout this book that come from my real life or are examples to be used in yours. These are not perfect templates but suggestions to help you craft your own wording. It does not mean that these conversations need to take place over text message. If you think the conversation is more appropriate to have over the phone or in person, please trust your own judgement.

If you have ever been insecure about the fact that you have never had that one go-to best friend, this book is for you. If you don't have a friendship group, this is the book for you. It's for you if you have been through a heart-wrenching

WE PAINT A FRIENDSHIP BREAKUP AS THE WORST OUTCOME BUT SURELY IT'S BETTER THAN PRETENDING TO BE FRIENDS TO THEIR FACE AND BEING INAUTHENTIC BEHIND THEIR BACK?

friendship breakup that you think about just as much as men think about the Roman Empire. If you constantly worry that all your friends hate you, then this is the book that will reassure you that you aren't the only one. And most of all, I hope you walk away from this book knowing that friendships deserve just as much of our time and energy as romantic relationships do, and just as much of a conversation as well. This is the space where you can have all the friendship conversations you have never been allowed to have.

UNDERSTANDING FRIENDSHIPS

WHY ARE FRIENDSHIPS IMPORTANT?

The reason I am writing a friendship breakup book isn't because I believe we should all break up and live life as isolated as possible. It's because I believe in the power of friendship and I happen to believe that friendship breakups are a necessary part of the conversation. Friendship breakups allow us to be in the best friendships and give us permission to change our minds if our dynamic is no longer healthy. By ending one relationship, we create more time and space to find a better match. In fact, I believe the breakup is proof of the power of friendship. Anyone who has been through a friendship breakup knows how devastating and painful it can be and yet it is the overwhelming love of friendship that makes me go back for more, knowing the risk of a potential ending and still wanting to try again with someone new.

In my dating book, *The Selfish Romantic*, I didn't need to write a chapter on why your love life is important because we already understand that romantic relationships are valuable. In this book, however, this chapter is needed because we still view platonic friendships as inferior. Laura Eramian, a social anthropologist and one of the leading researchers around friendship, explains that 'the hierarchy of intimacy' places friendship lower than romantic relationships.[1] All of this starts with how we define platonic relationships. It's embedded in the dictionary definition where it states it is a relationship marked by the absence of romance and sex. We say it in our everyday language too. When you want to start a romantic relationship, you might say, 'Let's be more than friends' as if it's a promotion, and then when you want to break up, you might say, 'Let's just be friends' as if it's a demotion. If we start with a definition of inferiority, it's no wonder it's shaped how we have viewed platonic relationships – but this is where we are going wrong. This was not the intention when the word 'platonic' was coined by Marsilio Ficino in the fifteenth century. Inspired by Plato, he spoke of a love that transcends bodies, and was therefore superior: 'It does not desire this or that body, but desires the splendor of the divine light shining through bodies.'[2] This is how we should speak of friendships, or at the very least we should stop comparing them to romantic relationships.

Friendships kept me afloat for most of my twenties. With my family living in a different country and not having a romantic partner for most of that time, they were my community; they were the people who picked me up when I was down and celebrated me when I won. Without exaggeration, they were my entire world. So much so that for a long time, I never contemplated living anywhere apart from London because I couldn't imagine my life without my friends in it; the idea of not being physically close to my friends terrified me so much that I never even entertained the idea. Every important story from my twenties is interwoven with friendship. To this day, when I watch my TEDx talk, I can hear my friend in the beginning cheer (look it up! It's the loud one at the start!). When I remember stories from my love life, they are often told through the lens of friendship. It's not that I remember a guy calling himself 'white sugar' while he tried to flirt with me. I remember that my friend and I were laughing so loudly about it that a waiter brought over white sugar. I don't remember the first dates as much as I remember the podcast-length voice notes that followed them. My Valentine's days have been dedicated to my friends since the moment they threw me a surprise party on my return from hospital. It's not some surrogate Galentine's day but *actual* Valentine's day, because platonic love is love.

If this is not your experience and friendship has always been an optional extra in your life, let me convince you why it needs to be a big slice of the pie that is your life. First of all, it increases your happiness. If you have a happy friend, it will increase your chance of being happy by an average of 9 per cent. If you are directly connected to a happy person, you are 15 per cent more likely to be happy; if you are a friend of a friend, you are 10 per cent more likely to be happy, and even if you are a friend of a friend of a friend, the impact on you is 6 per cent.[3] If that's not proof of how wide-reaching the effects of positive friendships can be, I don't know what is. It also makes a case for friendship breakups because if your friendship is unhappy, it decreases your happiness by 7 per cent. It is important to be clear that we are advocating for healthy friendships.

In terms of both mental and physical wellbeing, an

eighty-five-year Harvard study found that the largest predictor was the quality of your relationships, more so than blood pressure or cholesterol.[4] As a society that is so obsessed with health, you would think that we would prioritise friendships more. The science is clear: it's not the green juices or another Barry's Bootcamp that is going to make the biggest impact on your health, it's your friendships. It will increase your lifespan too! A meta-analysis across 148 studies indicated a 50 per cent increased likelihood of survival with stronger social relationships, the magnitude of which is comparable to quitting smoking.[5]

Friendships have been shown to boost physical health in so many ways, from helping us sleep better to even healing skin punctures faster.[6,7] People who have an adequate number of good friends also have lower rates of heart disease, fewer infections and illnesses thanks to a stronger immune system, fewer abnormal inflammatory responses to stress and lower rates of dementia.[8] And its impact is just as important on mental health. Research shows that people who have friends and strong social support are less likely to have depression.[9] Friendship has also been shown to make us more trusting, have more empathy and even make us less sensitive to rejection up to two years later.[10] People who enjoy close relationships are found to cope better with various types of stress, including job loss and illness.[11] A study by the psychologist David Halpern suggests that the presence of supportive relationships diminishes the exposure to stress, but again, it is important to emphasise that these positive effects are only linked to high quality friendships.[12] Ambivalent relationships (as opposed to supportive ones), characterised as having a

THE SCIENCE IS CLEAR: IT'S NOT THE GREEN JUICES OR ANOTHER BARRY'S BOOTCAMP THAT IS GOING TO MAKE THE BIGGEST IMPACT ON YOUR HEALTH, IT'S YOUR FRIENDSHIPS.

mixture of positive and negative factors, like frenemies, can lead to more stress, higher blood pressure and an increased heart rate.[13] The unpredictability of not knowing whether you will get support or a snarky remark not only negates the positive effects of friendship but actually results in negative effects and therefore supports the idea that friendships are important and that unhealthy friendships need to end.

In terms of the comparison to romantic relationships, a study found that friendship, especially in later life, is more protective of health and happiness than family or romantic relationships and that our friendships even impact the success of our romantic relationships.[14] Our romantic relationships and platonic relationships benefit from each other! When we are stressed, our cortisol level rises. Marital conflict can trigger unhealthy fluctuations in our cortisol, but it has been shown that the harm is buffered when spouses have adequate social support outside of the marriage.[15] Other research has emphasised this specifically in respect to women, demonstrating that those with social support tend to be more resilient to stress within the marriage.[16] Even if we are content in our romantic relationships, it has been shown that if friends disapprove, it weakens the chance of our romantic relationship being successful. Most interestingly, in heterosexual relationships, a husband's negative perception of his wife's friends is a greater predictor of divorce than a wife's disapproval of her husband's friends.[17]

In all areas of life – from our love lives to our health – it's clear that friendships are much more important than we give them credit for. I would even argue that friendship is more important because we aren't bound by obligation or responsibility. You aren't even bound by choice. If someone wants you, you have been chosen. They have nothing to gain other than friendship – not marriage, kids, sex or even society's approval, just having you in their life. You've been included because you are you.

THE MYTHS ABOUT FRIENDSHIP

In order to rewrite the definition of friendship, we need to recognise that what we have been taught is not accurate. When it comes to old adages around friendship, most are narrow and without nuance. It means we approach friendship with a very all-or-nothing style of thinking, which does not benefit our relationships. Growing up, whenever I was given friendship advice, I would take what they were saying as gospel, rarely considering the source. I wanted a rule book on how to be a good friend. I remember once being told to 'stop messaging first and see how many dead plants you are watering' so I stopped texting first to see how many people would notice and because I was young, I never paused to think about how unhelpful this way of communicating was. It is pivotal to liberate yourself from these outdated ways of thinking. This chapter helps us to tear down what we know so that we can start from scratch to figure out what kind of friendships work for us.

THE MYTHS ABOUT FRIENDSHIP

Myth: Best friend forever

I wish. According to research, we replace half our friends every seven years and when I look at my own life, that statistic checks out. As an author, phases in my life are often marked by the books I publish; I see each book as a time capsule. I have published four books, with this being my fifth, and if you look at my acknowledgements pages, they serve as graveyards of past friendships. This pressure of 'forever' doesn't benefit anyone because it means if the friendship ends, we consider our investment in that relationship a waste of time. Instead, I prefer to think of friendship as defined by Brian A. 'Drew' Chalker: 'People always come into your life for a reason, a season or a lifetime.'[1]

Myth: Friendships are meant to happen naturally

If romantic relationships take work, then why do we think friendships don't? We need to accept that friends don't magically land in our lap. Friendships take work to survive and be healthy. If we treat our friends as disposable, they will be. The maintenance of any relationship requires effort. This myth worsens the shame around loneliness because it makes us self-conscious about making effort and showing that we actually like someone. Putting in effort doesn't make you desperate. Within adulthood, we all have so many demands on our time and energy that friendship rarely happens by accident.

IF WE TREAT OUR FRIENDS AS DISPOSABLE, THEY WILL BE.

THE MYTHS ABOUT FRIENDSHIP

Myth: Friends don't fight

The truth is that any time two humans interact, there is a potential for conflict. When those moments arise, it's easy to worry that the friendship is unhealthy. The myth results in us either ending the relationship or avoiding the issue for so long that the friendship deteriorates anyway. Storms are inevitable and we need to trust that our friendships are resilient enough to survive the bad weather. Believe that your friend will care about your feelings. Remember, they want to resolve it too! When we fear conflict, we avoid the problems and that leads to our issues snowballing. Being prepared to address conflict early on gives your friendship the best chance because it gives you both the opportunity to change to make the friendship work.

Myth: Romantic relationships are more important than platonic ones

In a patriarchal society, the goal is to get married and to have children and therefore we are encouraged to place our love life at the centre of our universe. When we define our worth by how men see us, we ignore our female friends. Whether we want to admit it or not, living in a patriarchal world means we have grown up judging women more harshly and holding each other to a higher standard than we do men, so it would make sense that this would seep into our friendships and result in us giving our female peers fewer chances. It is so important to build a complete support system and the added bonus is that it actually benefits our romantic relationships. Most of us need more support than one human can provide. Not only does it mean that we put less pressure on one person to be our everything, but it means that when romantic relationships don't work out, we are not isolated from the world.

Myth: True friends are the ones who no matter how long it's been, will be there for you no matter what

This idea promotes awful communication strategies and encourages minimal effort, which can actually harm, not help. Can you imagine if we said this about romantic relationships? If a guy didn't message you for months and then reappeared, they would be called a fuckboy, so why is the same sentiment dedicated to the highest rung of friendship? I believe this gives us permission to make our friends our lowest priority and not feel guilty about it. This kind of belief endorses the idea that friends are the first thing to be dropped if you get busy with a partner or with a job and that they must be unconditionally understanding if they are a 'true' friend. I rebel against this. No one likes being taken for granted.

Myth: A good friend will bail you out of jail – a best friend will be sitting right next to you

There is this idea of complicity within friendship. We often talk about friendships in extremes with people either preaching that blind support is the goal or brutal honesty, when the reality is that true friendship should lie somewhere in the middle. The one sitting in the jail cell next to you is not making you a better person and we want our friends to hold

IF A GUY DIDN'T MESSAGE YOU FOR MONTHS AND THEN REAPPEARED, THEY WOULD BE CALLED A FUCKBOY, SO WHY IS THE SAME SENTIMENT DEDICATED TO THE HIGHEST RUNG OF FRIENDSHIP?

us to a higher standard. We don't want 'yes' men who will go along with every stupid idea and let us get away with anything. At the same time, we don't want the friend who will hang up the phone when we call from jail, and who disguises their insensitivity as tough love. We also don't want the friend who will sit in judgement and make snarky comments like, 'Well, you shouldn't have been so stupid then.' I believe the middle ground is the friend who will bail you out and support you through a difficult time in your life but who will also deliver the truth in the most compassionate way, which makes it easier to listen to. The one who will be able to say, 'I love you and I can't stand by watching while you ruin your life. How can I help you to build the life you want?'

Myth: If you have no friends, the common denominator is you

There are so many reasons why someone would struggle with friends, from the fact that they had a turbulent childhood to the fact that they have gone through a spell of bad mental health. I find it peculiar that this is the conclusion we jump to within friendship when we are much more understanding in our romantic lives. We all have a friend who has a messy love life, and where we acknowledge the broader context. We understand that if their parents had a messy divorce, it might impact their ability to find love, and we love them anyway. We might even love all their wild dating stories! Yet we never question if our parents had unhealthy friendships, which might impact our own platonic relationships. Research supports this, demonstrating that the quality of parental friendships is related to the quality of the friendships a child forms.[2] By labelling the human as the problem, we are turning guilt into shame, and shame is not an effective learning tool.

Myth: Romantic breakups are harder than friendship breakups

I do not believe comparing pain is helpful but when the pain of a friendship breakup is so unspoken and often undermined, we have to question why romantic breakups are given so much space and the conversation around friendship breakups is largely non-existent. While no human would like to go through either, in season eleven of *Married at First Sight Australia*, there was a rare situation where someone was going through a friendship and a romantic loss at the same time. Two participants on the show had been cheated on by their partner with their best friend, and in both cases, they said the fact it was their best friend was the most devastating part. In romantic breakups, we talk about how there is a shared future that you grieve, but that also exists in friendship. When you have been best friends with someone for a while, you also have similar conversations surrounding growing older together, having kids or getting married and when that friend was part of your life growing up, losing them can shake your identity in the same way a romantic breakup can.

Myth: If friendship lasts longer than seven years, it will last a lifetime

This statistic is currently going viral on social media, but this isn't where I first heard it. In 2012, both my best friend and I were doing a psychology degree when she told me this. We had indeed been friends for seven years yet we are not friends today. Upon the statistic resurfacing, I looked it up and found that it is a distortion of the truth. What the research actually found was that only 30 per cent of closest friends remained that way after seven years. That is not the same thing! Seven years is an oddly specific number but that number only exists because that's how long the study was. There is nothing special about the threshold of seven years.

This is not a comprehensive list of all the myths out there about friendship but I hope by highlighting a few, it makes you aware of how many friendship 'rules' we have inherited. Throughout this book, I am asking you to question it all. If you have beliefs about friendship, let's make sure they aren't outdated tropes but instead ones you have chosen that are beneficial to your life.

IN DEFENCE OF FRIENDSHIP BREAKUPS

I want us to think differently about friendship breakups from the outset. While I am not actively encouraging breaking up, I would like to destigmatise it so that we feel empowered to make the right decision without shame or embarrassment. I want to neutralise the concept of breaking up so that it is not an automatic condemnation of the person choosing to end the friendship. When we declare someone a 'bad friend' or a 'good friend' we speak of these labels as inherent traits, but if friendship is defined by the behaviours and actions of a person, it means that we can be a 'bad friend' to one person while being a 'good friend' to another. They are subjective terms.

Laura Eramian explains, 'People are putting a lot on friendship now, so it's really no wonder people are having trouble with it.' She explains that people want the old definition of friendship in terms of letting off steam and having fun but also the newer definition of being able to be more intimate, serious and to better understand themselves. She adds, 'If people are struggling with friendship, it's not because they're bad at it. It's because the expectations around the whole relationship have changed.'[1]

We understand that romantic breakups can be messy and complicated and that we rarely have the full picture and I would like just as much understanding to be given to friendship breakups. As Marisa G. Franco, author of *Platonic*, writes, 'As we minimize the significance of friends, we minimize the grief of losing them.'[2] In removing the judgement around friendship breakups, I also hope it means that as a society, we can raise the importance of such connections and therefore validate the heartbreak that comes with such a loss. I believe this all starts with more conversation around the topic. Alua Arthur once said, 'Talking about sex won't make us pregnant, talking about death won't make you dead,' and I want to extend that to say that talking about friendship breakups won't ruin your friendships.[3]

You aren't alone

It doesn't make you a bad friend if you have gone through a friendship breakup; it makes you the norm. Friendship breakups are more common than you think, and if you have broken up with a friend, you are in the majority. A study found that 70 per cent of our close friendships and 52 per cent of our social networks dissolve after seven years.[4] Jacqueline Mroz and Brooke Schwartz surveyed 152 women and found that 54 per cent had experienced a breakup with a female friend.[5] Even anecdotally, I have noticed it. In the last decade, whenever I write about friendship breakups, there is an outpouring in my comments section. Sometimes people will share stories and sometimes they will just say 'thank you for posting about this'. It is those people who capture my attention. I always think there must be such a deep and painful story that it resonates but shame breeds silence. Anytime I have been at an event and said I am writing a book on friendship breakups, I see it on the face of women. Their jaws drop. I have started saying, 'Do you have a story?' Everyone has a story. I have never witnessed so much vulnerability and pain intertwined. I've seen the real tears as they share a story of intimacy with me, a woman they have just met, because they are desperate to talk about it. Whether it's a woman who ended a thirty-five-year friendship over racist remarks or a woman who, in her words, was exploited by a friend who used her as a free babysitter. Every story I hear is complicated, full of emotion and, most of all, weighing heavy on their heart because most have never spoken about it.

Breaking up can make you a better friend

We stay longer in friendships than we should because we believe that's what a good friend does. I disagree. I am a better friend for ending a friendship instead of faking it. I am a better friend for choosing loss over passive aggressive bitching behind your back. I am a better friend to my other friends because it means I have more energy for them. The part that has never made sense to me is that we judge those who end a friendship when it is not working, but we accept it as the norm to gossip about a friend, talk badly about them or air all your personal issues into the friendship group. How is that better? With each friendship breakup, I have a mutual friend

WE JUDGE THOSE WHO END A FRIENDSHIP WHEN IT IS NOT WORKING, BUT WE ACCEPT IT AS THE NORM TO GOSSIP ABOUT A FRIEND, TALK BADLY ABOUT THEM OR AIR ALL YOUR PERSONAL ISSUES INTO THE FRIENDSHIP GROUP. HOW IS THAT BETTER?

who has stayed on and complains about them. The kicker is that what they are usually moaning about is the exact same reason why I ended the friendship, and yet through society's lens, I am the one who has a problem with relationships.

We are not doing the other person a service by keeping them in our lives out of duty, obligation or a feeling of debt. They deserve to have people in their life who truly value them, and if you are unable to provide that, you should let them go. Let's face it, when a friend starts to gradually pull away or acts a little off, you notice it. If you ask what's wrong and they say there is nothing wrong, it can feel frustrating when you know the dynamic has changed. Often we are deluding ourselves into thinking that we can stay friends without our behaviour changing. You might notice that you start talking to other friends about them or that you are flaking on them more than usual, and that's when you have to ask yourself, are you truly being a better friend by keeping them in your life no matter what? Wouldn't it be a greater sign of love if you voiced your issues and either gave them an opportunity to amend the situation or chose to mutually end the friendship? We have to change the narrative that ending a friendship is worse than maintaining a false friendship. In a false friendship, you are acting one way behind their back and another in front of their face, and ultimately you have to ask yourself: is that the kind of person you want to be?

The consequences of staying in an expired friendship

Controversial or not, I believe all friendships should add to your life – scrap that, *all* relationships should add to your life. When you stay in an expired friendship, resentment and anger comes out, and if you do not feel confident in expressing that, those emotions sneak out in passive aggressive comments and jabs disguised as jokes. You both know they aren't jokes but for people who avoid conflict, it's all too easy to ignore them. Kate Leaver writes in *The Friendship Cure*, 'I've watched people keep toxic, good-for-nothing friends in their life and suffer excruciatingly for it.'[6] We like to pretend that we can continue a friendship that is no good, but most of us are not good enough actors! If you are not processing your emotions internally or addressing them externally, you are in denial if you think it won't seep out. When I say that the likelihood is you will start talking about them behind their back, people often retort by saying 'well, I'll just stop doing that', but that's not how emotions work. If there is something unresolved, no matter how much you repress it, your behaviour will alter. The words you say, how you respond to that friend and your feelings towards them will shift, and if the other party has an ounce of emotional intelligence, they will notice that shift. Even if you were capable of pretending, another consequence is that when you leave their company, you will leave feeling drained because putting on a mask and pretending to be a person you are not is exhausting. You deserve a friendship where you don't have to pretend!

Your grief is valid

Society has a hierarchy of grief. We empathise more with the person who has lost a husband than the person who

WHEN YOU STAY IN AN EXPIRED FRIENDSHIP, RESENTMENT AND ANGER COMES OUT, AND IF YOU DO NOT FEEL CONFIDENT IN EXPRESSING THAT, THOSE EMOTIONS SNEAK OUT IN PASSIVE AGGRESSIVE COMMENTS AND JABS DISGUISED AS JOKES.

lost a boyfriend. We give people more understanding when they are going through a divorce than a romantic breakup and friendship sits lowest on the totem pole of 'deserved' grief. It doesn't matter if your romantic partner was in your life for two years and your best friend was in your life for twenty years, it doesn't matter if your best friend has held your hand through sickness, health and for better or worse, it still doesn't touch the sides of how much kindness we give to those going through a romantic breakup. Kate Leaver wrote about this in *The Friendship Cure*:

> We have been so utterly captivated by the breakdown of romantic love that we've practically forgotten to investigate how the heart aches when a friendship is, for whatever reason, over ... I hate the idea that people are aching over something that we as a society have not deemed worthy of our cultural interest.[7]

I want to defend not only the right to break up but the pain of breakups too. When we talk about grief, there is an automatic assumption about death, but grief can arise around any loss. It can occur when leaving a job, moving countries or when you realise your parent is not the parent you wish you had. Grief is a much heavier emotion than sadness and is often accompanied by apathy and a feeling of loneliness that seems all-encompassing. The grief exists because the love did too, and the depth you are willing to experience the grief will have an impact on how quickly you are able to move on.

SOCIETY HAS A HIERARCHY OF GRIEF. WE EMPATHISE MORE WITH THE PERSON WHO HAS LOST A HUSBAND THAN THE PERSON WHO LOST A BOYFRIEND. WE GIVE PEOPLE MORE UNDERSTANDING WHEN THEY ARE GOING THROUGH A DIVORCE THAN A ROMANTIC BREAKUP AND FRIENDSHIP SITS LOWEST ON THE TOTEM POLE OF 'DESERVED' GRIEF.

You can learn from friendship breakups

As much as friendships have made me who I am, I believe my friendship breakups have shaped me too. They have not only affected how I communicate with my friends but also how I deal with issues when they arise. One of the biggest lessons I have learned is that if you ignore issues and think they will magically resolve themselves, more often than not, they'll build up until they feel like they are too big to address. When my friendships have ended explosively, I often question whether it would have ended that way had I only set boundaries or communicated my issues earlier. As lovely as it is to have history with someone, we need to be cautious of when that history means the other person is keeping you in the box they remember you being in. Looking back, I don't think I could be the current version of myself if I hadn't had to let go of certain people. Elizabeth Day encapsulates this idea beautifully in *Friendaholic*, where she writes:

> If friendship break-ups were seen as a noble part of the necessary evolution of selfhood, and if it were more widely acknowledged that some friends will be lifelong, while others will walk by your side for a finite, but important, period of time, the whole thing would be a lot easier to deal with.[8]

Sometimes, in order to grow, you need to surround yourself with people who allow you to be the new version of yourself and will not hold you to past memories. There have been

IN DEFENCE OF FRIENDSHIP BREAKUPS

beautiful people in my life who have given me permission to change, but when I have to choose between them and myself, I will always choose to grow.

AM I THE PROBLEM?

When I get a book idea, the words usually fly out of me and the proposal is out in the world as quickly as possible. This book was different. I sat on this idea for over a year, and while I knew that this was an important conversation and one I wanted to have, something was stopping me. How would I talk about losing so many friendships without seeming like I'm the problem? Then it occurred to me: we never do this with romantic breakups. When a friend repeatedly breaks up with romantic partners, we might feel sympathy at times and at others laugh at their chaotic stories, but very rarely do we judge them. Yet with friendship, there is the repeated notion that you must be the problem, and I think it starts with the assumption that friendship should be easy. Friendship is a skill, and it's not always as natural or instinctive as we are led to believe.

I am not writing this book because I believe I am an expert in friendship – I'm sure my ex-best friends would laugh at the concept of me teaching anyone anything about friendship. I am writing this book because friendship has never been easy for me and I have a solid belief that I'm not alone. I have fucked up in friendship, at some points, irreparably. I believe that if there had been enough conversation on the topic, I could have learned another way to be – or even just thought about it earlier. I look back at my younger self with so much compassion: a person who was trying her best in friendship but just hadn't been taught how. Since I was never given a roadmap, my strategy was to people-please, overcompensate, bend over backwards and give until empty. This does not work. It's taken me years, training as a life coach and pursuing my own personal development to figure out how to forge authentic friendships. That is the place I am sharing from; I don't want others to go through what I did. Am I the problem or am I simply the person pointing out the problem?

One of the keys to life coaching is asking the right questions, and I think we are asking the wrong question. Not only because for a relationship to break down it requires participation from both people, and very rarely is the dissolution of a relationship one-sided, but also because by asking if I am the problem, we are personalising it. I don't believe one person can ever be the problem. A human can be a bad friend to you and still be a good person. Instead, let's ask what the problem is.

It took me a long time to believe that I was likeable, let alone lovable. It took me a while to realise that people actually wanted to be friends with me and I remember the exact moment when I realised that. I had been training as a life coach and, as part of our homework, we were told to ask someone we trusted, 'What is something that I need to learn that would greatly improve my life?'

My friend replied instantly, 'That people actually want to spend time with you.' I was confused. He continued, 'Every time I invite you anywhere you are so appreciative, it's like you are shocked I would want you there.' He was right. I didn't even realise I had been doing it, but it seemed I'd never really grown past the little girl who struggled to make friends.

'I guess I've always thought I'm only included because I'm so reliable,' I said. 'I'm the friend who always turns up, will pick up the phone instantly, the one you can count on.'

He then referred to someone else I knew: 'She's like that, right?'

'Yes,' I replied.

'And you still never invite her to things and never want her around, right?'

I nodded.

'So could it be that people actually want you around because they want you around?'

The way life coaching works is that once you become aware of something, you can work on it – and from that moment I did. I always believe that the way someone talks about themselves is telling and over the years, I caught myself going from saying 'I'm good in small doses' to 'it takes time to get to like me', until one day the words 'I'm easy to love' fell out of my mouth. Be careful about how you talk about yourself; you are listening.

The truth is, I have found friendship harder than most people; to understand why, we have to go back to my childhood. One that was filled with surgeries, hospital visits and, ultimately, the repeated loss of friendships. I went into hospital in the first years of both primary and secondary school, which meant twice in my life, I went through the difficult process of entering a new school and making friends, only to

BE CAREFUL ABOUT HOW YOU TALK ABOUT YOURSELF; YOU ARE LISTENING.

lose them again. I had originally settled in well to secondary school. And then, as is often the case when my life is going well, my health deteriorated and I was taken out of school in the middle of the summer term in year seven. In the remaining months, I would have five surgeries, adding to my total of thirteen, and among them was a brain tumour removal surgery, a surgery to fix my intestine after an intern punctured it, and one to insert a new tube from my brain to the rest of my body to drain the excess water in my head. When I walked into school on the first day of year eight, everyone stared at me as if I was the walking dead, and said as much.

'I thought you died,' said the most popular girl in the classroom.

The school had failed to inform the girls in my year that I had in fact survived the surgeries. All my friends thought I had died and they had moved on without me. Have you ever wondered what life would be like for your friends if you were to die? You know, in the movies, where you get to walk through your life and see how everyone is getting on without you? Well, I got to live it. I saw how my friendship group had divided and joined other groups in my absence and being twelve years old, I didn't have the language to communicate how hurtful that was until nearly a decade later. You only have to live through that once to know you never want it to happen again, and very shortly after that, being a good friend became my identity. Subconsciously, I must have decided that if I were to make new friends, I would do my best to keep them. On some level, I thought it was my fault that I had lost them. I would do anything to avoid losing my friends again – and making friends from this place isn't the way to find the best match.

AM I THE PROBLEM?

Elizabeth Gilbert wrote, 'We all have to learn how to walk into a party or a restaurant alone. Otherwise, we will be willing to walk in with *anybody* (or worse, walk out with anybody).'[1] I was willing to walk in with anybody. I would have you if you would take me; I just needed you to like me, and even that was flexible as long as you needed me. In that way, dating is quite similar. Unless you know what you are looking for, you will find yourself perpetuating the same pattern, and that's what I was doing in friendship. Every time, my heart would get trampled and I would ask, 'How is this happening again?' It was happening again because the way I was looking for friends hadn't changed. There are unwritten codes to friendship that we either learn in childhood or we learn later in life by doing it wrong first; I did the latter with a lot of trial and error because I didn't know how else to learn, and it fucking hurt.

Using the comparison of your dating life again, if you were not taught what healthy love looks like, you have to learn it yourself the hard way. It took me eight years of consciously being single and actively going on up to three dates a week to figure out how to navigate romantic love, but when it comes to platonic love, we are expected to learn it through osmosis. After all, when was the last time you decided to go on a friendship date? Within friendship, you are often already cemented and invested before you realise that the friendship is not ideal and therefore either you have another friendship breakup under your belt or you spend a lifetime dodging invites, ignoring texts and calling each other 'friends' without any actual friendship behaviour.

We have to accept that the way we make friends is shaped

by our life experience both for good and bad. My hospital experience might be the reason I cling on more than I should and want people's approval more than is healthy, but it is also the reason why when I write my friends' birthday cards, I fill both sides with sentiments 'just in case' I don't make it to the next birthday. It's also why I tell my friends how much I love them, miss them and am thinking about them more than most people. Growing up in a hospital gave me an acute awareness of my mortality, and I never want the people in my life to question what they mean to me.

I would also be lying if I didn't credit a lot of my friendship breakups to my personal growth. Change is likely the biggest cause of most of my friendship breakups – whether that's the unwanted change that emerged from my trauma or the intentional change that came out of going to therapy, getting a life coach and working on myself. If you view friendships as a contract, I had changed the terms and conditions. When you engage in a friendship, or any relationship for that matter, you sign up to a certain person. If you change into a completely different person, then that's not what that person signed up for. In my case, they signed up to a people-pleasing pushover who would say yes to everything and anything, and within a few short years they were friends with a very boundaried, strongly opinionated person who would not tolerate being treated badly. It's no fault of theirs (or mine) that I was no longer who they signed up for. Whereas in romantic relationships there are many conversations and tools to help you grow and change together, in friendship there is almost an expectation for you to stay the same, or at least remain similar enough to be recognisable. It's why the words 'you've changed' are used as a sword to end a friendship. Some of my friendships survived it and I've still not figured out the science behind what makes a friendship survive and what makes a friendship end, but being able to adapt seems to be the key. When friendships have the flexibility to stretch between closeness and distance, they seem to have more strength and durability.

It's also important to look at the wider societal issue of why we stigmatise those who have ended friendships. We judge other people's friendship loss because we judge our own. We smirk and go 'no wonder they have no friends' because we are secretly insecure about whether we are a good friend. I have cried many a tear knowing I am the common denominator and questioning what is wrong with me. No one can judge me for my friendship issues more than I have already judged myself. And that's why I want to talk about it because I don't believe I am unique and nor are my friendship breakups. I believe we have all been unkind to ourselves. Friendship breakups are covered in a cloak of shame that is perpetuated by the silence surrounding it, leaving us all feeling as insecure as each other. It isn't just the loss of friendships that is judged; if you don't have enough friends, you are also judged. You will also be judged for the type of friends you have. My behaviour in friendship has been far from perfect but there is a difference between behaving badly in a friendship and believing you are a bad person because a friendship ends – and I fear our society ventures closer to the latter.

NO ONE CAN JUDGE
ME FOR MY FRIENDSHIP
ISSUES MORE THAN
I HAVE ALREADY
JUDGED MYSELF.

ARE MALE AND FEMALE FRIENDSHIPS DIFFERENT?

Male friendships are weird. I discovered this in my last long-term relationship. One ex-boyfriend had a group chat for everything and even if he only wanted to talk to one person, he'd message the group chat. Not only did he not text them individually, but he rarely spent time with his friends individually either. When we ended our engagement, he messaged his group chats to acknowledge that we had broken up and said that he didn't want to discuss it. His friendships seemed to revolve largely around Xbox and sport and his smallest group chat had seven people in it. Early on when we were dating, he was confused by how much I went out for individual dinners. I value personal and intimate connections and couldn't imagine anything worse than being bugged by constant notifications in a group chat.

He could have been an anomaly, but research demonstrates something similar, suggesting that around 80 per cent of men say the way they socialise most is via playing or watching sports. Geoffrey Greif, author of *Buddy System: Understanding Male Friendships*, explains that men's friendships are largely based on 'shoulder-to-shoulder' interactions such as watching a football game or playing video games, compared to women who interact in a more 'face-to-face' way.[1] This has also been explained by suggesting that in male friendships, there is often a third object involved. An *Atlantic* article, 'Games Boys Play', explains that the introduction of a third object, whether that be a video game or sports, allows men to avoid intimacy: 'The common objective gives you something to talk about, and not having to face each other means you don't have to lay the full weight of your emotions on each other.'[2]

The difference in these interactions was most noticeable to me when one evening, my friend Freddie and I decided to set our friends up at a party. Freddie introduced me to Seb and I introduced him to Milly. Milly and Seb would end up going on three dates, with the third being my book launch, and after each date I would get a debrief. When I mentioned to Freddie that they had come to my book launch together, he was shocked. He didn't even know they were still dating. Months later, when Freddie came to my birthday party and I introduced him to Milly, he had no clue who he was talking to. 'This is who Seb was dating,' I said. It turned out that in the months they were dating, not only was a picture not shown, a name wasn't even mentioned. This lack of detail seemed to be a continuous theme and it is echoed in the research. A meta-analysis conducted in 1992 also verified that male friendships are less vulnerable than female ones. It made me question whether they don't talk about these things because they don't want to, or simply because they never had?

Women are better at the maintenance of friendship, whereas men do not feel the need to keep in touch. Men's

ARE MALE AND FEMALE FRIENDSHIPS DIFFERENT?

friendships are less supportive and intimate but then as a result they are less fragile. A study also found that what men look for in friendship differs greatly from women.[3] They value same-sex friends who are physically formidable, possess high status and wealth, and afford access to potential mates. This is in sharp contrast to women, who look for emotional support, intimacy and useful social information. Men also tend to have fewer best friends than women, which Robin Dunbar accredited to the difference in being able to mentalise: to make sense of ourselves and others. Since women are able to do that better, it has been suggested they are able to manage two intimate relationships, such as a best friend and a romantic partner, better than men can.[4] Dr Gindo Tampubolon found that 'Friendship between women seems to be fundamentally different to friendship between men. It is much deeper and more moral. It is about the relationship itself rather than what they can get out of it.'[5]

I do not like making sweeping generalisations based on gender because with every rule, there are exceptions. I know for example that my male friendships are exceptions to the rule as our favourite conversations are often deep and emotional, but when the research indicates a repeated theme, we must also question the stereotypes that are attached to it. Anne Morrow Lindbergh once wrote, 'Men kick friendship around like a football, but it doesn't seem to crack. Women treat it like glass and it goes to pieces.'[6] In general, society portrays the message that female friendship is harder work, more complicated and filled with greater drama, complete with bitching and backstabbing. The reality though is that while yes, female friendships are more intense, it is only

IN GENERAL, SOCIETY PORTRAYS THE MESSAGE THAT FEMALE FRIENDSHIP IS HARDER WORK, MORE COMPLICATED AND FILLED WITH GREATER DRAMA, COMPLETE WITH BITCHING AND BACKSTABBING.
THE REALITY THOUGH IS THAT WHILE YES, FEMALE FRIENDSHIPS ARE MORE INTENSE, IT IS ONLY THIS WAY BECAUSE THEY ARE DEEPER FRIENDSHIPS AND SO WHAT IS A STRENGTH IS ALSO A WEAKNESS.

this way because they are deeper friendships and so what is a strength is also a weakness. It hurts more when female friendship ends because it matters more. Their power means they are powerful in their demise too. And just like how the strength of female friendship has drawbacks, there are downsides to being more distanced. Men's relationships are seen as simpler because they are more superficial – there is no dramatic breakup because there is less care and fewer feelings to begin with. A 2015 UK survey found that 2.5 million British men had no friend they could turn to for help or advice in a crisis.[7] In a study on male friendship, when a researcher asked for the names and addresses of very close friends (someone you would call in a bind or ask for money), they found that many of these 'close friends' had not spoken in years and in a few cases, the close friend had passed away – and their 'close friend' did not even know![8] Most women I know would not call someone they hadn't seen in a year a friend, let alone multiple years, but that's because the word carries more weight – it means more. It is a status that you earn and you have to work to keep. While that might sound like an effort, having friends that are only friends by title also has an impact and we are seeing how the lack of deep platonic connections affects men now.

More and more men are struggling with loneliness and isolation because they do not have the companionship and friendship that women do. In turn, this often puts more pressure on romantic relationships because it's the only space men have to be open and vulnerable. With the partner as the receiver of all of this and without a support system in place, it leads to a lot of emotional labour on one person because they do not feel comfortable or safe enough to be that vulnerable with their peers. The same can be said about mixed-gender friendships.

When it comes to men and women being friends, we are seeing men benefiting from the kind of connections that women want but without putting the same level of effort in. Research supports this, showing that men find their cross-gender friendships more enjoyable and nurturing than their same-gender friendships.[9] This was not the same for women, who ranked their female friendships higher. Erin Rodgers explained this in a viral tweet which read, 'I want the term "gold digger" to include dudes who look for a woman who will do tons of emotional labour for them.'[10]

The age-old question around male–female friendships is whether a man and woman can truly be friends without anything romantic and sexual and frankly, I've always found it a boring question. If you can't have friendship with the gender you are attracted to then are bi people meant to have no friends? It's just a novel concept because for decades, men and women were not allowed to be friends. It is a relatively new concept for a man not to control who a woman interacts with. Nowadays, 80 per cent of adults have or have had a close cross-sex friendship, which is a huge shift from a few decades ago.

We should neither demonise female friendships for their complications nor praise male friendships for their simplicity, because it is more complex than this. There is no benefit to comparing which is better or worse; instead, we should draw from the strengths of both.

Men and women's friendships might be different, but they

don't have to be. We are seeing a more blended approach happening as 'bromances' grow more common and as our gender norms become less rigid. As long as we view emotions and deep conversations as purely feminine things, women carry the burden within romantic relationships and men are deprived of that connection in their platonic sphere. We need to normalise men being able to have platonic intimacy and make more space for male friendships to have as much depth as female friendships. Niobe Way, author of *Deep Secrets: Boys' Friendships and The Crisis of Connection*, believes the lack of vulnerability is rooted in the homophobia that exists in a patriarchal society, discouraging emotional intimacy as a way of emphasising manhood.[11]

This, sitting alongside the fact that our culture devalues adult friendship, makes me question whether it is devalued because it is seen as a more feminine thing, in the same way that 'chick lit' is seen as a lower tier of literature or 'rom-coms' as trashier entertainment. In a patriarchal society, anything revolving around women is automatically deemed less important. Vera Brittain writes in her book *Testament of Friendship*, 'From the days of Homer, the friendships of men have enjoyed glory and acclamation, but the friendships of women . . . have usually been not merely unsung but mocked, belittled and falsely interpreted.'[12] In a society that assumes heteronormativity, it is also likely why platonic relationships are seen as less important than romantic ones, if romantic ones mean women's relationships with men and platonic connections mean women's relationships with women. If I look back to boarding school, this message was ever-present, with those who had male friends seen as more popular and cool. If you were not able to attain a boyfriend to secure your status, then having male friends was the next best option. This is why I believe that prioritising female friendships, especially when in romantic relationships, is a small act of micro-feminism – because the women in your life are important.

WHAT ARE YOU LOOKING FOR IN FRIENDSHIP?

Before jumping into the depths of friendship and the issues that they bring, I want to normalise us thinking about values within friendship. Values are one of the keys that unlock the secrets to understanding ourselves. Once you understand your values, it is so much easier to know what you want in life and in this case, what you are looking for within your friendships. It's the age-old cliché of you won't know you've found it if you don't know what you are looking for.

Going into friendship without knowing your values is the same as playing *Monopoly* without clarifying the rules first. You call it the same name but have different ways of playing and you end up an hour into a game arguing because someone has landed on Free Parking and that means nothing to you but to them it means that all the money gets given to them. You both agreed to play but you agreed to play different games. This happens more in platonic relationships than romantic ones because of the vagueness and

GOING INTO FRIENDSHIP WITHOUT KNOWING YOUR VALUES IS THE SAME AS PLAYING *MONOPOLY* WITHOUT CLARIFYING THE RULES FIRST. YOU CALL IT THE SAME NAME BUT HAVE DIFFERENT WAYS OF PLAYING AND YOU END UP AN HOUR INTO A GAME ARGUING BECAUSE SOMEONE HAS LANDED ON FREE PARKING AND THAT MEANS NOTHING TO YOU BUT TO THEM IT MEANS THAT ALL THE MONEY GETS GIVEN TO THEM. YOU BOTH AGREED TO PLAY BUT YOU AGREED TO PLAY DIFFERENT GAMES.

WHAT ARE YOU LOOKING FOR IN FRIENDSHIP?

ambiguity built into the term 'friend'. At least in romantic relationships we have something of a rulebook on how to be a good romantic partner, but when a friend can mean both distant acquaintance and platonic soulmate, we are venturing out on a road to failure. Jacqueline Mroz writes in *Girl Talk* about a study she conducted with Brooke Schwartz where she found the top value women seek out in a female friend is support (22 per cent), followed by authenticity (17 per cent), loyalty (15 per cent), success (13 per cent) and being a good listener (10 per cent). The ones that sat lower included compassion, intelligence, humour, optimism and trustworthiness.[1] Some friends are looking for similarities and some people are looking for differences. Most of us are looking for a unique combination of both. Enough in common to have mutual interests and enough difference to keep it interesting.

Even if we look across language, different languages have different connotations. Greek has six words for love, so which one is appropriate for which friendships? Japanese has *nakama* to identify a best friend, Spanish has *camarada* for a dear friend, and Korean has *sarang* for someone you want in your life till you die. Within psychology, there is a concept called linguistic relativism which describes that how we speak and the language we use shapes how we see the world. This makes me question whether if we had more vocabulary for social feelings and our friendships, would that allow us to think about friendship with more complexity and nuance?

There are unwritten codes of conduct in friendship – whether it be the fact you must remember their birthday to picking up the phone when they call, but ultimately not all these things are important to everyone, and that's the place we need to start. If someone forgot my birthday, I would be more upset than if someone didn't pick up the phone, and that's because I value thoughtfulness more highly than reliability.

Within the life-coaching world, values are non-tangible higher-level generalisations that some might call criteria. When we look at the research, social scientists highlight that the values people consider to be of highest importance are loyalty, trust and warmth, with generosity and caring being other values that are a high priority.[2] Have you ever thought about how you would define friendship? When I seek to define friendship, I have always believed it sits in the knowing and understanding of each other. Friendship, for me, is found in the relationships where no preface or explanation is needed, when I don't need to explain my relationship with my mother to give context to the story I am telling or when I don't need to explain my upbringing for you to understand the importance of my health. A friend to me is someone who has that shared past and almost a mutual language through in-jokes and intimate details. It should be no surprise to you then that understanding is my number one value. Yet others will have a completely different definition from me that emphasises different aspects of companionship and intimacy. Luvvie Ajayi Jones described friendship on the *We Can Do Hard Things* podcast as 'taking some responsibility for that person's care',[3] which is something I had never personally considered, and when we look at studies from 1984, the defining characteristic of a friend was shown to be someone who 'volunteers help in a time of need'.[4]

WHAT ARE YOU LOOKING FOR IN FRIENDSHIP?

Each person is different and what is an important value to one person could be completely non-existent for another. For example, it is important to me that my friends are emotionally intelligent, but someone else's priority could be friends who are exciting and spontaneous. We all have different wants and needs, and this is the best way to illuminate what you are looking for in this area of your life. It can also help make sense of why something is upsetting you. For example, if your highest value in friendship is loyalty, you will worry more about people talking behind your back. In the event of a breakup involving mutual friends, your concern will sit more around who is taking which side. For me, loyalty is a value that was really important when I was younger but now, as much as loyalty is a lovely quality, I don't think it would sit in my top eight values and therefore I don't really care about it. This doesn't mean I'm disloyal or that I'm OK with people being disloyal to me but more that it isn't a guiding factor in my decision making. For me, loyalty is likely not high among my values because I have never had an issue with loyalty and I have always been quite loyal myself. With values, when something has gone wrong or been neglected, it tends to rise higher in our priorities. For example, someone who has a lot of money will likely place money lower on their values; there is a lower need for it because it is already fulfilled.

It is also important to note that we all have different definitions of values. This particularly happens with words like 'communication'. To one person, this could mean being in frequent contact but to another, communication could be about an ability to be emotionally articulate. Communication is actually quite a vague word. Some measure friendship by how often they talk and interact and others care more about the quality of communication. That sounds like a niche difference, but using the same word could display in very different ways.

To discover your own values, ask yourself, 'What is important to me in friendship?' If you answer something like 'sleepovers' or 'parties', push yourself further – those are not values. Ask yourself, 'What is important to me about sleepovers?' At which point you might answer, 'I like the cosy conversations.' Next ask, 'What does the cosiness give me?' and 'What does the conversation give me?', at which point you will find the value – for example, 'comfort' or 'intimacy'. Write as many values as you can down and then pick your top eight. If you are struggling to order them, ask yourself, 'If I could have intimacy but not comfort, would I be happy?' Then reverse the question to illuminate which is of higher importance. While knowing your values is important, the top eight are the ones that largely dictate your decisions and behaviour. Once you have your top eight, it will become easier to understand why some of your friendships aren't working, and when you look for new friendships, you'll have an exact list of criteria that you are looking for in a person.

Here is an example list you could end up with:

1) Understanding
2) Respect
3) Empathy
4) Emotional Intelligence
5) Honesty
6) Fun
7) Appreciation
8) Reliability

WHAT ARE YOU LOOKING FOR IN FRIENDSHIP?

Your turn:

1) _____   5) _____
2) _____   6) _____
3) _____   7) _____
4) _____   8) _____

Knowing your friendship values is essential for recognising when your friendships change and making sense of that happening. Sometimes you know something is off but you aren't sure why, and often it's because you no longer have one of your top values in common. This is also useful when it comes to how you want to engage with your friends. If your highest values are excitement and spontaneity, then having more task-oriented friendships or multi-person friendship groups will be a better dynamic for you, whereas if you prioritise intimacy and connection then you should place more emphasis on one-to-one interactions. Your values will then become the cornerstone for how to cultivate your friendships and will ensure you are finding friends who share them and align with your expectations. Most importantly, you can't communicate your values to your friends unless you know them yourself!

INSECURITIES
IN FRIENDSHIP

DOES EVERYONE HAVE A BEST FRIEND EXCEPT ME?

Meredith Grey and Cristina Yang. Fred Flintstone and Barney Rubble. Blair Waldorf and Serena van der Woodsen. Seth Cohen and Ryan Atwood. Rory Gilmore and Lane Kim. J.D. and Turk. Cher Horowitz and Dionne Davenport. Scooby and Shaggy. Poussey and Taystee. Otis Milburn and Eric Effiong. Brooke and Peyton. Grace Hanson and Frankie Bergstein. Leonard Hofstadter and Sheldon Cooper. Jill Zarin and Bethenny Frankel. Pacey and Dawson. Romy and Michele. Harvey Specter and Mike Ross. Tully Hart and Kate Mularkey. Woody and Buzz. Jack Pearson and Miguel Rivas. Thelma and Louise. Ted Lasso and Coach Beard. Penelope Featherington and Eloise Bridgerton. Chris and Kem.

Your person. Your go-to. Your number one. Your ride-or-die. Your platonic soulmate. Your everything. From the beginning of time, we have been taught that best friends come in pairs. After all, a best-friend-forever necklace only comes in two parts. The same way you will never be content with your love life if you are comparing it to the likes of *The Notebook, Love Actually* and all the other romcoms that set unrealistic expectations, you are never going to be content in friendship if you want your life to resemble *Sex and the City* or *Friends*. Much like how if we romanticise romantic relationships, our real partner will fall short, if you romanticise your friendships, your actual friendships will pale in comparison. We need to make more space between the perfection of *The Sisterhood of the Traveling Pants* and the bitchiness of *Mean Girls*. One of the shows that I think does female friendship well is *Grey's Anatomy*. I used to be envious of Meredith and Cristina's friendship, but then they get into a major fight and don't talk for the majority of season ten. It's a painful watch and it's hard to know whose side you are on at times. They show the pair's awkwardness around each other, the avoidance, the attempt from one side trying to mend while the other rejects it and then vice versa. They heal, they mend, and most importantly they go on to be the greatest love story on the show.

Growing up in school, everyone wants that OG bestie and I was fortunate to have one. Her name is Marissa and for the six years of primary school, we were each other's go-to, so much so that the teachers even decided to keep us in the same class for all six years since we had such a 'positive impact on each other' – we knew this because Marissa's mum was a librarian at the school. And as the story of best friends goes, we are still friends today – even a world apart. Since primary school in Hong Kong, our friendship has survived through my departure at eleven years old to England, and then her leaving for Australia at fifteen.

At that age, having your best friend forever was everything. When a teacher asked us to pair up, Marissa and I didn't even need to go around the room asking because it was so automatic. And then I left. I went to boarding school and finding a new best friend felt impossible. A lot of people had known each other from their previous school and I was in a new country with no familiar faces, and while I made friends, there was no clear best friend and I felt that every day in class. Not having someone to sit next to on the bus or pair up with for projects left me feeling like a lesser person. When the price of being seen as a loner was so high, it's no wonder that not having a partner was seen as such a social threat.

It was therefore a relief when I arrived at university and found Louise. My friendship with Louise was the closest thing to a romantic relationship a friendship could be without actually being romantic. We had rituals like buying each other Valentine's day presents (the weirder the better) and we had inside jokes like yelling 'turnip' at each other – neither of us can remember why. There is a special magic when you meet someone who you never run out of things to say to. I once saw an Instagram quote that read, 'You are the best person to hang out with because if I ask a ridiculous question like "A hippo is chasing you, what do you do?", you'll say something like "How big is the hippo?"' She was the embodiment of that quote. In university, we came as a pair and maybe that was the problem. When someone is your 'everything' or you are both seen as a half of a unit, it implies that you could not survive without them, or at the very least you are incomplete without them. Looking back, Louise and I were definitely more codependent than was healthy. As adults, we must unlearn this messaging that you need to be someone's number one to matter.

You are enough without a best friend

One thing I wish I was told when I was younger was that you are not defined by whether you have a best friend or not. We need to remember that just because you aren't their first priority doesn't mean you are not a priority. You are not a lesser person for not having a best friend and you are not less lovable. There is nothing wrong with you. Some people only have a best friend for a few years and some people find their best friend later in life. My dad met his best friend, my godfather, in his fifties. Just because you have not had that friendship yet doesn't mean it won't happen for you someday – and more importantly, let's stop assuming that everyone wants a best friend! I no longer have a best friend and I don't want one. If I'm being really honest, I don't think I have the time and energy to make someone a priority to that extent. I have a few good friends, and while I am open to someone becoming my best friend one day, I would need there to be boundaries that weren't in place with Louise. The truth is that that friendship ending was more her choice than mine. I would have never ended that friendship – I would have hung on as it deteriorated out of hope for a revival. By the end, I needed our friendship more than she did and five years on, I'm glad she did what I couldn't.

WE NEED TO REMEMBER THAT JUST BECAUSE YOU AREN'T THEIR FIRST PRIORITY DOESN'T MEAN YOU ARE NOT A PRIORITY. YOU ARE NOT A LESSER PERSON FOR NOT HAVING A BEST FRIEND AND YOU ARE NOT LESS LOVABLE.

I might not be anyone's number one any more but I am a few people's number three – and vice versa – and in many ways I prefer it. I get the closeness and connection without having to be as reliable or available. By having a few number threes, I have more room to make space for more people who meet different needs.

Are you best friends or are you codependent?

Codependency is a term to describe relationships where the boundaries between where you end and someone else begins are blurred, and therefore your opinions and feelings can seem to be shared. It is a learned behaviour that is often taught in childhood when boundaries were not properly established and the child felt a responsibility to caretake the people around them in order to feel love. If the child is not taught differently, this can continue into adulthood. If you have ever been in a friendship where when your friend felt sad, you carried that sadness too, that could indicate codependency. Having empathy is a beautiful thing, but when it is a codependency, it is empathy without boundaries. Often you end up thinking the same and echoing each other's thoughts and if one person differs from the hivemind, the other feels a pressure to conform and cave. Codependency often looks like putting the other person's needs and opinions above your own, and if one party in the codependency is more dominant, the one who conforms can feel an underlying resentment that won't be acknowledged as acknowledging those feelings could threaten the friendship.

For Louise and me, the codependency exhibited itself

in ways like I would unconsciously hesitate to make plans with others until I knew Louise was busy because if she was free, I'd want to spend our evenings together. On her side, she would unconsciously not invest in the person she was dating until he had my seal of approval because the thing about codependency is that the relationship must always come first for it to survive. The best way to explain it is that when you are best friends, you are able to maintain your independence – you put yourself first and them second. When you are codependent, you put each other first, at the expense of yourself. Therefore whenever your needs are not getting met, you feel the relationship must come before the individual and therefore you keep the peace. Doing so means you exchange your own peace for calm within the relationship – until the inevitable day when everything that has been swept under the rug resurfaces in an intense way. Unfortunately, a codependent friendship ending is never going to be a peaceful one; it needs to end with an explosion because it's the only way to get distance from one another. Intensity is needed to form the friendship and therefore it is needed to break it too.

As negative as that sounds, it's important to recognise that some people exist in codependencies for years without even noticing. There are many best friends out there who are co-dependent. They will have never noticed because it works for them and because their effort towards each other is mutual. Who's to say that's unhealthy if it is not causing a problem in their life? But for a codependent dynamic to stay problem-free, each person needs to be the other's everything, and it needs to be reciprocated equally. When this doesn't occur, or

A CODEPENDENT
FRIENDSHIP ENDING
IS NEVER GOING TO
BE A PEACEFUL ONE;
IT NEEDS TO END
WITH AN EXPLOSION
BECAUSE IT'S THE ONLY
WAY TO GET DISTANCE
FROM ONE ANOTHER.
INTENSITY IS NEEDED TO
FORM THE FRIENDSHIP
AND THEREFORE
IT IS NEEDED TO
BREAK IT TOO.

if one person starts to seek out more independence, problems can arise. Codependencies, in that sense, are extremely fragile. All it takes is one person making a new friend that comes close to the level of best friend, someone getting a job that means they have less time to give, one person thinking too differently from the other, one party gaining more independence and no longer needing the other for support or someone replacing their codependency with a romantic partner.

If you recognise that you and your best friend might be codependent, my best advice would be to discuss it. Start the conversation with curiosity, using open-ended questions like:

- Do you know what codependency is?
- Have you ever felt like we are too close?
- Are there times in our relationship where you wish you were more independent?

If these feel like weird questions to ask, then preface it with 'Can I ask you something weird?' If you are concerned that they will start to worry, add some context by saying 'I was just reading a book on codependency in friendship' before launching into the conversation.

To make your best friendship more sustainable, start putting boundaries in place. This could mean you processing an emotional event for a few hours before reacting to your kneejerk desire to call your best friend, or it could be that when you are out for lunch with other friends and you see a text from your best friend, you decide to put your phone in your bag, give your other friends your full attention and know that your best friend can wait a few hours.

Every friendship requires flexibility to survive and unfortunately a codependency does not provide that. By addressing the issue head-on, you can create enough space in the relationship to grow, evolve and be independent without your best friend taking the distance personally. You might be each other's number ones now, but that might not always be the case. Addressing the codependency before it becomes a problem means that if another person enters the picture, either romantically or platonically, your friendship will be able to adapt.

A support system is more sustainable than a number one

If I learned anything from my friendship with Louise and its eventual breakdown, it's that one person cannot be your everything. In the loss of my forever best friend, the most noticeable thing was that no one cared about the intricacies of my days any more. I had no one to tell when the meeting I had been worrying about had gone well or when my creepy neighbour had been creepy again – but I was in this position because I had only ever gone to one person. If I'd spread that out, I would have had more of a network. I am at a stage in life now where I know I am never going to be someone's maid of honour and I'm OK with that because as much as there are downsides to not having a number one, there are upsides too.

Even if you have your go-to person who sits at the number-one spot, you need number twos, number threes and ultimately a wider support circle so that when your forever best friend is busy or unavailable, you have other people to spend time with and there are others you can rely on. With all of us having less and less time and energy to look after ourselves, let alone another person, relying solely on your best friend will inevitably lead to disappointment. Sometimes our worst life events occur at the same time and you don't have much to give to your best friend, not because you don't care but because you are too busy keeping yourself afloat. One way to do this is to make a concerted effort to make plans with the other people in your life. Allow yourself to have more than one person who you can turn to for support.

Are they really your best friend if you can't be honest?

It's been five years since Louise and I have spoken, and while it is often still painful to think about, I still believe that best friend kind of love is special in the way that it is such a rarity to be so deeply understood. If you have that best friend in your life, a platonic soulmate, appreciate them because it's a rare kind of connection. Most importantly, if you want to keep them in your life, you need to communicate. No matter how hard it is. No matter how uncomfortable it makes you. No matter how much you don't want to. The pressure to be perfect friends often means that when fractures appear, they aren't discussed. Remember that when you bury an emotion, it is only a temporary delay until the emotion resurfaces again. If someone is your best friend, you should be able to talk to them about whatever the problem is and navigate the difficult conversation together. Best friends should be able to be vulnerable, deep and emotional with one another, and if you can't, that's a problem you are overlooking. If something feels too vulnerable to speak to your best friend about, then I would question whether that person is your 'best friend' in name only. A best friendship needs depth to deserve the title.

IF SOMETHING FEELS TOO VULNERABLE TO SPEAK TO YOUR BEST FRIEND ABOUT, THEN I WOULD QUESTION WHETHER THAT PERSON IS YOUR 'BEST FRIEND' IN NAME ONLY. A BEST FRIENDSHIP NEEDS DEPTH TO DESERVE THE TITLE.

WHY DO I HAVE SO FEW FRIENDS?

I remember the first time I became paranoid that I had too few friends. We were at lunch when someone in my year saw a younger girl eating alone and muttered, 'I could never do that.'

'Do what?' I asked, turning around.

'Eat lunch alone. I would rather not eat than look like a loner.'

I had never thought about looking like a loner until that moment. My friend went on to say that she didn't walk between classes alone either. She said it with a level of authority that implied what she was saying was fact: a social rule that I just hadn't learned about our school. That day an insecurity was born. Most people ate lunch as soon as they could at midday, but if you had an extracurricular activity, you might eat at 1.15 p.m. There were usually people there at 1.15 p.m. but the issue with the dining hall was that you had to walk in to figure out if anyone in your year was there, at which point, it would look awkward to walk out by yourself if they weren't. If, however, I had *two* extracurricular activities, I had to eat at 2 p.m., when the dining room would be empty, and so on Wednesdays I would not eat lunch. I would rather not eat lunch than look like a loner. It sounds extreme but is it such a reach when research indicates the pain of rejection activates the same neural pathways as physical pain?[1] Looking back, I realise that my friend was not declaring a fact – she was just insecure about her own perception – but because at that age we are so impressionable, I inherited that insecurity and held it as my own. I wish I had known what I know now, which is that that friend was never a friend. This was the same person who would then tell me the following week that I was a 'non', short for non-existent, and that if it wasn't for my brain surgeries, which had given me the nickname 'brain haemorrhage girl' (I did not have a brain haemorrhage), no one would know who I was. I wish I could tell twelve-year-old me that just because you have fewer friends doesn't mean you are less lovable and, most of all, that you aren't alone.

Popular people can be lonely. Cool people can be lonely. It doesn't say anything about your social skills or how lovable you are. Even Gayle King, a woman in one of the most famous friendships in the world (her best friend is Oprah!) said recently, 'You can know a lot of people but that doesn't mean you have a lot of friends and that surprises people.'[2] According to the Campaign to End Loneliness, in 2022, 25 million people in the UK reported feeling lonely. In 2021, 20 per cent of people reported having no friends, a significant rise from 2012 when that number sat at 7 per cent.[3] This data is echoed in America, where the number of people with no friends was four times higher in 2021 than it was in the 1990s.[4] I believe that one of the main reasons for this is travel. It is no longer customary to stay where you grew up for your whole life and therefore relying on the stability of knowing your neighbours and watching other people grow up around you is no longer the norm. Most of us have also lost the religious communities that used to be a failsafe when you needed connection. Combine that with technology and the fact that even when we are together, we aren't connecting effectively. As a culture we have been emphasising individualism more and more, and that greater emphasis on the self means we are investing less in communities. Robert Putnam, author of *Bowling Alone*, suggested it has led to the privatisation of leisure time, whereas in the past we would go out and socialise in order to relax.[5] Evidence supports this, indicating that in 2013 we spent six hours a week with friends, and now we only spend two hours a week. As a society, we are experiencing a loneliness crisis which was exacerbated by the global pandemic, with studies showing that our levels of loneliness have not yet lowered back to pre-pandemic levels.[6] Sixty per cent of people have not returned to pre-pandemic activities, with 35 per cent saying that socialising is less important to them and 59 per cent saying it is harder to form relationships after the pandemic. This is combined with the fact that three times as many people work from home, meaning that the workplace is no longer the easiest solution to making new friends. Social media then exacerbates all of this because it creates the illusion that you are the only one impacted by this loneliness crisis. Our phones fuel comparison, leading us to believe that we are the problem, rather than there being a very real problem in the world around how we connect. I hope by knowing that loneliness is a global problem and not an individual one, it can reassure you that your lack of friendship is not an indication of your lack of lovability and that it is not a personal failing of your own. It is a societal failing and an unforeseen consequence that has come out of us underestimating the importance of community.

We all go through transitional phases in life where we have fewer people around us than we would like and while some people are happy with few friends, if you are not, remember that it is temporary. Whether you have moved somewhere new, lost a bunch of friends because you are changing your own identity or have entered a new life stage that has left you feeling more separate, remind yourself that you are making space for new people.

Removing the shame

Having fewer friends can bring moments of embarrassment, whether that's not having as many people as you would like to invite to your birthday or wishing you could have bigger celebrations for the milestones in your life. I remember one year for my birthday, I only invited six people and there was a moment when I wondered whether people would assume it was because I only had six friends. The truth was that one of my friends had passed away and I had only found out two days before. I cancelled my bigger event and only invited the six people who knew and who I would feel comfortable crying in front of. We often see having 'no friends' as a personal failing and an indication of who we are as a person

I HOPE BY KNOWING THAT LONELINESS IS A GLOBAL PROBLEM AND NOT AN INDIVIDUAL ONE, IT CAN REASSURE YOU THAT YOUR LACK OF FRIENDSHIP IS NOT AN INDICATION OF YOUR LACK OF LOVABILITY AND THAT IS NOT A PERSONAL FAILING OF YOUR OWN.

rather than a situational problem that can be explained with a little context. When we internalise the problem, shame is created.

Shame is one of the largest hurdles around loneliness. It tells us that we are the problem and when we think we are the problem, we distance and isolate ourselves, which exacerbates the issue. The psychologist Robin Dunbar found that the maximum number of friends and acquaintances one person can keep within their social network is 150: Dunbar's number. Within that 150, we tend to have five very close friends, ten close friends, thirty-five friends and one hundred acquaintances, with an inner layer of 1.5 people (usually your romantic partner). We must remember that this is the average and therefore there are people who will sit above that and also those who will sit below it. If you are the kind of person questioning whether you have even met 150 people in the entirety of your life, it doesn't necessarily say anything about you. There is no perfect number of friends, and depending on the kind of person you are and the stage of life you are at, you will have a different sweet spot that works for you. We have to be cautious about comparing our number of friends because people enjoy spending their time in different ways. In an *Atlantic* article, 'How We Learned To Be Lonely', Arthur C. Brooks discusses how loneliness tends to be self-perpetuating and therefore in order to break out of the cycle, we need to try an '"opposite signal" strategy':

> Your inertia probably tells you that getting dressed and going to work will be a hassle, and that inviting someone over for dinner will be uncomfortable.

You should do these things anyway ... At first, your system complains bitterly, but if you push through the complaints, you soon find that you can exercise (or socialize) easily, because it has become routine and because you can feel how it improves your life.[7]

Essentially, the opposite signal strategy is a technique used to overcome our brain's natural negativity bias by doing the opposite of what your instinct tells you. Another solution to the shame around your number of friends is to combat it with empathy. Brené Brown, a shame researcher, said, 'If you put shame in a Petri dish, it needs three ingredients to grow exponentially: secrecy, silence, and judgment. If you put the same amount of shame in the Petri dish and douse it with empathy, it can't survive.'[8] If you feel shame around your lack of friendships, I implore you to do something that you won't instinctively want to do: talk to a friend about it. They might not have a solution or friends to introduce you to, but at the very least, it removes the shame. Recently I admitted to a friend that I had felt lonely the previous weekend, and she said she had been feeling the exact same way. She asked why I hadn't texted and I said I had told myself that it was Saturday night so she'd likely be out and 9 p.m. was too late to text anyway. She said she was actually in bed unable to fall asleep because of how lonely she felt. I hope that this demonstrates that it is not a 'you' problem but a problem that we are facing as a society.

WHY DO I HAVE SO FEW FRIENDS?

Alone vs. lonely

Before anyone tells you that you can self-care yourself into not needing any friends, let me jump in. Humans are sociable creatures, nothing compensates for in-person interaction and we need each other to not just survive but to thrive. What is also true though is that while you are in a temporary phase of your life with fewer people surrounding you, it is a brilliant opportunity to learn to enjoy your alone time. Rebuilding our network takes time, and in that period you cannot succumb to desperation otherwise you will attract people who will take advantage of your desire to make friends. When I experienced a significant loss of friends all at one time, I used it as a chance to get comfortable with the stillness that comes with a lot of alone time. I realised that the reason I was always keeping friends around was that I feared being alone. My issue with being alone was that it made my internal voice louder and until I actually learned to sit with the discomfort that came with feeling my feelings, I continuously filled my life with people to use as a buffer between me and my own brain. Only when I was forced to spend time with myself did I learn to enjoy my alone time. We think that the day we start to like ourselves, we will start spending time with ourselves, but actually it is the other way around. I have a list in the notes section of my phone titled 'The Best You' of all my favourite things to do. When I'm feeling down, instead of caving in to it, I will pick something on the list and treat myself like someone who is worth it! You need to spend time with yourself to discover the good parts of yourself. Make it an occasion. If you light candles

BEFORE ANYONE TELLS YOU THAT YOU CAN SELF-CARE YOURSELF INTO NOT NEEDING ANY FRIENDS, LET ME JUMP IN. HUMANS ARE SOCIABLE CREATURES, NOTHING COMPENSATES FOR IN-PERSON INTERACTION AND WE NEED EACH OTHER TO NOT JUST SURVIVE BUT TO THRIVE.

and put the side lamp on when friends are over, then do the same for yourself. If you would put crisps in a bowl when you have company rather than eating straight out of the bag, then do the same for your solo date nights. Making the effort you extend to other people is an easy way to tell yourself that you are worth the extra time and energy too! When you spend a lot of time alone, it is easy to tell yourself that no one loves you or cares. One way I combat this is having a 'happy folder' on my phone of screenshots and texts from loved ones. This folder then becomes direct evidence that my brain can lie to me. When you are lonely, don't believe your brain!

Quality over quantity

When we are in this phase in our life we can feel tempted to accept anyone who is willing to walk in, but this is when we expose ourselves to unhealthy dynamics and settle for friendships that might do us more harm than good. Kate Leaver writes in *The Friendship Cure*, 'Loneliness exists in the gap between company and companionship. It lurks in between the quantity and quality of our relationships.'[9] I concur. I feel the most loneliness in my life when I'm stood in a room of people who don't understand me. I recently went on holiday with a friend who I had rarely seen since she'd moved to America two years ago. I knew it was a risk as we hadn't spent extended time together since she had moved, but what I didn't expect was feeling so misunderstood that by the second day of a four-day holiday, I was wishing I was back home. It is better to have fewer friends than friends who you can't be yourself around. Having warm bodies around you is not the solution if those people undermine, criticise and ignore you. Of course, none of us want to be in the position where we have no friends, but it's also important to detach from the school-playground idea that having more friends is better. Instead, we need to validate the relationships we do have. Adulthood is not a popularity contest, and having fewer friends can mean higher quality friendships, because you have more time and energy to devote to them.

Stop waiting for friends to live the life you want

One day I walked past my favourite restaurant around lunchtime. I was hungry and just seeing the restaurant made me crave my favourite dish; my next thought was, *It's a shame I'm not with a friend so I can go in*. Restaurants do not have a minimum-of-two policy and yet I thought I wasn't allowed to walk in without a companion – but I forced myself to go in. I happened to have a book in my bag and so I sat at the table and read. Now, if I want to go to a restaurant, I will, whether I have company or not. More recently, I wanted to see the new *Inside Out* movie but most of my friends live across London and no one was free, so I went alone.

We feed into the shame of having no friends when we tell ourselves we don't deserve to do the things we love or live the life we want to live without other people there. I promise that no one is watching you and if someone does judge you, it's only because *they* would be uncomfortable sitting in a cinema alone and wish they had your confidence. The beauty of going out alone is they almost always have a seat for one. I have gone into restaurants that have month-long waiting lists and the moment I say 'just one', they can fit me in. The most ironic thing about curating your dream life is that you become someone who people want to be friends with more. Rather than seeing a life with friends as a starting line for your dream life, your new friends can slot into a life you've already created.

THE MOST IRONIC THING ABOUT CURATING YOUR DREAM LIFE IS THAT YOU BECOME SOMEONE WHO PEOPLE WANT TO BE FRIENDS WITH MORE. RATHER THAN SEEING A LIFE WITH FRIENDS AS A STARTING LINE FOR YOUR DREAM LIFE, YOUR NEW FRIENDS CAN SLOT INTO A LIFE YOU'VE ALREADY CREATED.

DOES EVERYONE HAVE A FRIENDSHIP GROUP APART FROM ME?

Do you remember when the lockdown was lifted and they announced we could hang out in groups of six? My first thought was, *Who has six friends?* and my second was, *Who has six friends that both like and know each other?* I never truly fitted in with a friendship group at school but as our year group was divided into twelve houses, you almost had one formed for you via the ten people you shared your house with. Within our house, the ten divided into two groups and within my group, I was always at the bottom of the totem pole. In my head it was better to be included than not, until one day, I woke up to discover I had been excluded. The five girls I ate breakfast, lunch and dinner with had been told to not speak to me and they did what they were told, not even passing the milk if I asked for it. It would take me months to discover what I had done. I had heard one of them lying to another and I told that person the truth. Unfortunately, the one who was lying was the head of the friendship group and when I confronted her about it, two months into the silence, she responded with, 'It was only meant to last a week but then it didn't seem to upset you in the way we wanted it to, so we just kept going.' Of course, it *had* upset me and while I hadn't shown it, being suddenly iced out and not knowing why left a scar around friendship groups for me.

If I think back to my first ideas about friendship groups, I can easily recall my teenage memories with my sister. My sister is twelve years older than me, and when I was fifteen I started staying with her for long weekends. I was at boarding school in England and because my parents lived in Hong Kong, she started being my 'guardian' any time we had a weekend out of school. Waking up on a Saturday morning, I was always offered three options, which revolved around her friends: going to the pub in Camden with one group, joining another for shopping in Portobello Market or hanging out at a movie with the third group. Like most younger sisters, I thought my sister was the epitome of cool, and these weekends shaped my vision of what my life in London would look like at twenty-seven. I loved that she could pick and choose which friendship group to hang out with and I dreamed of a day when this would become my reality too. My twenty-seven looked very different though. There was a pandemic and I spent the first five months of lockdown completely alone. I had two friends who I would FaceTime nearly daily, a couple more who would call weekly and many more who would text me back and forth. Obviously I was not gallivanting across London, but even if the pandemic hadn't happened, my sister's reality could never have been my own because I didn't have a friendship group, let alone three to choose from.

While it sounds pretty idyllic to be in my sister's situation, the truth is that by the time I was twenty-seven, I didn't want to be in a friendship group – any friendship group. I'd been there and done that.

The reality is that I never felt like I was lacking in the pandemic simply because a friendship group was absent. Research supports this, stating that as long as you have one reciprocated friendship, this buffers the negative effect of not being accepted by a peer group. They noted that it's possible to be popular in your peer group and not have any reciprocated quality friendships and therefore having a friendship group doesn't automatically correlate to having good friendships.[1] To this day, I don't have a friendship group and I want to normalise that.

Group dynamics are complicated

Spending most of my school years without a solid core group of friends meant that it was a relief when I arrived at university and our corridor of twenty-five people became a ready-made friendship group. We were so tight that we were referred to as 'The Bermuda Triangle': once you got in, you never got out. (Maybe we should have taken it as a sign that the geographical location most known for sinking ships would be the watery grave for our friendships sinking too. Although ours was a lot less mysterious.) The problem with being that close is that intensity can also lead to intense fights and eventually that happened. Looking back, this friendship group was one of convenience. Most of us had come into university insecure and worried that we wouldn't make friends so we latched onto one another more than we chose each other. I missed out on so many opportunities because this group made me so comfortable that I never put myself out there to make other friends – but this is likely what I needed at the time. When they go right, friendship groups give you a sense of community and can make you feel like you have a chosen family. They provide you with a sense of safety in numbers that serves as a form of protection against ostracisation or even being picked on. The issue comes when fractures start appearing. A large group of twenty-five is never all going to get along. You will have to navigate both individual relationships and group dynamics, and that can get complicated. Six months into university, we had to choose houses for our second year. We were a happy family until people started saying who they didn't want to live with. This was worsened by the fact that one of the girls in the group body shamed me, which led to a divide among the girls. The final fragment that changed our friendship group for ever was when one guy punched another. By this point, we were living in three separate houses, and without proximity on our side, we all had an excuse to never properly heal the rift that had occurred. The most illuminating lesson was that the 'popular group' that I had always been craving never looks the same from the inside as the outside.

Being the bottom of the friendship group

Throughout school, I always found myself attaching myself to vague friendship groups. I thought it would fix everything. The truth is that constantly competing to

DOES EVERYONE HAVE A FRIENDSHIP GROUP?

feel legitimate in the group can make you feel worse than having fewer friends would as it serves as a constant reminder that you are not good enough. When I first landed back in London after university, I was in a similar predicament. I'd been included in a friendship group somewhat by accident as three of my friends were part of the group, with the other two people being complete strangers. This resulted in my friends having to ask if I could come along, and while the other two always said I was welcome, at no point did they start extending invitations themselves. It was a clear message to me that while they were never going to say I couldn't come, they would have preferred if I didn't. Things changed when I went to one of their birthdays. It was a massive party with more than three hundred people (which explains why I was suddenly included) and I met Clover's best friend, Archie. He had been one of her childhood friends to such an extent that Clover used to call him her brother. Archie and I started dating, and the other two came to accept me as part of their friendship group. But when my relationship with Archie ended, I started noticing that I was always the butt of their jokes. Eventually I made a decision to stop hanging out with the friendship group. I still went for one-on-one dinners with the three I wanted to stay in touch with, but I opted out of the friendship-group dynamic and it was incredibly liberating. You shouldn't have to convince anyone to be your friend; while it requires work to maintain a relationship, now I would only join a friendship group where I had individual relationships with each person. I don't want a friendship group that comes with people I wouldn't pick

YOU SHOULDN'T HAVE TO CONVINCE ANYONE TO BE YOUR FRIEND; WHILE IT REQUIRES WORK TO MAINTAIN A RELATIONSHIP, NOW I WOULD ONLY JOIN A FRIENDSHIP GROUP WHERE I HAD INDIVIDUAL RELATIONSHIPS WITH EACH PERSON.

as my own friends and I don't want to be in a group where I am lumped in as a two-for-one sale. There is a difference between having someone in the group that you don't love and someone who you don't even like. These two people did not like me, I did not like them, and yet I told myself that enduring their company was worth it for the other three when actually I could still have those friendships on my own terms.

How to have a healthy friendship group

Recently, I was listening to Melinda Gates talk about how she has a 'truth council' of three friends that she has had for over thirty years who she consults before big life decisions.[2] It's easy to feel jealous that she's got such long friendships, but Melinda is fifty-nine years old and I am only thirty-one. I could meet my truth council tomorrow and by the time I am her age, I could also have friends I have known for almost thirty years. These are not childhood friends but friends she made in her thirties. It's never too late to find a friendship group but we want a healthy one! What is the solution to creating a healthy friendship group?

- **Remove triangulation:** Triangulation refers to a communication pattern where one person avoids direct communication with another and uses a third person as an intermediary. In other words, stop talking to the friendship group about a problem you are having with another person in the group. In one of my friendship groups in Hong Kong, one person had slept with another's boyfriend. I became the intermediary, mediating between the two. With hindsight, I should have told both friends to talk to each other directly.

> Hey! I understand why you are upset and I would be too. I think it would be more productive for you to talk to her directly. She is the person you have a problem with and therefore she is the only person who can help you resolve it. I love you both and I don't want to get involved. I hope you can resolve it and I will also be here for you if you can't.

- **Compliments over complaints:** Whether it is tribal mentality or a few big personalities holding sway within the group, it is easy to fall into a pattern of us vs. them, which breeds negativity. Instead, we want to create an environment for meaningful conversation and set a precedent as your group being a safe space for vulnerability. To resist the temptation of just being a sheep in a crowd, we need the confidence to lift our head above the parapet and say 'let's not do this, we are better than this'. We want our friendships to hold us to a higher standard and in order to keep the circle healthy, we need to protect it against the desire to expedite closeness through mutual hatred. Instead, envisage your group as cheerleaders, make praising each other the norm and foster a judgement-free zone.
- **Nurture your individual relationships within the group:** Hanging out as a group is wonderful but it's also important to allow yourself to have different relationships with different people in the group. Not only will it

lessen competitiveness if you can recognise that each friendship is different, but it will diversify the range of interests and hobbies that might be limited when trying to make a decision for the whole group. If only one other person likes kickboxing, it is OK to go to a kickboxing class just the two of you, and it's OK if you reach out to one person when you are upset, and not another. Not everything has to go in the group chat and spending time alone with each person will make your relationships within the group healthier. We have to remove the idea that if you choose to hang out with one person, you are purposely excluding all the rest and instead accept that when we are all different people, we will have different ways of connecting.

WHAT DOES IT MEAN IF MY FRIEND DOESN'T LIKE MY INSTAGRAM POSTS?

I have been through two pandemics. We all know the most obvious one, Covid, but I also lived through the lesser-known SARS pandemic in Hong Kong in 2002. There were many similarities between the two but the biggest difference for me was marked by the role of technology, particularly its effect on maintaining relationships. I was in year five at the time of SARS, and it all happened very suddenly. One day, I was excited about the fact my dad was coming into school to talk to the class about World War II and the next day school had been cancelled indefinitely. There was no warning and being nine years old, I didn't know that there was a virus sweeping the country. I was just bummed that my dad was no longer coming into school with me. The sudden closing of the school meant that no one had the chance to say goodbye and I wouldn't see my friends again until year six. Not seeing my friends for five months felt like a lifetime, and in the absence of technology the months felt like years. In 2020, even though I was locked down alone, I spoke to my friends more than ever before. Four-hour FaceTimes were a regular occurrence between me and my friends.

This, along with many other reasons, is why I refuse to be the kind of person who knocks the internet or laments how kids these days never look up from their phones. Instead, I am more balanced. Technology comes with both positives and negatives; we are more connected than ever before and that means if you are a child growing up in an unhappy home or in a part of the world where you are unable to be yourself safely, you can find like-minded people on the web. It's harder to feel alone in your problems because, with a quick search online, you will find a community of people worrying about the same thing and often providing solutions. Technology also makes finding friends easier. Half of the friends I have in my life today are a result of Instagram and while that might be more than the average person because a large part of my job is on social media, friendships that bloom online are becoming more common, whether they are born on social networking platforms or on apps designed to meet friends like Bumble BFF. Most of all though, I will always be grateful for how technology has impacted my hospital stays.

When I was hospitalised at eleven, the only method of communication was email and so for two months of my stay, I begged the nurses to let me access a computer. They eventually relented when I was able to walk again, only for me to open my inbox to no mail. More than two decades later, I can still feel the devastation of opening that inbox and feeling like

I was invisible. My next hospitalisation occurred when I was nineteen, and it's no wonder that I went into that hospital stay worrying that out of sight really did mean out of mind. It turns out that I needn't have worried, because with the rise in technology, being chronically ill was now an entirely different experience. I was never out of touch with friends and family for long because mobiles, texting and Skype existed, which made the distance between Hong Kong and Bristol seem negligible. Technology kept those relationships intact and when I eventually returned to university six weeks later, it felt like I had never left.

The convenience that technology brings also has its downsides. I believe it is this increase in accessibility that has translated to a sense that we are entitled to people's time and energy. Immediate replies have become an unspoken expectation, with delayed responses causing friction, and the ease of technology can also mean we neglect in-person interactions. A study found that technology has a negative effect on both the quality and quantity of face-to-face communication.[1] Research suggests that even the presence of a mobile phone deteriorates connection, leading to lower levels of empathy.[2] When Esther Perel was asked about loneliness on the *Pivot* podcast, she explained that modern loneliness masks itself as hyper connectivity, with us having a thousand virtual friends but no one to ask to feed the cat.[3] In my own life I have experienced this, where if I wanted to text a friend, there were loads of people I could message or DM, but if I wanted someone to accompany me to an event, I only had two or three options.

It is easy to convince ourselves that we are up to date on

our friends' lives simply because we are seeing their pictures in our feed and not checking in with the human behind the screen. Without asking our friends how they are doing, we believe the highlight reel and we are all left a little lonelier as we compare the reality of our lives to the curated online portrayal of theirs. Research has found that people turn to social media more when they feel lonely but that it actually has the reverse effect due to us comparing our lives to other people's. One way they found to reduce this social comparison effect is to actually engage with posts. They found that just liking the post did not have an impact but if you left comments, the two-way interaction can lessen the tendency to compare.[4]

Social media also makes it more obvious when you are left out as you can see evidence of the night you were excluded from. When it comes to teenagers, bullying no longer ends when the school gates close as so many children now have smartphones. As a life coach, I have seen how texting has complicated all kinds of relationships and friendships. If someone doesn't have boundaries with their phone and texts at all hours of the day, it creates a problem. Conversely, if someone takes five to seven working days to reply to your message, that can also have a negative impact on your friendship. Whatever your point of view is on technology, it is here to stay and so we have to learn how to navigate around it.

You are not entitled to 24/7 access to anyone

In friendship, understanding phone compatibility is as crucial as shared morals, values and interests. It might seem silly to end a friendship because they like to send podcast-length

IT IS EASY TO CONVINCE OURSELVES THAT WE ARE UP TO DATE ON OUR FRIENDS' LIVES SIMPLY BECAUSE WE ARE SEEING THEIR PICTURES IN OUR FEED AND NOT CHECKING IN WITH THE HUMAN BEHIND THE SCREEN.

WHAT DOES IT MEAN?

voice notes and you prefer in-person interactions, but if we view our phones as communication devices, it makes sense to see communication as a deciphering dealbreaker for friendship. This does not mean that you have to be similar in the way that you communicate but it does mean that if your relationships with your phones is incompatible, you need to be willing to accept the mismatch. For example, one of my good friends rarely replies within the same week and has sometimes gone over a month without replying to me. In fact, as I type this, I am meant to be seeing her tomorrow and I still don't know where we're meeting because she has not replied to my text from over a week ago. She's been like this as long as I've known her so I no longer take it personally, however there was a time I found it rude and disrespectful. To stay in a friendship and continue to be bugged by this was a recipe for suffering so I had to make a decision to either end the friendship or adjust my expectations. I decided to experiment with the latter. I told myself that it was unrealistic for me to expect her to respond at a pace that she has never responded at. I now know if I want a quick reply, she is not the person to contact. And that's OK.

One of the pivotal mindset shifts I undertook to keep this friendship intact was to understand that her reply speed did not dictate her love or care for me. I also recognised that it wasn't personal and she replied to everyone slowly. As I implemented stronger boundaries with my phone, I also became conscious of the fact that there was a part of me that was jealous of how much distance she had from her phone and so some of my annoyance was simply a reflection of that. In addition to this, I changed my own behaviour. Now I text her even if she hasn't replied to the previous message. I don't bombard her, but if I am waiting for an answer I will either call her or just text her again. For example, I will call her tomorrow morning if I still don't know where I need to go for our night out, and I know that I will get the answer then.

When I became a direct communicator, I changed the way I interact in friendships. I no longer seethe in silence when someone is doing something that annoys me. Instead, I will let them know.

> I need a reply on this please xx

The way someone communicates is often the way they like being communicated with and therefore they won't know that their way of doing things can be annoying to someone else. Think about it. If someone is a spam texter, they won't know that sending multiple texts in a row is annoying because if someone did that to them, it would be familiar. If phone incompatibility is getting under your skin, have a conversation about it with your friend.

When having a conversation about phone boundaries, it is important to emphasise the behaviour you want and not the behaviour you don't want.

> Hey lovely! I get overwhelmed when I get a lot of messages in a row and that means I take longer to reply. Next time, it would be great if you could wait for me to reply before sending another and that means I can get back to you faster – yay! Win, win! Xx

WHAT DOES IT MEAN?

> Reply to me plsssss. I need to let people know if you are coming. I know you hate your phone and I'm cool with it most of the time. When I need to make plans though, I need a faster reply so I can organise my life. Thank you!! Hope you can come! Xx

Conversely, you might be on the other end and have to set boundaries with friends around their expectations or let them know how you prefer to be communicated with.

> Hey! I can't be on my phone at work. Feel free to text me but I can only get back to you once I'm out of the office at 6pm xx

> Ahh, I'm rubbish at texts. I'm much better over the phone, can I give you a call at the weekend?

Ultimately, there are ways to lessen phone incompatibility – whether it be more frequent in-person meetups or finding a middle ground that works for both people – but in order to do this, both of you need to be invested in resolving the mismatch. Phone incompatibility need not be a dealbreaker, but if it becomes a consistent problem or your boundaries continue to be crossed then you need to look at that as a legitimate reason why the friendship might not work, even if it just means that you aren't as close as you once were. During the pandemic, the friends who were rubbish on their phones were more likely to be the ones I ended up losing touch with and conversely, the relationships where we communicated most on FaceTime benefited most from our time in lockdown. In a digital world, compatibility in real life must now also be paired with compatibility online.

Can Instagram be a friendship dealbreaker?

Another source of conflict involving technology is social media. I have seen far too many posts on social media declaring that if a friend doesn't like your posts, they don't support you and you should ditch the friendship. Except it is much more complicated than that! We complicate our friendships when we interpret likes, comments and follows to be an indicator of love. To some, you must not only be a good friend but a good *online* friend too.

I remember a friend once getting upset with me because I never shared her posts on my Instagram Story. She equated my actions (or in this case, inaction) as the equivalent of dating a guy who never wanted to be seen in public with her, and decided that meant I was embarrassed about our friendship. In reality, I rarely share anyone else's posts on my Story, even my closest friends. Being a life coach, I took her assumption to be a reflection of her insecurities and I suspected it might have touched a previous sensitivity. We had a conversation about it and before I stated these points, I asked about what she was feeling. Not sharing her Instagram Stories, as petty as it sounds, ended up being an issue in our friendship and one that would arise every few months. The more I asked questions about why this made her so upset, the more I felt there was an ulterior motive in her wanting our friendship to be so public. It seemed to be an avenue for her to grow her own social media pages through my audience. I felt our friendship was becoming more transactional and when I voiced this, she ended up distancing herself.

This incident speaks to a larger issue that happens on social media. We see behaviour and attach a meaning that is not necessarily fact and then find evidence to fit the meaning. She saw a lack of social media engagement and chose the meaning 'she is embarrassed by me'. Alternative meanings could have been 'she is busy', 'she isn't on Instagram a lot' or 'she hasn't interacted because she said congratulations in person' but when we are feeling insecure or in a bad place mentally, it is a lot easier to choose a meaning that will hurt us and reinforce something we are already worrying about. Once that meaning has been chosen, we then find supporting evidence and scour through the friendship and recall moments to confirm what we fear.

Within our brains, we have something called a reticular activating system which recalls pieces of information that are congruent to what we already believe. The human brain can process 11 million pieces of information every second, whereas our conscious minds can only be aware of forty to fifty pieces of information at any given time. What we are conscious of is therefore a tiny fragment of what our unconscious brain is aware of. How our brain decides what is vital information and what is not is determined through a filtering process. Information comes in through our sensory organs (our eyes, ears, nose, mouth and skin) and is organised by our unconscious using three filters: delete, distort and generalise. As the brain does not like cognitive dissonance, these filters act in accordance with the beliefs our brain already holds. In my friend's case, her unconscious mind deleted the fact that

I had recently asked how her projects were going, helped her brainstorm titles for her next book and checked in both in person and over text. Her unconscious mind might have distorted a look I gave her and now perceived it in a different light. The unconscious mind might take a singular incident and generalise so that they could tell themselves things like 'they always do this'. It's not that these events didn't occur but instead, her unconscious mind filtered events through the reticular activating system and only entered evidence into her conscious mind that were in accordance with her already existing beliefs.

Unfollowing your IRL friends

Some people view online friendship and real-life friendship as the same thing. I disagree. I believe you can love a person and hate their social media content. I don't care how much I love you, if you post diet content, I will unfollow you and it's not because I don't care about you, it's because I care about myself and my mental health more. Diet content is a no-go for me because of my past relationship with food and therefore if I unfollow, it's because of me, not because of you or our relationship. In real life, if you have a diet culture mentality, we can just agree to disagree. You can go to a different friend to talk about your diets and I can set a boundary and explain that I don't like talking about diets. On social media, this is not an option. It is not my right to dictate your content and therefore the only thing in my control is whether I choose to see it or not. I will not declare that I will be unfollowing you because doing so would be unnecessarily hurtful, but if

SOME PEOPLE VIEW ONLINE FRIENDSHIP AND REAL-LIFE FRIENDSHIP AS THE SAME THING. I DISAGREE. I BELIEVE YOU CAN LOVE A PERSON AND HATE THEIR SOCIAL MEDIA CONTENT.

you notice and ask, I will tell you the truth and reiterate how much I love and care about you and that the unfollowing is not a contradiction of that. The reason why I do not mute people is that I find it inauthentic. If I don't want to see your content any more, I'm not going to pretend I do. The mute button doesn't exist in real life and I believe in friendship, you should both be on the same page, so if telling the truth threatens the friendship then that's not a friendship I want. Of course, the truth should always be shared in a considerate way, but people don't click the mute button to save their friends' feelings, they do it to avoid the conflict. Stand by your decisions and feel confident in your choices so that you can back them up if the conversation arises.

Remember that you are in control of your social media, so make it work for you. If who you allow onto your online platforms ever impacts your mental health, then it is your job to do what is necessary to take care of yourself. Ultimately, your social media is *yours*. Your page means your rules and there are no right or wrong beliefs around social media. Much like phone compatibility, we might not always agree with our friends on how we should interact or behave on social media, but much like in the real world, we don't always need to agree on everything.

FRIENDSHIP WHEN LIFE CHANGES

WHY DOES MY FRIEND DISAPPEAR WHEN THEY GET INTO A RELATIONSHIP?

The day I found out that my fiancé had been cheating on me, I was out of London and needed to come back to the flat we shared the following night. Without even asking, my friends all gathered around me so that I didn't have to arrive at my flat alone. As mentioned, I don't have a friendship group but they still huddled together like a group, finding each other's numbers, texting each other and knowing which people I would want around me that evening, telling them the news, arranging a supermarket delivery and coordinating their arrival times. I found out in a public way, so I was on the phone to my publicist when I received a text from a friend I hadn't told the news to, saying, 'I just spoke to Taryn, I'll be over at 6pm xx.' They were all there and all I could think was, *Thank god I didn't neglect my friendships just because I had found romantic love.*

Of course, no one thinks their relationship is going to end the way mine did, but that is not the reason why you should invest in your friendships. The reason I hadn't neglected my friendships is actually because of the eight years of being single before that relationship. Anyone who has had a prolonged period of being single knows that the experience of being the 'single friend' sucks most because people drop in and out of your life according to their romantic status. They expect you to be there to pick up the pieces despite not making any time and energy for you while they were in the honeymoon phase. It feels awful, like you are replaceable and forgettable, and so when I was single, I vowed that I would never be that friend and I kept that promise to myself.

And it was hard. I didn't truly understand it when I was the single friend, but having been in a long-term relationship, I understand the temptation to be absorbed into your little bubble and let that consume your whole life. Robin Dunbar found that the addition of a romantic partner leads to the loss of two of your closest friends – so that feeling of your friend disappearing is not in your head; it is a very literal replacement. Without an active and conscious effort to do otherwise, the course of least resistance is to let your partner take up so much of your time and energy that you ignore your friends. It is important that we remember that in order to do this we have made the assumption that our friends will be there no matter what. We tell ourselves a story that they won't mind or notice the absence from their life without checking whether this story we have told ourselves to feel better about our neglect is accurate. The truth is though, in order to tell yourself this story, you are ignoring the fact that it's not just about them being a friend to you, you have an obligation to be a friend to *them*. When that absence is extreme and sudden, you can't know when you should be there for them as you haven't checked in, made regular contact or asked how they're doing.

Since I made an active effort to not be that person, it was shocking to me that there was still distance with friends when I got into a romantic relationship. Whether it was the fact that we had lost our bonding over dates and being single or the assumption that my partner would be there for me so they didn't need to be, it was displayed in small ways. When I was single and I would call, they would always answer with a 'Hey! Are you OK?' even if they then went on to say they were busy, just in case it was an emergency. When I got into my first serious relationship, that stopped; there was an unspoken expectation that if there was an emergency, I would call my boyfriend. The mutual caretaking that happens among single women in particular was an aspect I felt I had lost because we live in a world where we expect coupled people to rely on each other. Even with my concerted effort to not disappear, I felt the lack of closeness and I missed the previous connection we had. The irony is that all of this led me to reach out to my partner more than my friends and therefore it became a self-fulfilling prophecy. Now that I am single again, I can confirm this suspicion was correct. What's worse is that I think it's unconscious; most of my friends didn't realise they had pulled away when I got into a relationship and got closer when I was single again.

The other reason why getting into a long-term relationship was challenging for my friendships is that for the first time, I wasn't talking to my friends about the issues in my love life. I had a partner who I felt safe enough to talk to, so when we had an issue, I would address it with him directly. I understood that talking to your friends can create tension between them and your partner when they know intimate details about your fight. I remember when my former best friend got into her first serious relationship, she stopped talking to me about her sex life and one night I queried her on it.

'What do you want to know?' she asked.

'Nothing in particular, I just noticed we don't talk about that part of your life any more,' I said.

'I guess it's because there is nothing to talk about any more,' she replied. 'We used to talk about it because I was insecure about something or having an issue and that's not the case now.'

It made sense and it makes even more sense now that I've been in a long-term relationship. The part that went unsaid in that conversation was that the boundaries were also to protect his privacy. There is a shift when you resolve issues in a healthy relationship where you turn more inwards to your partner where you might previously have turned outwards to friends.

With the research indicating that the addition of a romantic partner leads to the loss of two close friendships, I understand there are time and energy constraints that mean we have to make decisions about the people in our life. Personally, feeling deep romantic love for the first time in my life suddenly made other relationships feel shallow in comparison. The deepening of my ability to love romantically meant the more superficial relationships in my life seemed unimportant. Maybe part of this was due to the fact that being in love does open you up in a way that you might not have experienced before, but until we put friendship on an even playing field with romantic relationships, it will never be a fair choice. I am of the belief that they are not in conflict with each other and you do not need to choose.

If your friend keeps disappearing when they get into a relationship, talk to them about it.

> Hey! I have noticed that when you get into a relationship, I don't hear from you as often and I miss you when that happens. It is starting to upset me when you drop off the radar when you are dating someone new and I wanted to let you know how I was feeling. I really value our friendship and consistency is important to me xx

Unfortunately, most of the time when a friend does this, they either don't notice or they hope you won't. Confronting it head on will give them an opportunity to change. To me, it is better to judge someone on whether their behaviour changes than on if they notice your silence. They might not notice, whereas if you have done the brave thing, now they know and they get a choice as to what they decide to do next. If their behaviour doesn't change, you need to ask yourself if this is a friendship you want in your life. If you want to keep this friendship, then the key is to accept that they will likely keep doing this and that you need to stop expecting them to change. You can't be shocked when someone acts in the way they have always acted!

UNTIL WE PUT FRIENDSHIP ON AN EVEN PLAYING FIELD WITH ROMANTIC RELATIONSHIPS, IT WILL NEVER BE A FAIR CHOICE. I AM OF THE BELIEF THAT THEY ARE NOT IN CONFLICT WITH EACH OTHER AND YOU DO NOT NEED TO CHOOSE.

WHAT DO I DO IF I HATE WHO THEY ARE DATING?

In a world where romantic relationships are seen as more important than platonic ones, I have never seen a friend chosen over the person that they are dating. While they might not eradicate you from their life immediately, the moment you voice discontent about their relationship, there will be greater distance. I would know; I have lost the two strongest friendships in my life to their boyfriends. One was a slow burn and one was overnight. Both those friendship losses sting to this day and the greatest lesson that came out of both is to keep your opinions to yourself.

I met Emily when she joined my secondary school at thirteen, but we didn't really become friends until sixth form when we were in the same chemistry class. In our final year at boarding school, we changed houses and ended up living together and this was the same year that Emily met Aaron. I loved hearing about her stories until one day, the stories started taking a turn. He continuously ignored her boundaries and when they got into a fight, he said, 'Well, you are too stupid to get into medical school.' So when they broke up upon arrival at university, I was the first person to say, 'Thank god, you deserved better! I never liked him anyway.' She even agreed. A week later, she decided to get back together with Aaron and that one comment of mine was never forgotten. In over seven years of friendship, I only ever saw Aaron once; she kept us separate, which was doable until they moved in together. By the time she was engaged, I was no longer in her life. If I could take that comment back, would I? Yes, mainly because it was unnecessary, but there is another part of me that questions how strong the friendship truly was. After all, the fact she felt she had to choose between us was in her imagination. She never even gave me a chance to be around him and therefore I was never able to learn enough about him beyond my initial opinions. If the only things you tell your friends about your partner are negative, don't be surprised when your friends don't like them.

With Jane, it was a completely different story. I loved Jonathan. He came over to our flat often, I'd known him well for years and didn't even mind when Jane brought him along for my birthday dinner. We got on so well that I didn't feel like a third wheel and he was welcome. Eventually Jane would move in with him and I was happy for them both, but on the night of their housewarming, it all went wrong. From the moment I arrived Jonathan was drunk. He was a notoriously bad drunk, so I fobbed him off. He started making comments about my family, divulging information that he had only known through Jane, and I felt hurt that she had betrayed my confidence. I went to Jane and she didn't believe me, insisting that he would never say that. My hurt grew but I decided since everyone had

WHAT DO I DO IF I HATE WHO THEY ARE DATING?

been drinking, I'd let it go and we'd talk about it the next day. As I returned to the living room, he was cheersing his glass for a speech and, in front of the whole room, offered me up to his best friend sexually before thanking everyone for coming. It was gross and I was mortified. What made it worse was that I'd previously kissed his best friend. The following morning I texted Jane hoping that Jonathan would say sorry and she continued to insist that Jonathan would never behave that way. I asked her why I would lie and she said I was jealous. The argument escalated over text, he denied what had happened and she believed him and then stopped replying. And while I hoped for weeks that it wasn't, that would be the last time we spoke.

Looking back, I don't know why I didn't pick up the phone. I guess I was too hurt. We had been best friends for eight years, living together for seven of them, and she didn't respect me enough to even give me a proper goodbye. We were as strong as a friendship could get and yet it was no match for her romantic relationship, no matter that I'd never had an issue with Jonathan and our relationship had been going on for twice as long as theirs. And the final straw was asking her boyfriend for an apology? Clearly the idea of keeping him accountable threatened their relationship too much. I hate that this friendship ended but I stand by the fact that I deserved an apology and I was unwilling to ignore his comments. By this point in my life, I had good boundaries. I wouldn't let anyone speak to me like that, and I wasn't going to make an exception for the sake of our friendship. What hurts me most is the fact that if he had apologised, I would have accepted it. Now that I've been in a long-term relationship myself, I believe this even more so. If my best friend told me that a boyfriend of mine did something like that, not only would

I believe her but I would also tell my boyfriend myself that it was unacceptable behaviour and that she deserves an apology. I would thank her for letting me know and I'd be embarrassed on behalf of my partner. Being in a healthy relationship, romantic or platonic, is about holding ourselves to a standard we would be proud of and I would not dismiss his negative behaviour just because it makes me uncomfortable to face it. In both of these situations, it is lazy to blame the guys. Sometimes it is easier to be angry at the partner but the reality is that the friendship wouldn't have broken if they didn't want it to. There were many other ways both of these friendships could have survived but the responsibility lies with the person who was your friend.

You don't know better than them

Before we launch into a tirade about our friend's partner, we need to take a step back and be self-aware. Is it that your friend is in a dangerous position, or is the partner just not your cup of tea? There is a difference. I remember when one of my friends started dating a guy that the whole friendship group hated. They would go on and on about him as if he was the worst guy in the world. When I asked them what was so bad about him, all of them would say the same thing: 'he's weird.' He was a bit of a geek and they didn't like that, so they made my friend's life difficult by continually voicing their negative opinions and failing to see how happy he made her. It wasn't that she was in an unhealthy relationship, it was simply that he didn't meet their standards of cool. I am so thankful my friend never listened. They are still together today, married with two kids, and it would take five years, but the friendship group eventually

WHAT DO I DO IF I HATE WHO THEY ARE DATING?

got on board. They realised that they were being judgemental and that being a little bit awkward was not a crime – but can you imagine if my friend had been swayed by their opinion and dumped this guy simply because her friends didn't approve?

The only two people who know what it is like dating the other person are each other and at the end of the day, what you are hearing from your friend is only part of the story and has already been filtered through their own perception. This is why it is important we learn to put boundaries around our opinions. Getting unsolicited opinions on anything from what we are wearing to our life choices is annoying but we need to be wary of believing that our opinion trumps everyone else's. We have all had a friend who defends their hurtful comments with 'I'm just being honest' when actually they are being unnecessarily unkind. Honesty never needs to be brutal, and if you feel like your friend needs to listen to your opinion, it can read like a form of entitlement. Sometimes we all need a strong word with ourselves and to understand that assuming you know better than your friends about their own life and their own relationships is undermining. It reminded me of a scene in *Grey's Anatomy*, where McDreamy starts dating someone new and McSteamy says, 'I don't like her. I'm sorry, but as your friend it's my job to say that I don't like Rose.'[1] Except it isn't. There was a time in my life when I would have believed it was my duty to let the other person know, but with a little bit of growing up, I recognised that it was arrogance to believe I had any right to declare my opinion as fact. Believe in your friend enough that they are capable of deciding things about their own life and that they have the strength and confidence to end a relationship when it is no longer good for them.

Mind your own business

Everyone hates unsolicited opinions and so this is an important rule when it comes to friendship. Start using this sentence more:

> Do you want my advice or would you like me to listen?

Your friends are not obligated to take your advice; they might not even want it. I know it's frustrating when your friend is dating someone you don't like, but people need to make their own mistakes and sometimes you need to make the same mistake over and over to learn from it. Learning from both of my own situations, I no longer give my opinion unless I am asked. When I *am* asked, I will then respond with:

> Do you want me to be honest or do you want me to be happy for you?

I will also say 'my opinion does not matter' before sharing my thoughts, because I truly understand that now. Since I've had good boundaries in my life, I have friends who also have good boundaries. I've actually had a number of friends respond with 'just be happy for me', and that's what I then proceed to do. I will comment on any positives I have noticed and keep any concerns to myself. If they do want my honest opinion, I will give it once but then I won't repeat it. When one of my friends recently broke up, she said I was the first person she called. I wasn't her closest friend, not by a long shot, but she called me because I was the only one who didn't judge her, going on to

YOUR FRIENDS ARE NOT OBLIGATED TO TAKE YOUR ADVICE; THEY MIGHT NOT EVEN WANT IT.

tell me, 'Even when you shared your opinion, you would always ask first.' She told me about how every time she would bring up her now ex, her best friend would reiterate how much she didn't like him and so she learned to stop mentioning him.

While I am not looking for blind support in friendship, I am looking for a friend who will walk through the relationship with me, rather than someone who is continually predicting the ending. The fact is that unless someone is ready to hear it, they will not take your advice anyway. Whenever I say this, I get people telling me stories of their friends being in abusive situations and feeling the need to step in. I have been in these situations too and I understand why you want to keep them safe, but if you continue to voice your negative opinions, it will be used against you. Instead, I would voice my concern once. Ensure the conversation is not brought up in an impulsive manner but an intentional one and deliver your concern with as much care as possible. After that, say, 'You already know my opinion, I don't agree with your decision. When you are ready to leave, I will be here to support you.' One of the ways that abusers maintain control over people is by isolating them from their family and friends, so if you speak negatively about them and your friend tells them, the abuser will be more motivated to get them to cut contact with you. More than that, when your friend is finally in a position to leave, they might not come to you for help if you have been repeatedly making comments about their partner. There will be shame around them not listening or fear that you might say 'I told you so'. As painful as it is to watch, we have to accept that our friends are allowed to make different choices than we would make.

WHAT DO I DO IF I HATE WHO THEY ARE DATING?

You are still allowed your own boundaries

Just because you are respecting their decisions and keeping your opinions to yourself doesn't mean you have to listen to endless rants about your friends' partners. I have taken those two friendship breakups and learned from them by setting boundaries. I had a friend who had a consistent habit of getting into unhealthy relationships. They would break up to make up, over and over, and every time she wanted to talk to me about it. It had reached a point where I felt complicit. Talking about an issue can give us the illusion that we are doing something about it when in fact she was repeating the same pattern over and over so I set a boundary.

> Hey lovely! I can't keep talking about this. You already know my opinion and I am not going to keep repeating myself. I have already stated that I believe this dynamic is unhealthy and I respect the fact that you aren't ready to do anything about it, and also I am unable to continue listening to it. I really care about you and it upsets me to keep hearing about it as I'm starting to feel like I'm complicit. It is starting to affect our friendship and our friendship is really important to me so if you need to talk about your love life, I would appreciate it if you could go to a different friend. I love you lots and I'm here to support you in every other area of your life xx

She understood and we stayed friends. I believe setting this boundary not only kept our friendship healthier but that it wouldn't have survived without it. Research has shown that this behaviour of extensively revisiting and discussing the same problems, known as co-rumination, while it can enhance friendship closeness, can be maladaptive and unhelpful, leading to higher anxiety and stress as well as having a correlation to depression.[2] It's easy to get the illusion that you are doing something about a problem simply by talking about it and therefore, I also now am boundaried in ranting about the people I am dating. There are things that I won't share out of respect for the romantic relationship and there are times when I will need to talk to a friend but I check that they have enough emotional capacity to listen.

> Hey! I need to vent, do you have the headspace? Xx

You can also set boundaries around how much time you have to spend with their partner. I once had a friend who would often invite her boyfriend without asking and even though I did not have an issue with him personally, I was unable to catch up with my friend properly. The next time we went to arrange a dinner, I clarified beforehand:

> Hey! You know I always love seeing Patrick but this time, I would love it if it could just be us two! I really miss you and I want to be able to talk to you about my date last night and think the details might be a little TMI for Pat! Xx

They have chosen to have that romantic partner in their life but that doesn't mean you have to see them all the time too. Similarly, we have to be careful to uphold boundaries around the information we share, as in the above example

WHAT DO I DO IF I HATE WHO THEY ARE DATING?

with Jane. It is often excused under the guise of 'I tell my partner everything', but if someone has not explicitly said that your partner can know, then it is respectful to ask first. I had this happen recently when one of my friends was dating a famous footballer. We were on FaceTime as I was walking to my flat and I knew my partner at the time was home so before I went in, I said, 'I'm just walking in, my boyfriend is home, are you OK with me telling him?' It was a quick and easy check for permission to share information and then she ended up telling him herself when I walked in.

Thinking back on my two ex-best friends, am I saying you should never share your opinion with a friend? No, but it means that you need to be prepared to lose the friendship if you do. You can package your opinion in the most boundaried and compassionate way and yet it is still the risk you take. And sometimes the risk is worth it. If I found out a partner was cheating on my friend, for example, I would tell them no matter what and I could live with that friendship ending because that would be the act of a good friend. Being a good friend doesn't always mean staying friends the longest.

ARE WE REALLY FRIENDS OR JUST COLLEAGUES?

It can be really hurtful to discover that the people that you considered friends were simply colleagues. This realisation hit me most in the pandemic. Without frequent events and the constant contact that our jobs provided, I was disheartened to see how many people in my life no longer seemed to care about the relationships that existed outside our work world. The one that surprised me the most was with one of my old publicists. She used to be the person I spoke to more than anyone else in my life. She was incredibly emotionally intelligent, so even when we had a call about work, simply asking 'how are you?' would lead to her insisting that she knew something was wrong and our quick work catch-up would easily dissolve into an hour-long chat about life and everything else in the world. Becoming friends felt like this amazing two-for-one deal until I knew it had come time to leave. Being honest, I delayed ending our working relationship for a year simply because I didn't want to let go of the friendship or hurt her feelings. When I eventually worked up the courage to tell her that it wasn't working any more, I cried for

ARE WE REALLY FRIENDS OR JUST COLLEAGUES?

three weeks. I had been her first client and I had said often that we were ride-or-die, but what I couldn't foresee was that the pandemic led to so many financial losses that it became unviable to stay at her agency.

She understood and we promised to stay friends and yet, even though I reached out, trying to get a date in the diary, without the convenience of work chats, the replies got less and less. Our date in the diary got pushed and pushed until I eventually stopped trying. I ended up seeing her at a party a few years later and instantly ran up to her and gave her a hug. She made a joke about how I had forgotten her and I pulled out our texts and showed her that I was the one who had been trying to make dinner plans. She apologised and insisted we would find a date and again, we never did – not for my lack of trying. I guess, much like a romantic breakup, if we weren't friends before, why would we stay friends after?

With each instance where this has happened, I believed them when they said we would stay friends and it's hurt every time we haven't. Laura Eramian and Peter Mallory have found that having two relationships with a person, like being both colleagues and friends, is one of the main three themes of a friendship breakdown.[1] Ever since then, I have preferred to keep my work relationships and personal relationships separate. It is easier and it makes it simpler when you have to end the working relationship. Maybe it is wiser eyes that come with age, but I look back at that time in my career, where I would joke about being her favourite and promise I would never leave her, and realise I was quite naive. I was unable to make decisions in the workplace with a clear head because I let my personal feelings get in the way and while I eventually always made the right decision, there was more heartache than there would have been if I had kept it professional from the start. I have no regrets about that relationship but the lasting impact of that friendship ending is that I am more cautious about befriending those I work with now.

Being friends with colleagues is hard because we are all so burned out – or have we got it the wrong way around, and we would all be less burned out if we had more friends at work? A study by Asana reported that 70 per cent of people have experienced burnout and that level of exhaustion tends to make us go into fight-or-flight mode to survive.[2] We react to the urgent or important and therefore without an active effort, friendship falls by the wayside. When we spend a third of our lives working, it's important that we have relationships to support us in our careers.

The perks of being friends at work

It is undeniable that when you are friends with a colleague, you get prioritised in a way that doesn't happen if you didn't have a personal relationship. It's the age-old cliché of men getting ahead at work because they are holding events at golf clubs or even strip clubs, leaving women left out of the social aspect of it. Cronyism – the appointment of friends to positions of authority, without regard for their qualifications – does happen, and I have been on both sides of it. In my work, there is a well-known fashion brand that only works with three influencers from the plus-size community. All three are friends with the head of publicity who makes the decisions when casting jobs. I know that I have lost out on opportunities because she invited me out to a girl's night a few times and I declined. Some people would say it would have been smarter to say yes, but I don't like pretending to be friends for the sake of it. I'd much rather befriend someone because we naturally get along, and while I accepted that turning my back on a personal relationship meant lost job opportunities, I was OK with that decision.

Whether people admit it or not, there are benefits to being friends at work. When I was my publicist's favourite, we were in communication more than any of her other clients and – even unconsciously – I think she prioritised me, pushing for more jobs for me and advocating more fiercely because of our personal relationship, but with all those benefits comes a cost. The practical cost was that I stayed in our working relationship longer than I should have and the emotional cost was that I was very hurt when our personal relationship did not continue. I have heard stories of people being penalised at work for not participating enough in the social side of the job or attending after-work drinks enough, but I am of the belief that this should not be a requirement. Yes, there will always be an element of networking, but the 'forced fun' of social events should be in the workday if you want your employees to partake and not during their free time. This is how the world should be, but it's also important to deal with how the world is, and because it does impact your work, I understand that it's too simplistic to say 'just don't go'. Instead, weigh up the pros and cons. If you do turn up and show your face for the sake of work, then own it and remember that you don't need to emotionally connect to everyone you meet. It is OK to keep them as surface-level friendships. If you do not want to attend, that is your prerogative. Make the conscious decision, knowing that you might be picked for a promotion more slowly or get fewer opportunities. This is the decision I have made in my own career because I believe if you are undeniably good at your job, they will have no choice but to keep working with you.

The difference between personal and professional

One of the key pieces of advice my publicist, Charlotte, gave me is to not confuse friends for people being friendly but unfortunately, by the time she gave me that advice, I had learned it the hard way. The issue with blurring the lines between personal and professional is unmatched expectations. The way to avoid this trap is to stay away from assumptions. When you work together you are lulled into a sense of closeness. Do not mistake someone being kind to you as them wanting more of a relationship and make the boundaries very clear. The solution I have found with any workplace friendship is mutuality. Research supports this idea, showing that relationships that mix your social life with your working world can increase the amount of conflict that occurs due to incompatible relational expectations – the title of colleague and friend can create extra confusion.[3] You need to both be on the same page and if you are, the office can be a great place to make friends. But these relationships get complicated when you confide in someone who you thought was a friend and then they share what you say with others because they only view you as a colleague and don't have the same concept of loyalty as you do. This is why it's important to check that your

DO NOT CONFUSE

FRIENDS FOR PEOPLE

BEING FRIENDLY.

views are aligned. I wish I could write a list of all the ways you can figure out whether your relationship is a working relationship or a true friendship, but every context is different. If you want to know whether your desire to be friends is mutual, err on the side of caution when communicating it.

> Hey, I know we are just colleagues but I am going to this event on Friday and I have a spare ticket. Would you like to come as my friend? Xx

Some relationships can make the leap from professional to personal, but in order to find out you need to be willing to take the risk of asking. It doesn't need to be said in an official or formal way but by assuming less, you can see where their headspace is at. They might reply saying that of course, you are friends – but you won't know until you ask. I have been friends with a few of my agents too. Because of the nature of the working relationship, it is easy to become close and therefore one way we try to be clear about not only our relationship, but the specific conversation, is by clarifying with 'Are you saying this as my agent or my friend?' They would often reply saying, 'As your agent, I would say this, but as your friend, I would tell you to . . . '

Ultimately, I don't believe there is any way to truly know if you are friends until you stop working together. There is a transitional period where you need to renegotiate your expectations and your boundaries because your relationship will change. For example, as friends, you could discover that they are a rubbish texter, whereas in the past they had always replied to you because they needed to respond to the work aspect of your communication. The difficulty some have with the transitional period is not wanting to acknowledge the shift. You need to confront the awkwardness!

You do not need to be friends with everyone

It is actually quite liberating to realise that you don't have to befriend every person you encounter and you don't even need to be liked in the workplace. If you have walked through the world as a people-pleaser, the fact is you are obsessed with controlling how you are perceived. Let go of what people think of you and you give yourself the freedom to move through the work world in a different way. If you weren't so busy trying to get everyone to be your friend, how would you react to that coworker who always dumps their work on your plate? When you are concerned with being liked, you say 'absolutely' and ignore the fact that it's making you exhausted and that it's not fair that you are having to do both your job and theirs. If you didn't care about being liked, would you be able to send this message?

> Hey! I'm quite swamped right now. How about I finish my stuff and I can let you know if I have time left by the end of the day? Xx

How would you negotiate your salary if you didn't care if they thought favourably about you? Companies profit off your desire to be liked. It's why companies like to call themselves a 'family', to foster the idea that we should be going over and beyond without financial compensation. Humans are sociable creatures and companies capitalise on the fact that it is

IT IS ACTUALLY QUITE LIBERATING TO REALISE THAT YOU DON'T HAVE TO BEFRIEND EVERY PERSON YOU ENCOUNTER AND YOU DON'T EVEN NEED TO BE LIKED IN THE WORKPLACE.

an inherent trait in all of us to want to be accepted by the 'in-group'. As such, the way to flip this narrative is to remind yourself that in every company, you are replaceable. It doesn't matter how much they love you, if they want to fire you they will. Focus on being respected more than being liked. The more we people-please in the workplace, the less we set boundaries and override our need for financial compensation. Having friends in the workplace is a brilliant perk but it cannot be such a large need that you dismiss the reason you are actually in each other's lives. And true friendships will only benefit from you standing up for yourself, setting boundaries around your time and energy and insisting on respect for the work you put in.

Should you work with friends?

You have probably heard of the phrase 'do not mix business with pleasure' and I stand by it. As much as I have worked with many friends, if I have the option not to, I try to avoid it. A study found that workplace conflict affects those who started as friends more than those who start with business relationships and then form friendships.[4] The report suggests it's because true friends are not motivated by the benefits within the relationship like money or status. Those benefits are inherent in a business relationship and that's where it gets complicated. I was recently working on a project with a friend. Initially, she told me small lies, repeatedly saying that we weren't working together and that she had been dumped from the project. I knew from the team I was working with that this was not true, but when I asked my friend, she insisted it was. She then asked me to help her on a new project,

COMPANIES PROFIT OFF YOUR DESIRE TO BE LIKED. IT'S WHY COMPANIES LIKE TO CALL THEMSELVES A 'FAMILY', TO FOSTER THE IDEA THAT WE SHOULD BE GOING OVER AND BEYOND WITHOUT FINANCIAL COMPENSATION.

failing to mention the project was in fact with the same team. It felt peculiar that she kept lying and I never understood her motive. What hurt most was that I was finding out this information from other people. The final straw was that the favour she was asking was a huge one. She wanted me to talk about a story of abuse and to publicly name the institution I was in at the time – something that I have never done. The subject matter was being treated with no sensitivity and the fact she knew how personal this story was to me was what upset me most. Our friendship never recovered from this breach of trust, and while part of me is grateful the friendship ended because our work relationship illuminated her lack of care, there will always be a part of me that wonders if we would have survived if we had kept work out of it. After all, we were friends for a decade before we happened to land in the same industry. If you would like to work with your friends, it's imperative you set the boundaries out before you start work. To be able to function as effective colleagues, you need to have even better communication than if you were just friends and be able to have frequent conversations to check in and make sure you are on the same page and know where the line is. If you don't have the kind of friendship where you feel able to do this, then adding a working relationship might be the straw that breaks the camel's back.

It's OK to have transactional relationships

Transactional relationships are demonised in our culture – looked down on as 'using people'. In my mind, if you are both using each other, then what is the harm? The only downside of a transactional relationship is when one person isn't aware that that's what they're signing up for and are blindsided when the personal aspect falls apart when the favours stop coming. I have personally learned this lesson the fastest in the influencer industry. There was a time in my life when I had more influencer friends than not, and I made the mistake of thinking all of these were true friendships. It would take me years to realise that most of these relationships were, in some form, transactional, and too often I would only recognise it when they gained more followers than me and no longer needed me (or my page) for support. It was like I ceased to exist. For a time, it made me really cautious to interact with new people in the industry and reluctant to make new connections, until I realised that there was actually no harm in these kinds of relationships as long as I knew what they were. What's the difference between two people who use each other and friends? In my mind, it's that the love, care and affection for the person doesn't depend on whether they say yes or no. Within transactional relationships, there is a tit for tat. I did this favour for you so now it's my turn. In true friendships, this shouldn't exist. Neither kind of relationship is wrong, but as long as you can tell the difference, you won't be blindsided by the mismatch. Now, I have many transactional relationships in my life. There are people I see at events and I get the benefit of knowing someone in a room when I walk in alone. There are people I invite to events and I get a plus-one out of it and they get an introduction to a new brand that they can work with. I might ask one of these people for a favour when I need a guest on my podcast, but then they also know they can ask me for a favour when it's their turn to promote their book. I've learned to detach the personal from the professional and I know just because the state of our relationship is transactional, it doesn't mean they don't like me enough to want more, it might just be what they need in their life at that time, or frankly that they don't have energy for more friends.

The average person will spend 90,000 hours of their life at work and that's a lot of time to spend without some sort of support from the people around you. Research has shown that social relationships might help mitigate the deleterious effects of burnout, so whether they are friends, or simply just friendly, they are needed. Having people to brainstorm ideas with, vent about work stress or explain something that is confusing helps improve our workplace experience, and maybe that's enough. Even if the friendship doesn't survive out of the workplace!

WHY DO WEDDINGS COMPLICATE FRIENDSHIPS?

Weddings have a way of letting you know exactly where you stand in someone's life and sometimes, I don't want to know. I don't want to know whether I am on the hen rung, or bridesmaid tier or maid-of-honour level. I just want our friendship to exist and be important. I don't want it to be compared. It's taken me years to learn that friendships are not designed to be ranked and yet weddings seem to dissolve all that personal growth. You grow up and realise that it's OK to have different friends for different occasions and that the people in your life don't need to be in competition with each other. That is, until we regress back into childhood and get segmented into cookie-cutter-shaped weddings and we're back to being put into a hierarchy of importance. I'm over it! I was so over it that my ex-fiancé and I had planned to elope and one of the largest motivators was because I didn't want to have to rank my friends. I didn't want to have to choose and nor should I have to. I'm also not unique – 45 per cent of couples named guest lists as the most stress-inducing part,[1] spotlighting the difficulty of navigating social politics around who to invite when it comes to wedding parties.

With so much conversation about your wedding being 'the best day of your life', it's hard to be honest about the downside. It's reported that 84 per cent of brides feel stressed, with over a quarter calling it the most stressful event of their lives.[2] Very early on in my twenties, one of my best friends took me for a birthday meal. We sat next to two women who were clearly having a heated conversation, and as their argument got louder, my friend and I, without saying a word, halted our conversation, getting sucked into theirs by our sheer nosiness. They had been each other's maid of honour and it had all ended with one of the maids of honour being uninvited to the wedding and this meal was the first time they were seeing each other since. I remember my best friend and I talking about it afterwards and being confused how you could go from being someone's maid of honour to not being invited at all. Being in our early twenties, we were baffled. Now, I understand it a lot better. In fact, before deciding to elope, I had already decided against having bridesmaids. I kept envisioning looking back at my wedding party photos and seeing women in my wedding party who were no longer in my life. Due to my past friendship breakups, there was a part of me that didn't want to frame these women as forever friends because I was so acutely aware of how quickly this could change.

BAD FRIEND

Are weddings that important?

I was the kind of little girl who dreamed of having a big white dress at a massive venue. But when I went ring shopping, I suddenly felt a U-turn in my feelings around weddings. I remember telling my sister that I wanted to elope instead and how we'd planned to be engaged for a few months before going to a courthouse and signing the papers. My sister asked me to pause. She said, 'Out of everyone I know, you are the person who has dreamed of that big white wedding the most. Are you sure that's what you want? Why the sudden change?' Seeing my friends going through weddings over the years had made me see the reality behind them, and being in love with my partner at the time made me realise that the marriage is way more important than the wedding. My strengths are not event organisation: it makes me really stressed and I have complicated family dynamics where the thought of getting my whole family together in a room fills me with panic. On top of that, I hated what weddings had done to my friendships. I resented that weddings had become trump cards. One of the moments that made me most feel like this was when my ex-best friend decided to throw her hen party on my thirtieth birthday weekend. Our mutual friend decided to go to her hen instead of my thirtieth and I couldn't understand why a hen was more important. The mentality that she only has one hen, whereas I have many birthdays, didn't seem fair because I only have one thirtieth birthday and I wouldn't be renting a house for the weekend for any other. She could change the date of her hen; I couldn't change the date of my birthday. And we were closer, she was my best friend, she

WHY DO WEDDINGS COMPLICATE FRIENDSHIPS?

wasn't even a bridesmaid and yet I lost out because weddings trump birthdays. Well, what if you never want to get married? Are all your events automatically second tier? Are we still living in a culture where we only prioritise marriage and kids? I believe it all starts with lowering the importance of weddings. They can be important without being the most important. It can be a great day without needing to be the best day of your life.

Are you as important to me as I am to you?

One of the ways in which weddings can be hurtful is that they illuminate when your friendships aren't mutual. If you are more important to me than I am to you, I would rather be blissfully unaware of that. I have been on the receiving end of not being invited to a hen party by someone who would have been my bridesmaid, and I guess part of my motivation for wanting to do my own wedding differently was that I didn't want to be the perpetrator of that pain. In that instance, I didn't actually mind not being invited to the hen party. I don't even like hen parties and I knew it was likely because her maid of honour hated me, but what cut me deep was that she never acknowledged this to me and she didn't feel confident enough in our friendship to be honest with me. Instead, she avoided seeing me for eight months and would go to our mutual friends to ask how I was instead. After her honeymoon, I addressed it with her. I sent her a voice note and then she decided to end the friendship. It's a very strange reality when the last time you see someone is at their wedding.

Maid of honour is a skillset – and I do not have it!

I don't want to be a maid of honour and if I were asked, I would say no. Newsflash: you can say no. When I have told people this, they have told me that this is not something you can say no to but considering I have literally written a book called *How to Say No*, I am here to tell you that you can. If someone asks you to do something, you can decline it – even if it's being a bridesmaid or maid of honour. The main reason I would say no is because I would make an awful maid of honour. It's not about closeness, it's about the fact that it requires a specific skill set and I do not have it. What boundaries have taught me is that I can appreciate the gesture; I can thank them for asking me and I can also decline because I know it's better for both of us. We have this idea that we should sacrifice for our friends in order to be a good friend and I disagree. Part of me is saying no out of selfishness, knowing that I would have an awful time and how bad I would be at it, but a bigger part of me is saying no because I think my friend deserves an amazing maid of honour who will love being that person for them. Is being honest not an act of love in itself? We get so wrapped up in the compliment of it that we forget that being a maid of honour or a bridesmaid is a job. There is a specific role that you are saying yes to and if you do not feel like you are capable of fulfilling the requirements, you are within your right to appreciate the compliment and decline. I will always appreciate the gesture and then I'm happy to celebrate my friend in another way. Want me to give a speech? Now that is a job I am suited for!

IF SOMEONE ASKS YOU TO DO SOMETHING, YOU CAN DECLINE IT – EVEN IF IT'S BEING A BRIDESMAID OR MAID OF HONOUR.

The hidden financial cost of weddings

In 2023, 60 per cent of weddings went overbudget, with the average wedding costing £20,700, up 12.5 per cent from the previous year.[3] With grander affairs, this seems to trickle down to the guests too. Most of the time, the issue isn't that your friends don't want to be there for you on your big day, it's the fact that the expectations for weddings, and therefore wedding parties, have got higher and higher over the years. Saying yes to being part of someone's wedding party or even attending their hen isn't just about your friendship, it is also about money. Weddings are getting very expensive! I went for lunch with one of my friends who told me that she didn't realise that signing up to be someone's maid of honour would entail such a financial cost. She'd expected to pay for her dress but all the extraneous costs added up, from goodie bags for the hen to organising decorations for the engagement party, and she felt awkward because the financial part hadn't even been mentioned. When someone is saying yes to being part of your bridal party, they need to know what they are saying yes to. The romantic notions of a wedding often mean we forget about the practical aspects, and as awkward as it can be to divvy out what you expect your bridal party to cover, it's better than leaving your friends in the position where they have to bring up the conversation themselves. Someone not financially prioritising your wedding does not mean they don't care about you. If you are throwing events abroad, whether it be the wedding itself, the stag or the hen, you need to understand that not everyone has the same disposable income as you and therefore we should not measure how much someone

SOMEONE NOT FINANCIALLY PRIORITISING YOUR WEDDING DOES NOT MEAN THEY DON'T CARE ABOUT YOU.

cares about your upcoming nuptials based on whether they can afford it. To one person, spending that amount to attend your wedding could be 2 per cent of their income and to another person it could be 50 per cent. While the monetary value might be the same, the personal cost is greater when it has a greater impact on what they will be able to afford.

Ultimately, when it comes to weddings, we have to remember you can do your wedding your own way! When I was thinking of having a wedding, I would say, 'At the end of the day, it's a party and if I'm throwing a party and I'm not having a good time, then why am I throwing it?' It's pivotal to keep this perspective in the face of it all. If you put a lot of pressure on a friendship, it will break, and that means we need to also look at reducing the pressure around weddings. You do not have to do things the way they have always been done. If you don't want to have bridesmaids or a maid of honour, then don't.

CAN OUR FRIENDSHIP ADJUST THROUGH FAMILIES, CHILDREN AND FERTILITY ISSUES?

The one thing that makes me scared about growing older is how few friends people of a certain age have. My parents each have one best friend and that's it. There are people they see at dinner parties once a year, but other than that, they see their best friends once every few months and that fulfils their friendship quota. Maybe it's the fact they live in Hong Kong, which is a small enough place that they will often bump into other people they know and have a ten-minute catch-up in the middle of the street, but is that really enough? Research backs up my parents' behaviour, showing that even monkeys become pickier with age and less sociable. Dr Alexandra Freund explored the tendency to have fewer friends as we get older and explained, 'This clearly tells us that we, as humans, are not unique in the way we age socially but that there might be an evolutionary "deep" root in this pattern'.[1] The original dominant psychological theory was that humans lose friends as we prepare for death and want to maximise the amount of time we have left with the people who matter, but since monkeys are not consciously aware of their own mortality, this suggests that our behaviour seems to be the result of deliberation, choice and losing stamina to deal with negative, or even ambivalent relationships.

One thing I have only really contemplated while writing this book is that my parents likely made sacrifices for me that took a toll on their friendships. If you have a healthy relationship with your parents, they would have prioritised you. It's strange to look back now and think that every minute they chose to spend with you was likely also a choice to not be with their friends. When you are a child, you don't realise your parents are also growing up at the same time as you. They likely have their own friendship struggles and it's only upon reflection I remember people in my life who I once called aunties dropping out of my world because my mum's friendship with them ended.

According to research, a dwindling of the number of friends you need as you get older is more common than not. A study found that the number of friends we have increases until the age of twenty-five, at which point our social contacts tend to decline.[2] Being in my thirties now, I am seeing this happen, but it makes me question whether this is a conscious decision or whether it is just a natural side effect of a society that places less emphasis on friendship than marriage and children. There is obviously a period where friendships become harder to maintain as the family you are building dominates your time and energy, but does that mean in later life we struggle to bounce back to our former friendships because of the decades in between where we let those connections dwindle?

I have seen my own friendships shift as my friends become parents and – especially for working mums – their weekends become precious baby time. The way we spend time with each other has had to change to accommodate a baby, and ultimately you must accept that you will see them less. On their side, it's not just the time constraint but there seems to be a preference for friends who are parents too, or at least friends who are in couples, which understandably leaves single friends a little left out. Your NCT group become the people you talk to the most, and the parents at the school gate are the easiest people to hang out with – but what about those who don't want children, can't have them or simply don't have them yet? Is being at different life stages a reason why friendships drift apart?

When their happy moment is your pain point

There is nothing worse than strangers having a full-on PDA session in the street when you've just gone through a breakup. You don't blame the stranger but you'd hope your friend wouldn't do the same. Sometimes though, the timings of friendships don't align and that can be really tough to navigate. In my own life, I remember dreading making the call to tell one of my best friends that I'd got engaged. She was the first person I wanted to tell, but I knew it would also be a painful call because she'd just broken up with her boyfriend of three years. We had got into our relationships within a few weeks of each other, so to have hers end in the same week that mine advanced to the next step must have been bittersweet for her. As a good friend does, she didn't make the call about her and I made a mental note to check in later. Later would never come, as the next day I found out my fiancé was cheating and again, she was the first person I wanted to call, but this time for a different reason. Fresh out of a breakup, I thought she would be the person who would be most understanding if I decided to stay. I believed she would look at it with more nuance as she'd been navigating the decision of whether to break up or stick it out for months. With another friend, my engagement fell at a time when she was feeling left behind in her life. She had expressed to me how she wanted to freeze her eggs to give herself more options, but that as all her friends were in long-term relationships, she couldn't help but worry that we'd all be in a different life stage soon. Who knew that in a month's time I'd be spearheading a group chat called 'All the single ladies' and I would be adding her to it along with my friend fresh out of a breakup. The way we navigate these ever-evolving life stages is by giving each other the permission to feel all of our feelings, even when they conflict. We said our feelings aloud and by not burying them that kept the friendship healthy because we didn't take them personally. I understood that a friend could both resent my engagement and be over-the-moon happy for me. You can be both. Humans are complex and we need to make space for the nuanced emotions. It doesn't mean they don't love you or care about you. Instead, humans are inherently self-centred as we interpret everything through our own lens: one that becomes more rigid the longer we are alive. I was reminded of this as I scrolled down my newsfeed and saw a colleague had posted her wedding photos. My first thought was, *That was meant to be me this summer* and my next was *What beautiful photos*. Is it bad that the thought about myself came first? Or should we stop judging which order our thoughts appear in and just let the tangled emotions exist at once? I was at an event recently where a woman a couple of generations above me said, 'Oh and it doesn't end!' She'd just become a grandmother and she was sharing the pictures with all her friends because he was only a few weeks old but she said that soon she'd only share it with a few friends because she knows it's hard for her friends who are widowed, especially those who were widowed young and didn't have time to have children so wouldn't be having grandchildren either. When I left the event, she made me promise that I would include it in the book because 'us older women struggle with this too!'

Your friends aren't disposable

Of course your friends are less important than a child that is physically reliant on you to keep them fed, watered and generally alive, but it doesn't stop them from feeling shit that they have become expendable with age. Julie Beck describes this well in an *Atlantic* article: 'The voluntary nature of friendship makes it subject to life's whims in a way more formal relationships aren't. In adulthood, as people grow up and go away, friendships are the relationships most likely to take a hit. You're stuck with your family and you'll prioritise your spouse.'[3] Living in a patriarchal world that only celebrates marriage and motherhood entrenches this 'voluntary nature of friendship' but I believe that mentality is flawed. We might not notice the impact our friends have on our life because we take them for granted – but if you would notice if they were *not* there, you should notice when they are!

Friendship is expected to fill the gap. In the video game *The Sims*, there are meters for your needs: Hunger, Bladder, Energy, Fun, Social and Hygiene need to be fulfilled in order to keep your Sims content. If you have ever played, you know the first two that get neglected: Fun and Social. It makes me think we only make room for friends if we have perfect mental health, have enough sleep, don't have too much work and have spent enough time with our family and partner – but of course, adulthood means you never reach that point and so friendship drops lower and lower in importance as our lives get busier. If we consider our love lives though, there were times when I was exhausted but my boyfriend at the time had planned a date night and I would still go without any complaints because my relationship was important to me. Even now, there are nights I have planned a date and I still go, even if I don't want to, because my love life is important to me. There are times you don't want to do something and yet you still do it. But are we doing that for the friends in our life too? If you wait until everything is perfect in order to make space for friends, that point will never exist.

In Sheila Heti's novel *How Should a Person Be?* she discusses the concept of invariables: people who are fixed in our lives and must remain so. With the way the world has set up adulthood, our invariables are usually our romantic partners. When you are thinking about where to live or what job to do, you take into consideration your romantic partner – your invariable – but you generally don't factor friends – variables – into these decisions.[4] I would say that I have had two friendships in my life that were invariables. I could not contemplate moving abroad because both of them lived in London and the idea of being further from them scared me so much. The difficulty is that they were invariables to me but I was a variable to them because both chose to move away. This happens because friendship doesn't have a framework where we can say, 'Hey! I take you into consideration when I make plans about my life because I want you in it' like romantic relationships do, which means we end up in a situation where they treat your friendship like a bonus, even if you have centred your life around it. Is it any wonder though that women treat friendships like a bonus when we have such a hard relationship with letting ourselves enjoy things? We live in a world that says we must stay productive, so if all a friendship is adding to our life is love and laughs, no wonder it is considered frivolous. I've already made the case for why friendship is not just frivolous, but because it's worth reminding you, life is long and when it comes to friendships over the age of seventy, an Australian study found that their social circle predicted their survival into their next decade, so never let your world become one person.[5]

Being the child-free single friend

I have so much empathy and compassion for mothers and also am really grateful that as a society we are having more of a conversation about how becoming a mother can lead to a loss of your identity, or at the very least a re-evaluation of who you are and what matters to you. We even have a word now to describe the physical, psychological and emotional changes you go through: matrescence. One of the facts that I have shared with my mum friends is that human babies are born quite prematurely and so their reliance on the mother is quite unusual as a species. Robin Dunbar speaks about that from an evolutionary standpoint: 'We're trapped by the fact that we produce premature babies that are only half developed when they're born.'[6] This results in a very long period after birth in which the baby is completely helpless and completely reliant on the mother. If babies could be born already mobile and had the ability to feed themselves, like monkeys, then the human gestation period would need to be twenty-one months.

I recently asked one of my friends who was a mother whether she gets upset when someone doesn't remember her kid's birthday or didn't make an effort to meet her child when he was born and she replied very simply, 'If someone is getting upset about that it's because they have forgotten what it was like when they were the single one, before they had kids. They have to remember it's not their kid and when you were at that life stage, it was just another annoying child.' I have always been quite maternal – so much so that for most of my life I wanted to work with children – but even for me it was a relief to hear this. I actually didn't realise until I asked the question that I don't know when her kid's birthday is. Ultimately, what I took from her response is that it's about mutual respect – so, single friends, don't roll your eyes when the new mum in your life shares yet another photo of her child. New mums, don't snap at your childfree friend when

CAN OUR FRIENDSHIP ADJUST?

she says she is tired. They know it doesn't compare to your sleep deprivation. Let's all have a bit more appreciation for different life stages.

Let's be real, there are few solutions at this life stage. The friend with a child has less time and the ones without tend to have more. One has more flexibility and one has less. Those things can't change but one thing that can fundamentally help the friendship is to take the time to understand their point of view. You can do this by being upfront and asking, 'Did it feel hard when I called you to tell you I was engaged and you'd just gone through a breakup? I know you were happy for me but it's also OK if other feelings came up.' When I asked my friend this question recently, she admitted she was worried that the different stages would tear us apart, and I wouldn't have known that if I hadn't asked. Asking about your friendship and checking in with a question like, 'How do you find our friendship since I have become a mother?' can make you feel quite self-conscious, but when you approach the conversation before it leads to a fight, it can allow you and your friend to voice feelings in a more constructive manner. Don't try to fix your friend's feelings and instead just listen and validate what they are saying. To acknowledge how the other person is feeling is underestimated, but taking the time to listen to your friend's point of view is a simple way to show you care about what they are going through. That acknowledgement and feeling of being seen and heard can work wonders!

FRACTURES IN FRIENDSHIP

HOW DO I SUPPORT MY FRIEND THROUGH MENTAL HEALTH DIFFICULTIES?

When I was diagnosed with PTSD from my surgeries in my final year of university, I lived with three of my friends who did their best to understand but ultimately couldn't. Choosing to live together was already a decision where we had made the best out of bad options, but as the year went on, housemate issues became worse and worse. The fights started when they forbade me from having my boyfriend over. We had met on Tinder and they were scared of dating apps – they said by bringing a stranger into the apartment, I wasn't just putting myself at risk but all of them. I returned one day from lectures to see him sitting on the doorstep after they had kicked him out. When exam season started, it became even more unbearable. My PTSD was in full force and I was still struggling with the diagnosis. My everyday experience was waking up and crying and it terrified me that for months I didn't seem to be able to stop. I felt like I was losing myself, I was too scared to talk about it and I could barely even leave the house, let alone be a part of the university experience with my housemates. Some of my friends handled it better, convincing me to get help and reassuring me that no matter what happened they would be there for me, but my housemates took another approach: tough love. They told me I just needed to leave my room more, it might help if I go back to Slimming World and go on a diet, and one even asked me why I was still crying about something that happened ten years ago. They would often affirm my worst fear, insisting that they 'just wanted me to go back to being the happy, smiley person they know'; these comments often made me feel like our friendship was conditional on me performing happiness. Now I can look back and see that they were doing the best they could with a situation in which they were out of their depth. At the time though, it cut deep. The final straw was when they banned me from having phone calls in the house. As I found it hard to talk to them, I started calling other friends. They took issue with this as they said I was speaking too loudly and they were revising for their exams. The next day I packed up and went to London. I stayed there for the remainder of the term to revise for my final-year exams, only returning on the day of the exam to pack up and move out. It was on this day that we had the argument that ended our friendship. I have always regretted that day, not because of what was said but *how* it was said – screaming and crying at a pitch that was largely inaudible. I was horrified at how I spoke to them, and after storming out of our flat, I vowed never to speak to anyone like that again. This was the moment that made me realise I really needed to address my PTSD, because I did not like the person I was becoming. Even when a friendship ends, I want to be able to leave the situation feeling proud of myself, and I was not proud of how I spoke or acted in that argument. I always believe in taking accountability and no matter what they did or how they acted, I know I could have behaved better. If I had the resources I do now, I could have let them in more and helped them understand what I was going through so they could support me more, but you can't know what you don't know and the only option we have is to do better next time. Looking back, I see these three friendships as a casualty of my mental health, and while they take some blame for our friendship ending too, I accept that if I had been in a better headspace, I would have not only dealt with the ending better but likely would have addressed the issues that had been building up. I do not regret ending those friendships but I do regret the way they ended. I have learned from these experiences, taking the lessons into future friendships when my mental health has struggled.

Do not take silence personally

Sometimes it isn't about you. Sometimes you are not the friend a person wants to come to with their mental health problems and that's OK. In the situation above, I didn't want to talk to my housemates but there were two friends who I did rely heavily on. Maybe that's because one did psychology with me so I thought he would be more equipped to handle the situation, and the other was older and handled vulnerable information with more maturity. My choice in confiding in them was not a slight on my other friends, they just seemed to be the people who could help most in that moment, in the same way that I am not always the person my friends come to when they want to get back with an ex. I can be quite blunt and direct and while I have improved at having boundaries when giving my opinion, I am usually the last one to find out when a friend gets back together with a negative influence – but I also tend to be the first one they call when it goes tits-up and they need a shoulder to cry on. I'm also the go-to when they are ready to break up but need to work up the courage to actually end it! It isn't always personal. We can't escape ourselves and as a result, as humans, we can be quite self-centred. There is even a term for it: The Spotlight Effect. It is the psychological phenomenon that leads people to believe they are more noticed than they actually are. It's not the fact that a friend is thinking about you and actively choosing not to speak to you about what is going on in their life; it's much more likely that they weren't thinking about you at all. For example, for someone to ignore your text, you might think that they have gone to reply and actively chosen not to. Instead, it could be they saw it when they were in the middle of a meeting and forgot, or they got distracted thinking about the many things that consume our brain in the phase of life called adulthood and your text dropped out of mind – it was not a conscious decision to ignore it – it wasn't about you at all! Choosing those two friends was an active choice but not choosing other friends was not, and it wasn't an indication of our closeness. As a friend, I am OK with not being the person there for you because as your friend, I want you to choose for yourself who can best support you. I will always let you know that I am there, but I won't take it personally if you don't take me up on that offer. It's taken me many years to realise this. It started with recognising that the amount of information you share or have access to doesn't measure the importance or closeness of a friendship, and that someone else's relationship doesn't threaten ours, it strengthens ours. We don't want our friends to choose us because they have no other choice. Instead, we want them to have a complete support system so that they have different people to go to for different situations and the choice to decide the best person for each situation.

Distance is a reason to check in

I know it can feel really painful when a friend stops checking in but sometimes it is because someone needs to be checking in on them. I had a moment like this during the second lockdown. I had done the five months of the first lockdown alone and the second lockdown had hit me really hard. All the months of isolation had caught up with me and I pulled away from everyone in my life. I am a person who replies to texts in seconds and my friends joke that I answer the phone after one ring, so it was a big shift for me as a person. Everyone was largely dealing with their own shit and so most friends didn't notice – and that was OK because I was using all my time and energy to look after myself and they were using all their time and energy to look after themselves. I understood

WE DON'T WANT OUR FRIENDS TO CHOOSE US BECAUSE THEY HAVE NO OTHER CHOICE. INSTEAD, WE WANT THEM TO HAVE A COMPLETE SUPPORT SYSTEM SO THAT THEY HAVE DIFFERENT PEOPLE TO GO TO FOR DIFFERENT SITUATIONS AND THE CHOICE TO DECIDE THE BEST PERSON FOR EACH SITUATION.

if I wanted help, I needed to reach out and I didn't want to. I was OK managing on my own but I also didn't have capacity to be there for anyone else. One friend, however, took it as a reason to take issue with our friendship. What started as an 'I miss you' text resulted in him saying that he put more effort into the friendship than me and that he was always the one initiating. This wasn't accurate; he had clearly taken the last month of low effort and generalised it to our entire relationship. It hurt that his first instinct was to call me a bad friend instead of asking 'Are you OK?' If your friend suddenly disappears, it might not be about you. It might be something that is happening to them. Constance Wu explained this perfectly when she was on *Late Night with Seth Meyers*. Constance was on a show called *Fresh Off the Boat* and received a lot of backlash and was 'cancelled' for expressing her disappointment that the show had been renewed for another year. The internet read it as her being spoiled, ungrateful and out of touch with the reality that so many actors would be thrilled to be on a successful show. What has since come out was that she had to continue to work with a senior producer who was sexually harassing her. She talks about how it led to a dark time as she wasn't just hated publicly but within the industry, and was very much painted as a diva who thought she was too good for the show when she was dealing with something much worse. She said, 'I think it's important that we engage in curiosity and empathy before we go straight to judgement, because if somebody does something out of character for them, it usually means something is going on in their life.'[1] For me, it's instinctive to actually ask 'Are you OK?' when a friend

IT HURT THAT HIS FIRST INSTINCT WAS TO CALL ME A BAD FRIEND INSTEAD OF ASKING 'ARE YOU OK?' IF YOUR FRIEND SUDDENLY DISAPPEARS, IT MIGHT NOT BE ABOUT YOU.

pulls away rather than being annoyed at the distance and accusing them of being a bad friend.

Your mental health is not an excuse

Mental health can explain why you act the way you do but it never excuses it and that's a very fine line to tread. Hopefully my previous story about PTSD demonstrates that I practise what I preach and take accountability for how I behaved when I was at my lowest, owning that I was responsible for the demise of certain relationships. Being on the receiving end therefore puts me in a position where I have a lot of empathy and extend as much patience as possible to my friends, but unfortunately there are still times when you have to accept you can't help someone who won't help themselves. When the pandemic came, one of my friendships was already in a difficult place. We had taken a break from each other for a few months and been able to return to our friendship with a little more distance, but then the lockdown hit her mental health hard. One of the final arguments in our friendship happened when she called me in the middle of a breakdown. She was in a state where I was worried she was going to hurt herself so I asked for her address as she was staying with her new girlfriend. She hung up abruptly. I called back and for the rest of the day she didn't pick up. All day I called her, panicked and concerned she was about to do something rash and, being mid-pandemic, I felt helpless that I didn't even know where she was so I could help her. She called me back the next day and told me that she had only hung up because her girlfriend had come home and that everything was fine, but our friendship was never the same. Our friendship no longer felt safe. She had picked me up when she needed me and dropped me when she no longer did, with no care or concern that I'd spent the last day imagining the worst. Years later we met up and I told her how scary that day was for me, especially because I was in the pandemic alone with no support of my own. I shared how that day had a profound impact on how I operate in friendships as it left me in fear of ever being someone's first call in a crisis. She understood why our friendship never really stood a chance after that and recognised that sometimes you are so deep in your own shit, you don't have the ability to realise the impact you are having on others around you. She shared with me that our friendship breakup was more painful than any romantic breakup she had been through and I shared with her how painful it was to watch someone who I love so much do so many things to hurt herself and how I'd reached a point where I realised I couldn't want the change for her more than she wanted it for herself and I had to let her go. For years I wondered if I did the right thing but over that lunch, she reassured me that I couldn't have done anything different or made her realise it sooner than she did. She eventually went on to make the changes she needed to make and with the benefit of hindsight, we could also recognise it was the kinder thing to go our separate ways.

We need to find the line between understanding that mental health is a reason for behaving badly and also not using it as an excuse. I accept it is a very fine line. We can't be their therapist but we want to be their support. We can hope for them to change but know we can't want that more than they want it for themselves. We don't want to leave someone at their most vulnerable and yet we also don't want to jeopardise our own mental health to try to save theirs. It's complicated and for each person, where their limit lies will be slightly different.

IS LIVING TOGETHER GOING TO END THE FRIENDSHIP?

I believe the fastest way to break a friendship is to go travelling or to live together. And in reality, travelling is just a mini-version of the experience of living together. Having gone to boarding school from the age of eleven, sharing rooms with up to eight girls, I was young when I realised how differently people live. In a way, dorm-living was easy because there was a hierarchy based on year group: what the older girls said, we did. It was only in my final year, when we moved into ten separate houses, that things started to get complicated, and I believe that was due to sharing communal space. We would have fights over mess in the kitchen, people leaving plates in their rooms and even people being left out. Each house consisted of ten people, so there were always people you knew less well, and the sense of competitiveness was palpable. In university, I first lived in halls and then in houses with four other girls and then three other girls, and then my eventual move to London meant a housemate of five years before

IS LIVING TOGETHER GOING TO END THE FRIENDSHIP?

finally living alone for a few years before my now ex-fiancé moved in. It's fair to say that I have had extensive experience in this area. Here are the few things I have learned.

You aren't easy to live with either

Thanks to my university experiences, I learned that you have to be willing to let some things go, like the fact your housemate who has a room above the kitchen has really loud sex and her boyfriend drinks all the milk. There will be things that annoy you but remember that there will be things that annoy them too. For example, it wasn't until I pointed out to my housemate that she never emptied the lint out of the dryer that she pointed out I use the kitchen table as my coat rack. We both tried to make a conscious effort to improve, but since humans are creatures of habit, I eventually learned to forgive the lint and she stopped mentioning my coats. There are some things that don't need to be said and there are some things that will be deal breakers. The lint was annoying but someone stacking unwashed dishes in the sink was a deal breaker. I had a housemate who did this in university. I asked her multiple times to stack the dishes on the side so that people could still use the sink and it never changed, so after that year was up, thanks to that and many other reasons, I knew we couldn't live together again. Psychologists explain this as responsibility bias: the tendency to overestimate our contributions compared to others. Researchers Michael Ross and Fiore Sicoly asked couples to estimate the percentage of housework they did. If one person had said they had done 60 per cent, the other, if accurate, would say 40 per cent, but instead they found three out of four couples had figures that exceeded 100 per cent.[1] While the research was around romantic couples in living situations, the same can be said for platonic housemates, as responsibility bias still exists. This bias is driven by our need to see ourselves positively, but more importantly, it's because of information discrepancy. We have more information about what we are doing in the household than what our housemates are doing, and because their contributions aren't all witnessed, we assume they don't exist. Adam Grant, author of *Give and Take*, explains, 'We see all our own efforts, but we only witness a subset of our partners' efforts.'[2] While the author is talking about romantic situations, living with a housemate will have the same effect.

Talk about money

Money comes up in friendship even if you aren't living together. It can wear on a friendship if a friend is never paying you back or conversely if they are so pedantic around money that when you owe them £10.11, they actually want the 11p. We can read into this and judge them for it or we can accept everyone has different financial circumstances and maybe it's more to do with their finances than our friendship. Think about the *Friends* episode 'The One with Five Steaks and an Eggplant', where the three friends who make a smaller income admit that they feel pressure to go out every time anyone wants to celebrate and that they can't afford it.[3] We have to accept that people have different budgets and even when budgets are the same, people will still choose to spend their money in different ways. One of the fights I had in university most often was around heating. Two of our housemates refused to turn the heating on and viewed it as a waste of money and me and my other housemate didn't think we should have to wear a coat, jumper, gloves and scarf inside. In one of these arguments, I made a point that my housemate could just go on one less night out to turn the heating on since she went out five nights a week and bought multiple drinks each night, but ultimately heating was not her priority and I couldn't force it to be. Eventually, I offered to cover the extra cost, but we still failed to make any progress. We never came to a resolution and the resentment hit an all-time high when our heating bill ended up being £200 less than what we'd allocated. Having conversations about money shouldn't just be about what you can afford but also what your priority is, because as in this example, my housemates could all afford it, but they were choosing to spend their money on their social life. The discussion can't just be an initial one but a continuous one. You won't discover some issues until living together, and if I could go back to that situation I would have set my boundaries more firmly. It's important to be respectful of the fact you are all paying rent and therefore you all should have a right to at least voice your preferences where compromises and flexibility are in place.

Set boundaries before they are broken

When I first moved in with my friend in London, I was fresh from a devastating friendship breakup, and I asked my housemate if she could not bring over my ex-friends. I told her that I hoped one day I'd be OK with having them around but for the moment I really needed to feel safe in the apartment and not worry about arriving home to find them being there. She agreed and after two years of living together, she said they were coming to her birthday party and asked if it would be OK if she also invited them to the predrinks in our flat. I agreed; I knew it had been a big ask at the time and I was really appreciative that my friend had been so understanding. Setting expectations on this before we moved in was the key to this working. This, to me, was an act of friendship, because while it probably wasn't fair for me to ask that, she had been respectful of the fact that it was my space as well as hers and I wanted to be respectful of the fact it was her home too. People don't know your boundaries unless you set them. Make decisions on whether you are going to share groceries, have a common kitty and get as specific as possible. For example, ask if they are the kind of person who will eat another person's food without asking or if they forgot an ingredient and borrowed yours, would they be sure to replace it? In the communal areas, how will access to the TV be split? When you have friends over, will the other person be welcome or would you prefer to have the communal space to yourself? One of the other key areas to set boundaries around is how often partners will come over and how much they will be entitled to. In my second-year house, there was a guy who ended up dating four out of five of us. It caused a lot of drama and upset each time he moved on, so as a house we certainly had to set boundaries. There is also probably a teenage lesson in girl-code here, because I can confirm he was not worth it!

IS LIVING TOGETHER GOING TO END THE FRIENDSHIP?

Good friends don't always translate to good housemates

When my housemate of seven years moved out of our flat, my initial plan was for someone else to move in. We had a great seven years together so I was keen to repeat the process. As the timing worked out, two friends needed a place to stay for a week, and despite only living with them for a short amount of time, our friendships were seriously tested, and now I am reluctant to let anyone stay with me. Most recently, I let someone stay towards the end of the pandemic and along with a positive Covid test and a lax attitude to the pandemic, it left a permanent stain on our friendship as I believe that's how I got long Covid as she was the only person I saw at this time. When you live with someone, you see all the sides of them. Just because you are good friends doesn't mean you will make good housemates.

We know that one of the most trying times in dating is when you first move in together, so why don't we assume the same when it comes to living together as friends? One of the key things that I realised when my partner at the time moved in was to separate relationship issues from housemate issues. For the first three months of living together, we were fighting constantly, but when we went away for Christmas we went from fights every day to none at all. It was then I realised that we were fighting about the laundry or the dishwasher or how he was hogging the TV. The relationship itself was not the problem, and that realisation helped us to navigate the housemate struggles. It's the same in friendship: if you can be very clear in distinguishing housemate issues

WHEN YOU LIVE WITH SOMEONE, YOU SEE ALL THE SIDES OF THEM. JUST BECAUSE YOU ARE GOOD FRIENDS DOESN'T MEAN YOU WILL MAKE GOOD HOUSEMATES.

IS LIVING TOGETHER GOING TO END THE FRIENDSHIP?

from friendship issues, not only will it be less personal when conflict arises, it also means the friendship has a greater chance of survival.

WHY ARE FEMALE FRIENDSHIPS FULL OF COMPETITION, JEALOUSY AND GOSSIP?

I only have one guilty pleasure in life: *The Real Housewives*. I rarely have any guilt around my pleasures but this one makes me feel guilty because it embeds the message that women are bitchy, talk behind each other's back and reveal each other's secrets. The show unfortunately perpetuates the trope that jealousy and competition are the foundation of most female friendships. Watch it for too long and it's easy to become convinced that all women are gossip girls, but that is not the truth and we need to be wary of normalising this because having friends who encourage this mentality can have a detrimental effect on our self-esteem. Women are not inherently competitive, jealous or bitchy. We learn these behaviours because as a society we do not give women permission to be direct and therefore we learn these indirect communication methods. Only when we understand why we're behaving in

WHY ARE FEMALE FRIENDSHIPS FULL OF COMPETITION?

this way can we become conscious of it; it is within our power to change. It has been shown that young girls and boys are equally aggressive but societal messaging teaches girls to revert to more indirect methods of aggression. From early childhood onwards, girls compete using strategies that minimise the risk of retaliation and reduce the strength of other girls. Girls' competitive strategies include avoiding direct interference with other girls' goals, disguising competition, competing overtly only from a position of high status in the community, enforcing equality within the female community and socially excluding other girls. In other words, young girls learn that women are penalised for being aggressive so they resort to other tactics to gain power. This reminds me of when Bebo was invented: you had to choose your top eight friends and that is one of my earliest memories of passive aggression. If your friend was annoyed with you, you'd find out because your ranking had lowered and it was then your job to figure out what you'd done wrong. In a patriarchal world, women already have less power, and therefore there is less room for us. This is supported by research done by corporate consultant Judith Briles, who found that women business executives are more likely to behave unscrupulously towards other women than their male peers.[1]

Your friends are not your competition!

I first learned that my peers were my competition in my secondary school. Friends would not help each other with homework and one of my closest friends even stole my textbook when she lost hers, not caring that I was getting told off weekly for losing my things, or that at the end of year I was charged for the lost textbook she had taken. Very early on in that school, I learned that friendship meant nothing when it came to academic achievement, and the teachers weren't subtle about it either. They ingrained into us that you weren't the best unless you were better than the rest. It doesn't matter if you both got an A*; if someone else got 1 per cent more, you had failed. I remember getting upset one day when one of my friends refused to help me with my homework when I was really stuck and she had explained that GCSEs were marked on a bell curve, so if I got a higher grade, it would push her closer to the percentile cut-off point. You'd think it would end with academic achievement, but as soon as we started having socials with boys' schools, the competition only worsened. Cressida in *Bridgerton* describes it well: 'It has been difficult to find a husband. It had been more difficult still to find a friend ... The season has a way of coming between young ladies, pitting us against one another. I suppose I've fallen prey to it.' Eloise responds by saying, 'You are right, society does not seek to forge affections amongst us.'[2] Despite this being set in a fictional world and a different time period, I related to it because as girls in a boarding school with limited access to boys, there was an air of seeing each other as direct competition when it came to finding a boyfriend; the attainment of a romantic match was a status symbol that would deem us worthy.

I had a real-life Eloise. From very early on, Eloise was a story-topper. If I told a story about doing well in class, she would top it with a story of her doing better. If I said a guy was interested in me, three guys were interested in her. It was such a running joke that we had all heard the story that

WHY ARE FEMALE FRIENDSHIPS FULL OF COMPETITION?

Eloise's best friend's godmother had directed an episode of *Friends*. Any chance she had, she would pull it out as if it were her own accomplishment. Ultimately, we all knew it was coming from a place of insecurity, so in school we all ignored it. But it persevered into university and then into adulthood. The problem with life is that if you don't address your problems, they don't stay the same, they become more extreme, and by the time we were twenty-six, it was becoming almost unbearable. We had gone to a friend's wedding and I asked my friend to take a photo of me. Eloise barged in, took the phone out of my friend's hand and said, annoyed, 'I don't know why you didn't ask me. I do this for a living.' She did social media for an entertainment company. An hour later, I was taking another photo, with a friend this time, and – annoyed again – she said, 'Why don't you want a photo with me?' I tried to keep calm. 'Eloise, just because I want a photo with Lily doesn't mean it is a personal slight to you. You are welcome to get in.' The final straw came when Lily told me that she'd got a new job. Eloise jumped in and started talking about a compliment a boss had given her. I'd had enough. 'Eloise,' I said, 'I was just listening to Lily talk about her new job. Can we give her a moment to celebrate her massive accomplishment?' Eloise stormed off, muttering something about me being rude.

In order for healthy friendships to exist, sometimes it's about you, and sometimes it's about them. You need to be able to balance both, otherwise it becomes a one-sided friendship. When each conversation turns into a competition and someone is incapable of giving the other attention, it becomes hard to have your separate moments. It is easy to make space for both people in a friendship, but there isn't always space for both in the same conversation. One way to unlearn competition is instead to reach for connection. Rather than boasting that you are being given an award, when you are friends with someone, tell them instead about how you are stressing to find a dress for it. Unfortunately, our difficulty with competing in female friendship is likely to do with what we have been taught about women. To unlearn this, a great exercise you can do is to finish this prompt:

Women are ...

My friendships with women are ...

What was your instinct? I don't want to know what you wanted to say or what you corrected yourself with, but rather what your first thought was. Was it bitchy? Difficult? Once you become conscious of your limiting beliefs, we can seek to address them.

I taught myself to stop competing with my friends with the mantra 'there is enough space for everyone'. This mentality stems from a scarcity mindset that only one of us can win, and that's not true. When your friend succeeds, it doesn't mean you lose. When your friend wins, you want to give the praise and acknowledgement that you would want if it was your win. If a friend gets attention, you will get your turn too. Another key part of the process was letting go of the idea that I had to strong-arm every single opportunity into my life. This helps me focus on my own lane and remember that my friends aren't the ones competing in the race with me; they are the ones on the sidelines, cheering me on, offering me water at my pitstops. Just like I am for them!

Jealousy will infect your friendships

Friendships are often the yardstick we use to measure whether we are ahead or behind in life.

If you are the first in a friendship group to get married, it is easy to tell yourself that you are ahead, but then you go to book a girls' trip and realise the hotel is too much of a stretch financially and suddenly you are behind. Research has shown we compare ourselves to our friends more than strangers and we primarily tend to compare ourselves to friends of the same sex.[3] The problem is that with comparison comes jealousy. Comparison is usually accompanied with a one-up mentality or a one-down mentality, and either way, it is awful for friendships. I learned this the hard way with Nina. Nina and I had been best friends for a few years. She had visited me at university in Bristol and I had visited her at her college and we had even gone to visit another friend together in Cardiff. While we were there, our friend introduced us to three guys from her friendship group and quite naturally, we all split off into pairs. It wasn't romantic – Nina was in a relationship anyway – but it was a great night and we swapped numbers at the end of it then went our separate ways. It would be years later that I would go to our friend's birthday party and one of the guys from that night was there – Jake, the one Nina had been talking to. I hadn't really got to know him all those years ago but the moment I walked in, he started flirting. I ended up having to leave early to have dinner with Nina. While I was on the Tube, Jake had added me on Instagram (both my private and my business), Snapchat, LinkedIn and messaged me on Facebook. I replied joking that he had missed out Twitter and we had a back and forth about how keen he was being. I arrived at dinner excited to tell Nina but her response was, 'You are reading into it. Jake is just a flirt.' I was hurt and because I didn't have a lot of confidence at the time, I also thought that she might be right. It fed the voice in my head that said, 'Who are you to think he could actually be interested in you?' so I played it off and said, 'Yeah, maybe, so we will just see.' Jake and I would continue to talk on Snapchat for the next couple of months and I started to like him. The next time I told Nina, she started talking about how he had flirted with her all those years ago. What confused me was that Nina was in a relationship: the same relationship she was in when we were in university. Nina was the kind of person who was so stunning that before I had even introduced my university friends to her, they had seen a picture of her on my Facebook and had friend requested her. While she never overtly said it, it seemed like she was shocked that a guy who was interested in her could also be interested in me. I spoke to a friend about it and said, 'It's almost like she sees me as the . . .' I paused and my friend finished the sentence '. . . fat friend.' My jaw dropped. It felt so gross that I couldn't even say it myself, but it shocked me even more that my friend knew what I was about to say. She continued, 'I've noticed it before but I didn't want to say anything. She's always thought that she's better than you but it felt unnecessarily unkind to say it.' It was a hurt that I don't think that friendship could ever have recovered from. I confronted her about why she thought it was so unbelievable that Jake would like me and she denied it but that comment, even though it did not come from her, coloured a lot of the past between us. What hurt the most is that even though her beauty had always been obvious to me, she had been really insecure when we met and I had spent hours telling her how beautiful she was. It felt more hurtful that the same friendship that had built her confidence was now pulling mine down. In a conversation with Melinda Gates, Oprah Winfrey said that 'you cannot be friends with anyone who has a hint of jealousy about anything that you are doing',[4] and I am inclined to agree; it blocks their ability to be happy for you. I actually believe that to counter this, the best thing you can do is admit it. It can be really hard to get vulnerable and admit to your friend that you are jealous. It is important that you don't make it their problem to fix, but if you name it, you'll find it becomes easier to come out from under the guilt. You can recognise the jealousy, hate that you feel that way and also be happy for your friend. Emotions are complicated and many can exist at once. Jealousy is a normal human emotion, but if someone is not self-aware enough to process it instead of project it, it will ruin a friendship. If you are the jealous friend, the solution is to transform that jealousy into inspiration. It is not about your friend; it's a clue to what you desire in your own life.

Time to stop gossiping

'Did you see Michelle got a tattoo? How the hell did she get so popular?' There was a text on my best friend's phone from someone we went to school with. My best friend had come

IF YOU ARE THE JEALOUS FRIEND, THE SOLUTION IS TO TRANSFORM THAT JEALOUSY INTO INSPIRATION. IT IS NOT ABOUT YOUR FRIEND; IT'S A CLUE TO WHAT YOU DESIRE IN YOUR OWN LIFE.

WHY ARE FEMALE FRIENDSHIPS FULL OF COMPETITION?

to visit me at university and we had been pre-drinking when her phone pinged. I looked over and caught my name. Why was this woman who I wasn't even friends with going out of her way to stalk my Facebook photos and decide that my new tattoo did not fit into her image of me, let alone that I was unworthy of the new popularity that I'd found at university? With age and maturity, I know it was likely because the transition to university hadn't gone as smoothly for her, but back then it hurt and it made me wonder what else had been said to make her feel so comfortable to say that to my friend.

When it comes to talking about other people, there are times when you will need to talk to a friend in order to process a situation with another friend externally. You want their opinion because you are unsure how to deal with it. This is not the same as gossiping. The difference is the intention. If you are talking about someone with the intention of being mean, getting people on your side, spreading information that is not yours or being judgemental behind someone's back when you wouldn't say it to their face, that is gossiping. If you are going through a friendship situation and you need to talk aloud to someone who understands it, that is processing externally. When we talk about gossip, we talk about it in a very gendered way and as a society, we believe that women bitch more than men. Gossip is actually an evolutionary behaviour that allowed us to keep informed about our in-group in the past, and therefore would increase our chance of survival. A study suggested that gossip is used as a tool by women to regain some of their power as a repressed group.[5] Research might show that stronger bonds can be made over a mutual dislike of another party but while they might be stronger bonds, they most certainly aren't healthier. As a result, we learn that life is easier if we skirt around the issue and voice our frustrations to someone other than the person we have the issue with. I want to make a case for us to do friendships differently. Life might feel easier as an indirect communicator but when you are direct, it gets simpler.

Shine Theory

Let's talk about the antidote to bitching, gossiping and competition. One of the biggest highlights of my career is doing the phone-in segments on *This Morning* where I give life coaching to callers from the audience. What few people know though is that the opportunity only came because I met a woman at an event who is a doctor on the show. I had messaged her to ask for some advice around management. I wanted to change my team because I was looking for someone with more broadcast experience but she didn't know that. Before I could mention it, she said, 'Have you ever tried TV? You'd be great! Let me send an email!' and that's how I first got booked on the show. Every time I try to give her credit, she refuses it. 'It's all you. They keep booking you because you are good,' she says, and I remind her that I could have been the best in the world but if someone hadn't opened the door, no one would ever know.

There are many women who have helped me to get where I am. Megan Crabbe is another – whenever she couldn't do a job, she would recommend me, and I've been her plus-one for events I couldn't get into myself. This was all Megan. I've never known a woman to hand over so many opportunities

I WANT TO MAKE A CASE FOR US TO DO FRIENDSHIPS DIFFERENTLY. LIFE MIGHT BE EASIER AS AN INDIRECT COMMUNICATOR BUT WHEN YOU ARE DIRECT, IT GETS SIMPLER.

and every time she did it, she made me want to be more like her. I am a better woman because of her. Not everyone is like Megan though. An influencer recently moved my name tag off her table so I was sat between an empty seat and a wall. I've also had supposed friends speak badly about me to the brand we were working with and only found out later. I believe women like this are the minority. I choose to believe that because I want to live in a world where if someone gives you a hand up, you don't forget to reach back to help someone else up too. Aminatou Sow and Ann Friedman, authors of *Big Friendship*, coined the term 'Shine Theory', stemming from a conversation in which Aminatou said, 'I don't shine if you don't shine.' They sum it up by saying, 'Shine Theory asks that we replace that impulse of competition with one of collaboration.'[6] They write:

> We came to define Shine Theory as an investment, over the long term, in helping a friend be their best – and relying on their help in return. It is a conscious decision to bring our full selves to our friendship and to not let insecurity or envy ravage them. It's a practice of cultivating a spirit of genuine happiness and excitement when our friends are doing well, and being there for them when they aren't.[7]

It reminds me of Oprah Winfrey and Gayle King, Tina Fey and Amy Poehler or how Cameron Diaz and Drew Barrymore turned up when Lucy Liu was getting her star on the walk of fame. Even going further back, Marilyn Monroe helped Ella Fitzgerald secure a gig in a nightclub that refused

IF SOMEONE GIVES YOU A HAND UP, DON'T FORGET TO REACH BACK TO HELP SOMEONE ELSE UP TOO.

to book her because she was Black. She personally called the owner of the club and said she would book a front-row table every night that Ella performed. Sow and Friedman discuss how we – particularly marginalised folks – are led to believe there is a scarcity mindset and only enough space for one of us; Shine Theory tries to counter that. This kind of mentality has also been proven to pay dividends! Adam Grant found that those who are unafraid to share their knowledge and resources with others are most likely to succeed in the long term.[8] They are aware that this is easier said than done though: 'It's not a failure of Shine Theory to feel a twinge of jealousy or envy sometimes, but it's how you act on those feelings that matters.'[9]

Being treated this way when I entered the influencing world completely changed me as a person and, as a result, changed how I operate. Whenever an influencer talks to me about brands, jobs or money, I will share my fees transparently with anyone, no matter how well I know them. I will make a point to actually say the number even if we have just met, because the only people who benefit by us not sharing numbers are the companies. Yes, that person can use that number to undercut me, but they would be undercutting us all. I only became aware I was undercharging because someone had the kindness to share their fees with me. The next time I pitched, I tripled my fee and it was accepted immediately. Entering the working world, you can't know what you don't know and I'm so grateful for the people who had my back.

WHY DOES PERSONAL GROWTH MAKE YOUR FRIENDSHIPS GROW APART?

Everyone changes over the course of their life, but people who pursue personal development, go to therapy or have a life coach change more. As a life coach for over a decade, I have noticed that the people who work on themselves tend to have a higher body count when it comes to past friendships. Any time you change, you take the risk that the people around you might not like that change. That growth does amazing things for the individual but it can be quite testing for friendships. Humans like the familiar and therefore when your friend starts changing, unconsciously you might want them to return to the person you know because it feels safer. Their change makes you unconsciously aware of how you can change too and if you don't want to make changes in your own life, that can be really confronting. It's easier to convince them to stay the same than to do the hard work of changing too. Sometimes the people around us benefit from our unhealthy patterns, lack of boundaries and inability to prioritise ourselves. Sometimes the motivation to keep your friends in the box you've always known is due to a fear that you will lose them and so while it sounds really negative to say you aren't happy when a friend starts to change, it can actually be out of wanting that person in your life so badly that you are scared. It's hard to imagine the changed version of them still being friends with you because you don't know them yet, but in order to have the healthiest friendships, and not just the longest, we need to give people permission to change and go through the difficult adjustment process.

When I started setting boundaries in my own life, there were people who went along with the process. There might have been a bit of a push and pull while we tried to discover our new dynamic but ultimately they adapted. And then there were the people who didn't. It's why now one of the main things I warn people about when they start implementing boundaries is to be prepared for friendship loss. If you start losing friends, you can start thinking you are making the wrong decision and retreat back to your people-pleasing self. Instead, we need to remember that if someone doesn't respect our boundaries, they don't respect us – and that's not a relationship we want in our life. Yes, it's hard, but they were likely friendships that are dependent on you not having needs and letting them treat you however they want. I know because I went through it. In the space of five years, I went from being a pushover to being known on the internet as 'The Queen of Boundaries'. With that change came such a large amount of friendship loss that I called it 'The Mass Exodus'.

WHY DOES PERSONAL GROWTH MAKE YOU GROW APART?

And I couldn't blame them. With most of those friends, when we met, I was a people-pleaser; in a very short space of time, I became the opposite. The irony is that I lost myself trying to please everyone and then I lost everyone when I started being myself. Losing so many people at once was incredibly painful but looking back, they were not people who treated me very well and it got to a point where I would chose myself over any friendship. I would rather be the person I was becoming, someone with boundaries, than stay a people-pleaser to keep them as friends. Your friendship should not be conditional on you staying small. If the friendship is reliant on you not setting your boundaries, that's not friendship, that's simply attachment.

You are allowed to feel that way

When you grow, the friends around you might not grow in the same direction and some of them will really miss the old you. They are allowed to feel that way and sometimes the best way to navigate the shift is to communicate that and bring them along with you on the journey. The first time I set a boundary with a friend, he said I was acting weird and that something was wrong with me. I refused to explain because I was learning that you didn't need to justify your boundaries and I ended up hanging up quite abruptly. When you are learning something new, like boundaries, you won't always do it the right way the first time. It's much more likely that it will be clumsy, messy and confusing – and my first boundary certainly was. It would take me a few more weeks to realise that from his perspective, who I was becoming was shifting

THE IRONY IS THAT I LOST MYSELF TRYING TO PLEASE EVERYONE AND THEN I LOST EVERYONE WHEN I STARTED BEING MYSELF.

really rapidly, and so one night, I explained to him that I was on this journey of learning to set more boundaries and that it had been really difficult but if I was acting differently that was why. This conversation gave him an opportunity to ask questions, learn more about what kind of boundaries I was setting, why I had suddenly had an interest in it and ultimately become more supportive and understanding when I put my foot down in situations that I normally wouldn't. There is a saying that is said to have originated from a Confucian philosopher, 'Tell me and I forget, teach me and I may remember, involve me and I learn' – so I involved him and it worked. We are still friends today and while it took a few years of pushing, pulling and giving each other some distance when this new normal became trying for our relationship, we figured our way out and now I set boundaries with him all the time. Not all friendships adapt though, and as much as friends are allowed to feel sad or upset at you being different, you are also allowed to feel sad that people don't want to join you on your personal growth journey, especially if the changes are having a positive impact on your life. It's not that they don't care about you but sometimes people benefit so much from your lack of personal development work that they are unwilling to do the work to adapt. Unfortunately, there were people who took advantage of my need to please and suddenly setting boundaries put a mirror up to their own behaviour.

Social identity theory

According to social identity theory, we pick people based on who *we* are, not on who they are, so if you have a certain

YOUR FRIENDSHIP SHOULD NOT BE CONDITIONAL ON YOU STAYING SMALL. IF THE FRIENDSHIP IS RELIANT ON YOU NOT SETTING YOUR BOUNDARIES, THAT'S NOT FRIENDSHIP, THAT'S SIMPLY ATTACHMENT.

WHY DOES PERSONAL GROWTH MAKE YOU GROW APART?

identity, you pick people who affirm that and make you feel supported. If your identity changes, then you are more likely to change your relationships because they don't support your identity. This explains why a single person is more likely to choose single friends or when someone becomes a new mum, they will look to find new-mum friends. When one of my friends was pregnant, she spent time on Peanut, an app for mothers to make friends. I was really happy for her but also wanted to do a friendship check-in and asked her if she felt she couldn't talk to us about the parenting part of her life. She said it wasn't that, it was more that she wanted to have friends for her child that were of a similar age. Now though, I think it's simply social identity theory at play. Her child is now three and while I don't think it was a conscious or deliberate decision, most of her friends are mum friends and she sees me and the rest of her school friends a lot less.

Social identity theory doesn't just apply to life stages, it also applies to our mindsets and mentalities – whether it's shifts from therapy or changes in your social awareness. For example, at university, I had a friend called George. George was a great support for me specifically in terms of my body image and our friendship gave me a lot of the confidence in my appearance that I have today. We stayed friends after university, but then one day, he left a comment on my public Twitter. I had been growing a following online and so my followers started replying to him, not knowing he was a friend. In 2014, I was becoming more vocal about body image and I found myself learning more about social justice and ultimately realised that the world was a lot bigger than the small subsection I had grown up in. I became passionate about being part of the change and started advocating against the discrimination that plus-size bodies faced. I also became aware of how much internalised racism I held from being a person of colour growing up within a largely white circle. Since I had never spoken about this before, I hadn't realised George held such different views. One day I had posted about the lack of racial diversity in the media, particularly in advertisements, and he commented saying that since people of colour only accounted for 4 per cent of the UK population, then they should only be 4 per cent of the media. I messaged him privately in an attempt to educate him and discuss how over 2 million people deserve to see themselves in the media and the long-term impact of not being seen or feeling invisible, but from the start, I knew this conversation was going nowhere. It illuminated views that I couldn't unsee. We tried to have the conversation one more time and then I blocked him for a comment he left on my page. Being a socially aware person had become part of my social identity. It became part of what I look for in the people around me, and knowing I already had someone in my life that was so opposed to my views was jarring.

There is a larger conversation about whether you should let 'politics' come between friends and the risk that we are in danger of becoming echo chambers if we isolate ourselves from anyone who thinks differently, but ultimately it spotlighted a point of view about humanity that I was so uncomfortable with that I did not want to be friends with that person. It wasn't about his 'views' as much as it showed a lack of empathy, compassion and an inability to see outside of yourself long enough to recognise people who have faced much more discrimination or oppression. We talk about not letting the political get in the way of the personal but I believe the political is personal. I can accept that I was the one who changed and therefore according to social identity theory, who I was looking for had changed as well.

Will I have any friends left?

Going through the loneliness period that accompanies major change in your life is painful. It felt like I was responsible for the lack of people in my life and, because I wasn't further along in my personal-development journey, I blamed myself. Now, I can say that for each friendship loss there was mutual responsibility. I made the decision to be different and they also made the decision not to seek to understand. Years on, I can tell you that when a friend leaves your life, you create space for new people to enter, and it wasn't the 'light' at the end of the tunnel but the very dark periods in my life that taught me that. When my dad was diagnosed with cancer, I might have had fewer people in my life, but I had people who showed up. None of the people who were there for me were old friends, they were people who had only known me for a bit more than a year, but they all showed up in a way that I have never known in friendship. All the hard work during my 'mass exodus' paid dividends in ways I couldn't even predict because by starting new friendships on even footings and not on the premise that I would do everything to keep them in my life, I actually found reciprocation in friendship. When I was in that loneliness period, I often wondered if having people was better than having no one – that any friendship, no matter how bad it was, was better than being alone – but

BAD FRIEND

I can say it isn't. The loneliness is not going to last for ever. You can see it as your life being empty or instead see it as creating space so that when the right people come along, you are open to receiving them. Ultimately, it's a positive sign when you have expanded so much that you no longer fit into spaces you used to.

HOW TO BREAK UP WITH YOUR FRIEND

CAN I STILL FIX THE FRIENDSHIP?

When I got engaged, I was in the middle of a friendship issue. Three weeks earlier, my friend had sent me a voice note asking if something was wrong and I had replied saying there were a number of things that I had been upset about but I was holding off on talking to her until she was back from her honeymoon. I had intentionally held off on bringing up issues when she was planning her wedding, rightly or wrongly so, and as a result, the issues had added up. She had sensed the distance and in hindsight, it would have perhaps been better to be honest from the start but at the time, my mentality was to not upset her newlywedded bliss and that since these issues had been building up for over a year, it wasn't urgent enough to affect her honeymoon. My voice note was left unread for three weeks and so when I went through my phone to tell my friends about my engagement, I hesitated on her. I chose not to call as I wasn't telling everyone directly anyway and was going to announce my engagement on social media the next day. That post would result in me finding out via a follower that my new fiancé had been cheating on me and me abruptly ending our engagement less than twenty-four hours later. It would be three weeks before I publicly announced it. When I did, it became a much larger national story than I expected, so much so, even ex-friends reached out, and yet she didn't. Two days later, I got a text. She didn't acknowledge the engagement or that my life was visibly falling apart on a national level and instead stated that I had clearly decided she was a bad person and that the friendship was over but that if I wanted to sort it through, she had sent me an email. The email was ten scrolls long and included facts, dates and pedantic details about everything I had said in the voice note. She had taken sentences I had said like 'you then reached out to me for the first time in ages' and used the word 'ages' to prove the timeline between our last two interactions. This was not productive and more than that, I was already at breaking point. That day the press had printed my dating profile, a picture of my ex and I was going on national television the next morning to address it live on air. If the breakup hadn't broken me down enough, the public aspect of it really put me through the wringer. The text ended by saying that no matter what I decided, she would always wish me the best. I replied simply.

> If you wished me the best, you would ask how I am right now.

The thing that struck me as peculiar is that I had never once said that she was a bad person, and when she declared that I had decided our friendship was over, that was furthest from the truth. If I wanted it over, I wouldn't have voiced the issues in hope for a resolution, I would have just ended the

CAN I STILL FIX THE FRIENDSHIP?

friendship. You should go into communication around trying to fix the friendship, seeking to understand the other's position as much as possible. Her response, that I had decided she was a bad person and that it was clear I didn't want to continue the friendship, irritated me. Who was she to decide that for me? You do not get to declare how I feel or what I have decided. If you have decided to end the friendship, that's fair enough, but don't tell me how I feel about you, just ask. I then stated that I thought the friendship was now over as it seemed cruel to not even acknowledge what I was going through. At this point, she had waited six weeks to reply, so why did she have to do this now? More than that, if a friend had got engaged and we were in the middle of a fight, I would have put the fight aside and said, 'Hey! I saw you got engaged, I know we have things to sort through but congratulations and I'm so happy for you!' The saddest part about our interaction is that when I replied, pleading that I couldn't take much more than I was managing right now, she had blocked me.

> ... if you wanted a friendship you would have put aside our fight to say congratulations on my engagement three weeks ago and you definitely wouldn't have sent that text or email while my whole world was falling apart in the most public way. I have had four ex-friends reach out, and you, someone who is meant to be my actual friend, just kicked me when I'm very visibly down. I cannot have a conversation about us right now, a human can only take so much. I genuinely am on the verge of breaking and I cannot manage one more thing xx

So if you are curious about what I was doing the night before I went on live TV to address my ex-fiancé cheating on me, it was calling a friend to talk about this because this cut me deeper than anything else. It's a brutal realisation that unfortunately not everyone who hurts you cares.

Susan Shapiro Barash explains that friendship breakups can hurt more than romantic ones because:

> a woman who experiences this feels so unanchored. Women expect their female friends to provide a support system: these friends understand their feelings in a way that a husband or child or one's mother may not. Thus, when the friendship falls apart, it feels particularly unsafe, as if there is nowhere to turn.[1]

In her research, she has said 80 per cent of women would feel more upset about breaking up with a best friend than a boyfriend. I couldn't understand the cruelty. I poured my heart out on the internet, exposing myself to complete strangers online, and none of them made fun of me or took the piss, but the thing that hurt most came from a friend who couldn't put aside her own shit to be there for me in my time of need. When we get into a conflict with a friend, how they handle it is revealing, and sometimes it is the fight itself that ends it. The actual issue that started the fight was fixable, it was a series of misunderstandings that had built up over time, but the fact she chose that timing, ignored the very crucial context she was sending that message within, and couldn't prioritise what I was going through was what ended the friendship.

NOT EVERYONE WHO HURTS YOU CARES.

Normalise working on the friendship

In a 2022 study conducted by Kinneret Lahad and Jenny van Hooff exploring online advice given around difficult friendships, they concluded that even though most online platforms agree that friendship is 'an important personal tie, there is very little encouragement to "work" on these relationships. As such, these discourses offer a reductive, disposable approach to friendship ties that overlooks the complexities and lived experiences of friendship relations.'[2] And I agree. We don't make room for bickering or tiffs in friendship; fights often escalate before they need to. Not every friendship fight needs to be devastating or even big. Within romantic relationships, we have normalised fighting – we even expect it – and I wish we could do the same with friendship. In my book on boundaries, *The Joy of Being Selfish*, I wrote about an incident with a friend where she had called me unforgiving. When I was doing the press tour for that book, interviewers would often ask me about it. 'That's such a bad friend!', 'How rude!' or 'What a mean person,' they would say. I was shocked by this reception, as I had included it as an example of how humans mess up. I set my boundaries, I told her that name-calling wasn't productive to the conversation we were having, she apologised and we moved on, but something about how it was being portrayed in interviews made me realise how ironically, as a society, we are quite unforgiving with friendship. According to a study conducted by MidAmerica Nazarene University, nearly 50 per cent of couples attended some form of counselling with their spouse.[3] Couples counselling or marriage therapy are well-known options if you hit

COUPLES COUNSELLING OR MARRIAGE THERAPY ARE WELL-KNOWN OPTIONS IF YOU HIT A ROUGH PATCH IN YOUR ROMANTIC RELATIONSHIP, BUT WOULD YOU DO THE SAME IF YOU HAD A FRIENDSHIP PROBLEM?

a rough patch in your romantic relationship, but would you do the same if you had a friendship problem? We dedicate date nights for our romantic relationships to ensure we are spending quality time together and we understand that if we don't make time for our partner, it's easy for our romantic relationships to fall by the wayside. But we don't seem to understand that platonic relationships require work too. Much as ruptures occur in romantic relationships, they occur within friendships, so we must put just as much effort into the repair. Laura Eramian states there are a lot of contradictions around how we talk about friendship. We believe we should be able to say anything to a good friend but 'the one thing that you're not supposed to talk about is the state of the friendship – it's supposed to be one of the easier, less serious relationships that provide you a refuge from the difficulties of other relationships'.[4]

There have been examples in the media of friends going to therapy, like the pop group McFly when their band hit a rough patch, or Ann and Aminatou in their book *Big Friendship*, but if both of these scenarios didn't also overlap into their working life and create a financial incentive to fix the friendships, would they have gone to the same lengths? Too often in friendship, we don't do the hard work of trying to fix our relationship or give the other person the time to change their behaviour. In one instance, I had a friend cancel on me six times in a row. When we made plans the seventh time, I set a boundary and said that if she cancelled again the friendship was over. The day before our dinner I got a message saying, 'Oh, I thought it was Thursday, not Tuesday.' I followed through on the consequence I had set and ended the friendship. She thought I was being ridiculous but I told her that my time was really important to me and now she had become disrespectful. When I had set the boundary she had clearly not taken me seriously, but with it being the seventh time, it was clear that she was not prioritising our friendship in the same way I was. I had declined work events and suggested an alternative night for a date in order to see her, and yet none of that was taken into consideration whenever she cancelled. For her, I was a friend who could be relied upon no matter what. She called me up at the last minute and expected me to drop things, and she would turn up unannounced; this behaviour illuminated the fact that my consideration was never reciprocated. I am the kind of friend you can rely on at the last moment and I will do my best to be there for you with little notice, but I had reached a point in my life where I was only willing to do that for people who prioritised me in the same way. When you set boundaries, you should only ever set consequences that you fully intend to follow through on, otherwise it becomes an empty threat and, more often than not, the other person will respect your boundaries even less. Obviously, setting a consequence where the relationship is over is a last resort. In the beginning, you can set more minimal consequences, like I will leave without you if you are more than twenty minutes late, but after the seventh time, it needed to be a more serious consequence. My time has become more precious with age, so treating her time as more important than mine became a red line.

BAD FRIEND

Sometimes distance is the answer

I don't like making all-or-nothing decisions unless I have to because humans are complicated. Within friendships, this means there must be a middle ground that isn't just ending the friendship and that middle ground is creating more distance. We all have instances where we have drifted from a friend naturally but what we discuss less is when you make a conscious decision to create more space between you. A few years out of university, one of my best friends and I were spending so much time together that it felt like we had lost our boundaries. We had started fighting endlessly. She viewed it as us bickering like sisters and didn't see an issue with it, but I don't bicker with my sister and if my sister started doing this, I would set boundaries with her too. There was a complacency growing in our friendship where she always expected me to be there, took my time for granted and would turn up hours late and decide on my behalf that I didn't mind. The final time was when I wanted to book a new restaurant opening but you had to pay upfront for the table. I told her that it was expensive and that if I booked it, she had to commit to it a few months in advance and couldn't cancel. I asked her three times to check that she had put it in the diary to avoid our usual pattern of her forgetting about our plans. She agreed and, in fact, told me to stop nagging her. The week arrived and I got a text from her asking whether I wanted to hang out. She had forgotten we had already made plans and I told her that it was starting to become annoying how unreliable she was because if asking three times for her to put it in her diary couldn't guarantee she would follow through, I didn't know what else I could do. She took issue with the word 'unreliable' and I wouldn't apologise for it. At this rate, she was so unreliable and now she'd left me in the position of having paid for a table for two with no one else to come with me. I told her I needed some space and she said that if I took space from the friendship, it was over. That was her choice. I reassured her that I still wanted to be friends but that we had been spending too much time together and with more distance, I was hoping we could have more boundaries and return to respecting our relationship. Her response was that she doesn't take breaks from friendship and so we stopped being friends. We have seen each other a few times since our friendship ended – we have polite conversations and she reached out to check I was OK when my engagement ended – but part of me has always wished she could have at least given the distance option a try.

When it is time to call it

The best way to figure out whether you should end a friendship is to do something in life coaching that we call a 'future pace'. Close your eyes and imagine your life in a year. Picture where you are, how you are feeling, what is happening and then imagine telling your friend about something good going on in your life and then imagine telling them something bad. See how they respond, notice how you feel in the moment. Then I want you to imagine something different. Go into a year from now and imagine your life without them. Picture your birthday without them in attendance; are they missed? How did you feel about ending the friendship? Did it feel like the right call even if it was a hard conversation? When you imagine your future, is your life better with or without them? This will give you a clue as to what the right decision is.

Do you have more or less energy after you see them? Some people use the analogy of radiators vs. drains. Radiators give us energy whereas drains suck it out. I share that with the caveat that I don't think people are inherently radiators or drains; a radiator to one person can be a drain to another. In terms of energy, I started noticing this most when I was writing my first book. My day was largely consumed with writing and because I work alone, I would schedule lunches with friends. Some days, I would come back from lunch and be fuelled with creativity and inspiration, and some days I would come back and want to have a nap. I started noticing that it was much less to do with what I was eating at lunch, or whether I'd slept the night before, and much more to do with the company I was keeping. Being around the right people should give you energy.

Of course, there are times when friendship hits a rough patch and there can be periods where you have to accept that your friend is in a bad headspace or in a particularly miserable mood. In these instances, look at the friendship from a big-picture lens and ask yourself if the good outweighs the bad. Last year, I went on holiday with a friend and from the moment we landed, she was in an awful mood. To be honest, she was even in a bad mood in the airport and we'd run out of things to say before we had even got on the plane. I asked her what was wrong and whether she wanted to talk about it and she said she was just tired but a few days into the trip, nothing had changed. I left the holiday feeling disheartened that the travels we had been looking forward to for months ended up feeling like walking on eggshells for a week, but this was one trip out of a decade-long friendship. I zoomed out, looked at our friendship as a whole and gave her the benefit of the doubt that maybe she was going through something she wasn't ready to talk about yet. The next time we went for dinner, she was back to her usual self and we stayed until the restaurant closed, catching up, and the friend I knew had returned. To this day, I don't know what was different about that trip but I'm glad now that I didn't end a friendship over one bad encounter. Ending a friendship should be a considered decision. If someone has been there for you for a decent length of time and you valued the friendship at some point in your life, that person deserves to be given a few chances. When it becomes a prolonged problem though, you have to do the hard thing. If every time that person calls, you look at your phone with dread, that friendship is already over. If you don't look forward to seeing a person, or hesitate over whether you can cancel, then you already want out. If you find that you always leave your encounters feeling worse about yourself, then that's a clear warning. More times than not, when someone asks if they should end a friendship, they already know the answer. What they are actually hesitating over is doing the deed. This is where you must be honest with yourself. Remember it is also not fair to them to maintain a friendship where you are dreading time together and resenting their company. Liberate them as well as yourself!

IS IT EVER ACCEPTABLE TO GHOST A FRIEND?

I'm going to be honest with you. As I write this chapter, there is a friend I have not replied to because I know we need to have a hard conversation that might end in a breakup, and so I am avoiding it. I am telling you this because it's important you know that while there is a right way of doing things, it doesn't always mean I do the right thing and even if I do, it doesn't mean I find it easy. I have been avoiding it because I'm scared. I don't want this friendship to end, I just want to have an important conversation about something that really hurt me, but I know from experience that sometimes what is only meant to be a discussion results in a decision to end the friendship. It is that fear that sometimes makes us choose the easier option of avoiding the conversation, and we must not do that. We are allowed to take our time and to pause on replying to a text to choose the correct words, but we must eventually say something. In this case, I'm taking my time to decide how I want to go about the conversation but I know that this weekend, when my mind isn't focused on this book, I am going to sit down, say what

IS IT EVER ACCEPTABLE TO GHOST A FRIEND?

needs to be said and hope that the fallout won't result in the end of a friendship.

Let's start with being clear in defining ghosting. There are times when a friendship ends without the need for a conversation. Sometimes you drift apart and sometimes you pull away and the other person does too. In these situations, it is mutual. It would be a little odd to initiate contact with someone you haven't spoken to in months only to tell them that you don't want to be friends. In my book, that would be unnecessarily unkind. You've already drifted, both parties are equally satisfied with either the end of the friendship or increased distance. Ghosting is when one person is left in the dark, often seeking a conversation, and the other is intentionally avoiding them and has used silence to convey the message. If you ask the person who is ghosting, they always have a reason and know why, while the person who is being ghosted has no clue. Ghosting is symptomatic of someone who has bad communication in general. As personal as it feels, it is not about you. It is about their inability to communicate and it is cowardly. If a friend has ghosted you, it won't be the first time they have done this to a person, and unless they do work to change their avoidance, it won't be the last. Most importantly, if a friend ghosts you, it will likely not be the only example of poor communication within your friendship.

In recent years, ghosting has seemingly become the default way to end a friendship, since we are not equipped with the language we need to have difficult conversations. We can all agree that ghosting is unacceptable in your dating life – whether you do it yourself or not, we know it is wrong. If we find it unacceptable to do that to a person who we have only

GHOSTING IS SYMPTOMATIC OF SOMEONE WHO HAS BAD COMMUNICATION IN GENERAL. AS PERSONAL AS IT FEELS, IT IS NOT ABOUT YOU. IT IS ABOUT THEIR INABILITY TO COMMUNICATE AND IT IS COWARDLY. IF A FRIEND HAS GHOSTED YOU, IT WON'T BE THE FIRST TIME THEY HAVE DONE THIS TO A PERSON, AND UNLESS THEY DO WORK TO CHANGE THEIR AVOIDANCE, IT WON'T BE THE LAST.

been on a few dates with, why do we think it's acceptable for long-term friendship? I believe ghosting is the most common way to end a friendship because we have not normalised breaking up with friends. Most people are in monogamous romantic relationships, so in order to date a new person, you need to end it with the one you are with. That doesn't happen in friendship. You can have as many friendships as you want to, so if you are choosing to end it, it often feels more personal. Even Michelle Obama said that slow ghosting is the way to go when you no longer want to be friends. She admitted that she did this when she moved to the White House. She talks about how life is like climbing a mountain and how your friends can join you on that journey but that some people 'lost oxygen [and] couldn't make the climb'.[1] While I agree that some people are not always going to be there for the whole journey, I strongly disagree when it comes to how she chose to end it. People slowly ghost and then go to their other friends, moaning, 'Urgh, why won't they get the message?' They won't get the message because you've not sent it! You're expecting them to read into your behaviour and that's immature. Your friend deserves better. Liz Pryor writes, in *What Did I Do Wrong?*, 'Women's love and commitment to one another is abounding, yet when friendships end, we show little to no respect or honor for that which has enriched, supported and even prolonged our lives.'[2] I know it's scary to have the conversation, and if you tend to avoid conflict this will feel really intimidating, but I'm saying this less as a life coach, and much more as a person who has struggled to have this conversation too. I am not preaching to you about how it should be done; I'm advocating for a change in

PEOPLE SLOWLY GHOST AND THEN GO TO THEIR OTHER FRIENDS, MOANING, 'URGH, WHY WON'T THEY GET THE MESSAGE?' THEY WON'T GET THE MESSAGE BECAUSE YOU'VE NOT SENT IT!

IS IT EVER ACCEPTABLE TO GHOST A FRIEND?

friendships that I would like to see. I'm asking you to be part of the change where we see friendships as valid relationships that deserve closure and clarity. We need to rewrite the narrative that ghosting friends, or slow ghosting, is ever acceptable.

Are they actually ghosting me?

The hard part about ghosting is the uncertainty. Are they ignoring my texts intentionally or did they just miss it? The reason ghosting is hard to decipher is that while we all live with phones in our hand, we have also all had instances of accidentally missing a text. Ghosting becomes complicated because the intention someone has exists in their head and we are not mind-readers. The unknown leaves room for someone to project their own reasons which opens us up to more miscommunication. Whenever I bring up the conversation of ghosting, I have people bringing up abusive situations as a reason to ghost. If there is yelling, screaming or name-calling, you still don't need to ghost. All it requires is a firm boundary.

> I will not be spoken to like this and this conversation is over.

If communication persists when you have asked for it to stop, then you can end the relationship.

> I have asked you to stop and because you haven't, I will be walking away/blocking you.

When I have been in situations like this, it has made me feel more powerful to set my boundaries and determine the standard by which I am treated. In situations where you are in harm's way, do what you need to do to get to safety – it is not my right to tell you what that is.

It is better to be told than to be left guessing

Ghosting is cruel because it leaves one party confused. If they have ever meant anything to you, they deserve that closure. Often when people ghost, they tell themselves that it is the kinder thing to do in order to make themselves feel better about it, but the truth is that most people ghost because they are scared and unable to have a difficult conversation. Caving to the fear of a difficult conversation as opposed to facing it directly means you are making the cowardly decision. Yes, it is uncomfortable. Yes, it is scary. But it is still worth the discomfort to communicate to your friend how you would like to be communicated with. If you want healthy, communicative friendships then it starts with you and you need to treat them how you want to be treated. If you have ever been ghosted, you will know how awful the pain is and that it is worsened by uncertainty and confusion. We need to lower the bar and stop expecting to have perfect conversations because this is what leads us to running away from the conversation. Be scared when you do it. Let it be messy. A clumsy conversation is still better than no conversation at all.

IS IT EVER ACCEPTABLE TO GHOST A FRIEND?

What if you are the one being ghosted?

It takes me quite a while to notice when I am being ghosted because in general, I am confident in my friendships unless someone gives me a reason not to be. My life is also too full to spend it tracking who has or hasn't replied to me. If someone doesn't reply to my message and I need to ask them something, I will often send another text with what I need to say. Most of my texts aren't of huge importance, so if a friend misses a 'how are you?' text and then I get asked to an event and I would like to invite them, I will just send:

> Hey! I got a plus-one at an event next week? Do you want to come? Xx

Within my friendships, this is quite normal, and I don't need an apology about the missed 'how are you?' because I won't have even realised until I opened up the texts again. Similarly, if you miss my call, I don't need a return call; I'll just ring you when I next want to talk to you. In this regard, I am quite low maintenance and so when a friend was ignoring my DMs and hoping I would notice, I didn't for months. I was replying to her Instagram stories and in her head she wasn't responding, but in my head they didn't need a response. It was only when she sent me a text telling me why she was upset with me a few months later, explaining why she hadn't been replying to me, that I noticed. The lesson in this is that you should tell people when you are upset because they might not know.

But if you think a friend is ghosting you, it is best to confront them.

BAD FRIEND

> Hey! We haven't hung out in a while, how are you doing? I am wondering if there is something up? X

> Hey! I miss you. I have noticed some distance and that our relationship has changed. Is there anything you would like to talk about? If I've done something, I would like to know!

> Hey! I haven't heard back from you in a while and I wanted to check in. I really value this friendship and if something is bothering you, I would love to talk about what is going on?

Ultimately, if they still don't reply, you have to accept that you can't make someone care. Sometimes when you ask a friend what is wrong, they will tell you it's nothing but continue to act differently. In those situations, you can't force someone to open up if they don't want to. Most of the time, it is because your friend is conflict avoidant – they are too scared to get into a proper conversation so they will do whatever they can to avoid it. People who are conflict avoidant are also communication avoidant. You can ask them a second time but ultimately, to fix a relationship, you need both people to make an active effort to change things. If someone wants to ignore the problem, it is hard to force them into a conversation they don't want to have. You should only want to be friends with people who will communicate with you and give you the opportunity to apologise and correct your behaviour when you misstep. People mess up in friendships; we need to give our friends enough time to give them a chance to improve.

PEOPLE WHO
ARE CONFLICT
AVOIDANT ARE ALSO
COMMUNICATION
AVOIDANT.

HOW DO I TELL THEM IT IS OVER?

If we can agree that ghosting is not the way to go, what's the alternative? The answer: having a direct conversation about how your relationship has changed. I believe that if you've had any respect for your friendship, you should also show respect in the ending. After all, you cannot ask for communication if your own communication is lacking. Kate Leaver writes:

> Because we do not have the tools to properly deal with the friendship breakup, we fumble along on our own. We haven't agreed upon a tactful or proper way to do it, so everybody's just bloody going for it in whatever way they can. That has resulted, if you ask me, in an epidemic of poorly executed friendship breakups. People are getting away with all sorts of behaviour that we've already vetoed in a romantic breakup scenario.[1]

Because we so rarely discuss friendship breakups, even the idea of having the conversation can be a foreign one and

IF YOU'VE HAD ANY RESPECT FOR YOUR FRIENDSHIP, YOU SHOULD ALSO SHOW RESPECT IN THE ENDING.

sometimes the issue can be a very practical one of lacking the language around it. In romantic relationships, we have ready-made phrases that get doled out, whether it's 'it's not you, it's me' or 'I just don't feel a spark'. With this friendship language absent, it can be hard to know which word to put in front of another in order to express what you mean.

A decision vs. a discussion

There will be times you will be unsure whether you want to end the friendship but you know that a certain issue needs to be discussed. Sometimes in discussing the issue, the friendship can end, either because of how someone reacts or subsequent situations, but if you are entering a conversation having already made the decision that the friendship is over, then you need to make that clear in the communication. If you have made your mind up and you are clear that you want the friendship to end, then also be clear that this is not a discussion you are trying to initiate, it is a decision. When you are communicating the decision, there might be issues that arise because the other person is seeking understanding and closure but it is not a debate about whether you are ending the friendship or not. Out of respect for our prior relationship, I will always do my best to give them as much information as possible without delivering anything unnecessarily hurtful, but I draw the line at rehashing past arguments. Let past issues lie because if a friendship is not continuing then they don't need to be resolved. Use phrases that close the conversation instead of opening things back up.

HOW DO I TELL THEM IT IS OVER?

> You are allowed to think that.

> It's a shame you feel that way.

> This is why I am saying the friendship is no longer working.

When I communicate the decision, I do my best to also communicate my thanks and gratitude for our friendship and wish them the best for the future. I have been through enough friendship breakups to know though that while this is the optimal way to do it, what would ideally happen doesn't always come to fruition. In these instances, you are only in control of your words and your behaviour. I always keep at the forefront of my mind that I want to leave the conversation with my head held high, proud of how I behaved and knowing that my side of the street is clean.

You do not need to be brutally honest

This is not the time or place to tell your now ex-friend every single thing they did wrong and what you hate about them. This is going to cause unnecessary hurt and you have to ask yourself if it would serve any purpose. If you already want to end the friendship, then you don't need to insult their character. In these moments, it's important to understand that just because you think something about a person doesn't mean it is a fact. You can think they are rude but there will be someone in the world who won't find them rude. You can think they are arrogant and someone in the world will perceive

IF YOU ALREADY WANT TO END THE FRIENDSHIP, THEN YOU DON'T NEED TO INSULT THEIR CHARACTER. IN THESE MOMENTS, IT'S IMPORTANT TO UNDERSTAND THAT JUST BECAUSE YOU THINK SOMETHING ABOUT A PERSON DOESN'T MEAN IT IS A FACT.

them as simply confident. These words are all subjective and throwing names and insults means ending the friendship with more animosity than there needs to be. Stick to the facts and remove the stories. Here's the difference.

FACT: You borrowed money and never paid me back.

STORY: You took advantage of me financially and didn't care about how it affected me.

You can give them the reason for the friendship ending without adding unnecessary detail.

REASON: I can no longer trust you and trust is important to me in friendship.

UNNECESSARY DETAIL: When you lied to me about the group holiday I wasn't invited on, I stopped trusting you and then you told our mutual friends information about my sex life that was none of their business.

The problem when you give unnecessary information is that it will put the other person in the position to defend themselves and that's when it turns into a discussion. They will start justifying why they did it or insisting that they didn't do it and that means you won't have the finality you want in choosing the end of the friendship.

How do you say it?

When doctors learn how to tell a loved one that the patient has died, they are told they must say the words 'they are dead' or 'they have passed away'. Those words are needed for clarity and so in the face of shock, they have no hope left. While the context is different, I believe the same goes for every hard conversation. Clarity is kindness, and you need to actually say in some form or other that you no longer want to be friends. In a world where women are so rarely given permission to be direct, this can seem harsh, unkind and blunt, but if we want to live in a world where we are able to be as direct as men are allowed to be, then we need to be part of the change. Depending on the state of the friendship and logistics like where they live, you can decide for yourself whether this is a conversation best done over text, over the phone or in person. I am not the kind of person who demonises written communication because I think sometimes, especially in an ending, it leads to more productive conversations as the ability to take space between replies can lead to kinder responses. In terms of the actual words, everyone has their own style. The example text messages are included in order to help you create your own versions but it is important that you personalise each message to the person you are talking to, whether it's including the specific fight that caused an issue (e.g. 'you were really hurtful when you brought up my difficult relationship with my mum during our fight') or being specific in thanking them for support at a particular time in your life (e.g. 'I couldn't have got through the pandemic without our friendship'). Boundaries get a lot of stick online for being cold

HOW DO I TELL THEM IT IS OVER?

and detached with people making jokes about how it sounds like professional language with a 'I will get back to you in five to seven working days' vibe, but that's because it's hard to give examples with the personal part included. The examples below demonstrate that endings can come in various forms and it can be messy at times.

> Hey! I know I've been quite distant for the last few months and I'm sorry for that. I didn't know how to say this so I pulled away and that wasn't right. I have decided this friendship isn't working any more because it seems like our points of view on the world are too different. I found our conversation in the park about diet culture really difficult and the lack of care when I voiced my upset really impacted my ability to trust you. At this point in my life, I am sensitive around this topic due to my eating disorder and I hope you can understand, I need to prioritise my recovery. Thank you so much for all our years of friendship, you really supported me through some tough years in school and I will particularly love our memories from living together. Take care of yourself and I'll be rooting for you from afar! Xx

> Hey! Thank you for your message, unfortunately I will be unable to attend your birthday as there were a few things that happened last time we hung out that didn't sit right with me. It made me realise we don't have the friendship we used to and I think it's best we just end the friendship now before it gets more hurtful. I understand you are going through a lot in your life but it is not OK how you

> spoke to me. Since you have refused to apologise or take responsibility for what happened, I can't move on or pretend like it didn't happen. I really appreciate the times when you have been there for me, especially while my mum was ill and I will always be grateful for your support during that period. I hope you have the best time on your birthday and best of luck for the future! Xx

> Hey! I am ready to talk now. I had to take space in the middle of our last conversation because it felt like the discussion was becoming unproductive. Some of the things you mentioned really caught me off-guard and I can't be friends with someone who believes I am that kind of person. I believe friendship includes giving someone grace, and in these instances you have assumed the worst of me and not given me the chance to explain. It felt unkind and I am hurt that you didn't give me the opportunity to even present my side of the story. This friendship is not working for me any more. I appreciate you being there for me in the past and take care. Xx

Do it scared

Communicating in this way will be new and different and can be terrifying. I remember there were times when I would send a text like this and then throw my phone across the room or put it on flight mode. If you keep waiting for the right moment, you will never have the conversation. It's not about the right moment, it's about the right intention. In life coaching we talk about how you have your comfort zone, your stretch zone and then your panic zone. These conversations are putting you into your stretch zone. It is going to be scary because you are doing something new, but just as you don't have to do it perfectly, you can do it scared. You don't need to wait for the fear to pass, and the fear doesn't mean you shouldn't do it. Feeling scared doesn't mean you are doing the wrong thing, it is just your brain trying to protect you from the potential rejection, hurt and heartbreak. Fear is not a reason to stay in a friendship. Elizabeth Gilbert often talks about letting fear be in the car, just not in the driver's seat.[2] You are allowed to feel scared; what you mustn't do is let your fear be the thing that makes the decisions. Embrace the uncomfortable conversations and the good news is, the more you do it, the easier it gets.

FEAR IS NOT A REASON TO STAY IN A FRIENDSHIP.

THE AFTERMATH OF FRIENDSHIP BREAKUPS

WHY DO I FEEL SO GUILTY?

The first time my life coach, Michelle Zelli, suggested consciously ending a friendship, my response was 'I can't do that'. When I went back over the friendship over the last decade, I remembered how my friend had been there for me when I was hospitalised and even threw a surprise party on my return. She supported me through my PTSD and my brain was filled with examples of how she'd been such a good friend to me for so long. The problem was that the friend I remember was not the friend I knew today. The friend I knew today had been neglecting our friendship for months. She would ring me weekly with a new work crisis, calling me as she left the office and venting about the problem on her walk home, only for her to arrive home just as it was time to ask about me. 'I know we haven't spoken about you but I just got in so can I call you back tomorrow?' she would say. That call wouldn't come, until the following week when a new work crisis would occur. This continued for months, and at some point I started feeling used. I had become her free life coach, or actually, her business coach, but it felt like that was all I was good for. I confronted her about it a few times and each time she acknowledged how rubbish she had been but made no effort to change her behaviour. Eventually, I grew tired and wanted to call it quits. Even though I knew we didn't have the same friendship we used to, I still felt guilty about the idea of ending it.

It felt like I owed her for our shared past. I shared the guilt with Michelle, explaining that I felt I was indebted to my friend for the years of friendship she had given me and she rebutted with, 'But for all that time she was an amazing friend to you, you were an amazing friend to her, so surely you're equal?' That was true but my self-esteem wasn't where it is today. I was so focused on being a good friend, I never questioned whether she had been a good friend to me. I hadn't just been a good friend to her, I had been a best friend. I had been the kind of best friend that dropped everything for her multiple times in my life and while I wouldn't define that as good friendship now, I often prioritised her to the detriment of myself. The guilt still lingered though. 'Don't I still owe her?' Michelle acquiesced: 'OK, if you owe her, how much time do you owe her? Weeks, months or years? How much does all that friendship equate to in time?' That hit me where I needed it to. How is it fair to her if I stay in a friendship simply out of feeling indebted? Our friendship was not a debt that needed to be repaid because I had paid in my reciprocation at the time. After all, do you think you should stay friends with someone because you feel sorry for her? It's sad when a friendship isn't the same as it used to be but hanging on to memories in the hope that the friendship will return to its previous state is an illusion. Emotions are healthy but making decisions based on that emotion is not.

I WAS SO FOCUSED ON BEING A GOOD FRIEND, I NEVER QUESTIONED WHETHER SHE HAD BEEN A GOOD FRIEND TO ME.

Why do we stay?

Research by Laura Eramian and Peter Mallory across studies from 2016 to 2024 has shown there are five top reasons why people will stay in touch with difficult friends: they would rather tolerate an imperfect friendship than be seen as someone who cuts people off, they see petty disagreements with friends as an opportunity to work on self-awareness, they've been friends for so long and their lives are too entangled, they see intrinsic value in being challenged by a difficult friend, and their own stubbornness to make the friendship work.[1] When you have invested so much time in a person and put the energy into building a connection, you might feel a resistance to ending the friendship as it will have all been a 'waste of time'. This leads to deciding to stick it out, pouring in more time and energy in the hope it can fix it. This is known as the sunk-cost fallacy – our reluctance to tap out of something we have poured time and energy into leads to investing even more in the hope of making our investment worth it. There is a tipping point where the maintenance you are spending on car repairs outweighs calling it quits and just getting a new car. Ending a friendship does not mean the time and energy invested was a waste. You benefit from the time you were friends and you benefit from the learnings through the ending. Combat this mentality by remembering that the longer you delay the breakup, the more the sunk cost. It is never going to get easier, and a year 'wasted' in a friendship is better than two years. We need to remember that if we stay, we are not doing them a favour either. It's kinder to them to not fake a friendship. The reason guilt and shame arise is

IT'S SAD WHEN A FRIENDSHIP ISN'T THE SAME AS IT USED TO BE BUT HANGING ON TO MEMORIES IN THE HOPE THAT THE FRIENDSHIP WILL RETURN TO ITS PREVIOUS STATE IS AN ILLUSION.

because, as women, we are taught to endure. We are taught to put everyone else first and forget about our own needs. Think about how the women most praised in society are those who are givers. The issue is if you are a giver and you have no boundaries, you will give so much you will have nothing else left. You will give until you are drained. Empathy without boundaries is unhealthy.

Appropriate and inappropriate guilt

Every emotion exists to teach us something. For example, anger lets us know when our boundaries are crossed. The purpose of guilt is for our unconscious mind to flag when we are not behaving according to our morals and values. For example, if you are stressed and you snap at a friend because you are too busy, you should feel bad. When I went through my first long-term relationship breakup I had an immense feeling of guilt. I had a realisation that I had never truly been there for any of my friends in a breakup, or at least, not in the way that they had shown up for me. The guilt propelled me to reach out and acknowledge it with each of them. Some accepted the apology, some insisted that I actually had been there for them and some truly didn't remember. Guilt will arise to say 'Hey! Don't behave like that', and that would be appropriate guilt. When you apologise, the guilt subsides. If you don't listen to the guilt and instead listen to your ego, that guilt will likely sit there for longer and you might express that guilt internally by being mean to yourself or resorting to numbing strategies like getting drunk to suppress the bad feeling. That guilt exists to encourage you to do better and

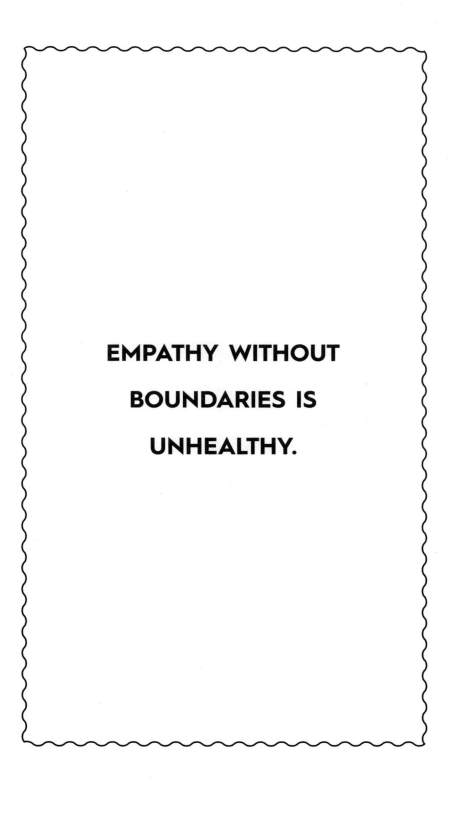

therefore it is the appropriate emotion. Inappropriate guilt is when you haven't done something wrong but you feel like you have, and this is the case when it comes to friendship breakups. You have not done anything wrong by ending a friendship. The guilt I felt above when ending the friendship was inappropriate. I was doing both of us a service by admitting what we both knew. One way to let inappropriate guilt go is to say it out loud, as it helps it to leave your body. It helps move the emotion and I will often do this alongside a swiping motion with my hands. Put the heel of your palms against each other with your fingers pointing opposite ways and then brush your hands against each other in opposite directions until your fingertips brush as you repeat the word 'guilt'. We need to teach ourselves that we don't need to feel bad if we haven't done anything bad.

Shame around putting yourself first

Shame is a derivative of guilt and if you do not have strong self-esteem in place, guilt can spiral into shame. The difference between guilt and shame is that guilt is about your behaviour and shame is about you. Guilt says, 'I did a bad thing'; shame says, 'I am a bad person.' If you have ended a friendship and now believe you are a bad person for doing so, this is because it is tapping into an old wound – you *already* considered yourself a bad person and that feeling is reinforced. It can be helpful to look back into your past and recall the first time you felt like or were told you were a bad person. Recall the specific age – it will likely be before the age of seven, as these early years are most critical for development – and float into your body at the time. Hear what you were hearing through your ears at the time, remember what you were feeling and then speak to that part of you. What did that little child need to hear from you? Did they need to hear that they are loved? Did they need to hear that they are a good person? Let them know that they can let all guilt and shame go. Tell them they are good enough as they are. Heal that older part of you and the current pain of shame should help relieve itself.

HOW DO I STOP REGRETTING WE EVER MET?

Sometimes a friendship can break so hard that you wish there was an 'undo' button. I've had this feeling once and I hope it never happens again. I wish I could rewind to the moment we met and choose to talk to someone else instead. The devastation they created was not worth the time we shared. The friendship was not worth the friendship breakup. I now worry about the secrets they know and I've even declined an event or two because I know they will be there. It's strange how the friendship you end up regretting the most, sometimes doesn't make sense. It's not always your longest-standing or oldest friend, it can be the friendship ending with a lack of closure or confusion that means your brain is unable to let it go. Our brains are meaning-making machines and when we cannot complete a story, we can get stuck in a loop and find it hard to close that chapter. In the one friendship I regret, my friend accused me of things I had never done and then declared that I was a bad person. It felt like she was projecting onto me because no matter how much I insisted that I had never done what she was accusing me of, she wouldn't believe me. She had lumped me in a category of people and it felt like I was paying for the sins of someone else. The friendship stings even though, weirdly, it lasted less than a year. It was intense in its creation and it was also intense in its burnout.

Let them think what they want about you

This friendship was the ultimate lesson in realising you cannot control your reputation, and if people want to believe bad things about you, they will. She would go on to spread rumours about me and tell many people in our industry to not work with me and the part that devastated me most was that the lie she had created was about a part of myself that I'm very proud of. I know I have good morals; I pride myself on being a good person who has never gone out of their way to hurt another, and the rumour she was spreading was about me being vengeful and vindictive. This ex-friend accused me of seeking to ruin people's careers and wanting to get people cancelled. This couldn't be further from the truth. I have always believed that cancel culture just leads to more shame and people not learning and growing. I told her this and even showed her pages in my previous books where I talk about how cancel culture leads us all to becoming less forgiving and we need to make room for humans to fuck up. But despite the evidence, she didn't want to hear it. It left me feeling so deeply misunderstood by someone who I thought knew me. Her perception of me was entirely wrong. Stop explaining yourself to someone who is determined to misunderstand you. If someone doesn't want to hear it, you can't force them to listen, and in that friendship breakup I had to accept that it was not my job to change her mind. The only solace I found is that I believe any person who has actually interacted with me will know it's false because it's just not the person I am. I refuse to be held accountable for something I did not do and I will not apologise because my apology would be fake.

Sometimes people choose to believe the story that you aren't who you say you are because it's more interesting. As they say, never let the truth get in the way of a good story. I had to make peace with the fact that I might be the villain in someone else's story and they are allowed to have their perception. While I had to learn this lesson the hard way, it has paid dividends for the rest of my life. I am able to be more unfiltered online because I am less precious about my reputation, I have more space in my brain and heart because I don't try to control what people think of me any more and, as a result, I am so much freer. Living your life according to other people's opinions is a straitjacket. It confines you because you are deciding your life around something you can't control. Let go of their opinions by doing what you want and realising that the world does not stop.

I know we all want a quick fix in order to stop caring what people think, but the truth is that realisation and empowerment come after taking action, not before. What would a person who didn't care about other people's opinions do? Go do that and – no matter how you feel – ta-da, you are that person because you have done it. Now rinse and repeat! Keep going until you can look back on your life and see all you have accomplished without the weight of worrying about being judged or misunderstood. Remember, even if you do

STOP EXPLAINING YOURSELF TO SOMEONE WHO IS DETERMINED TO MISUNDERSTAND YOU.

everything right, there will be someone in the world that will believe you have done something wrong. You can't control their narrative about you and they are allowed to have their own narrative. There is beauty in the sentence 'You are allowed to think that.'

Transform regret into learnings

Sometimes we can only learn from experiencing and in friendship, unfortunately, that means we can only learn from having loved and lost. Just because a friendship ends doesn't mean it was a failure. Just because your love didn't last doesn't mean it wasn't true. When we wish away the friendship, we are also wishing away the opportunities for growing, evolving and doing better next time. I credit so much of why I am a good friend now to having done it the wrong way in the past. We all make mistakes. To replace the regret with learnings, there are a few lists you can create. The lists become reminders whenever that feeling of regret churns in your stomach; they give you something physical to read and reread to help you let it go. They are also something you can return to and reflect on how much you have grown within friendship.

- **Every reason why you chose to end the friendship:** This list is helpful if you ever regret your decision. With time, we tend to either romanticise or demonise the person. This is a way to keep the reality in check because neither is helpful. Romanticising it just makes us feel worse about ourselves and demonising them means we aren't taking accountability for our part in it. Marisa G.

LIVING YOUR LIFE ACCORDING TO OTHER PEOPLE'S OPINIONS IS A STRAITJACKET.

Franco writes in *Platonic*, 'When endings are explosive, we rewrite the friendship, see it as perpetually defunct, our friend as treacherous all along, ourselves as naive parties',[1] but the truth is we are not naive parties and we played our own part in the dance. We want to preserve the memory and the truth of it as much as possible.

- **What were the warning signs you ignored or didn't want to see?** I do not like the concept of red flags because it can lead to victim-shaming and sometimes there were no warning signs. Sometimes things only become warning signs in hindsight and with the benefit of a pattern forming. It is normal to not take action on every single moment of concern because we are all human. To throw away every connection because of one concerning moment would mean we would never form relationships, but since hindsight is twenty-twenty, let's benefit from that. It is important you notice warning signs so that you can make a different decision next time.
- **What could you have done differently?** This list may include some things from the warning signs list but also can be detached from that. For example, one of the things I do differently now is to not bottle things up until they become larger issues. I had to learn this lesson a few times, but now I know that it is important to speak up sooner and that it's not as big a deal as my brain is telling me it is.

HOW DO I STOP REGRETTING WE EVER MET?

People leave their fingerprints on you

One thing I have come to accept is that every person who walks into your life, whether they stay or not, leaves fingerprints on you. It could be the way that you pronounce a word weirdly because it was a joke that you both shared, or a sensitivity around a certain word because that was the word thrown your way in the final argument. Interacting with humans involves risk: the risk of getting hurt, of heartbreak and yes, the risk of regret – but maybe there is something beautiful about the idea that we are the sum of all the people we have ever encountered? For better or for worse, we walk away from friendships different. We cannot go back to the person we were before, so wishing we could is not only a waste of time but a waste of the positive impacts. Even when a friendship has ended in destruction and devastation, it will have left positive imprints too, otherwise you would have never stayed friends. With one friendship, which still stings in my heart when I recall it, I really struggle to see the positive. At that time in my life, I was desperate for friends and I had let her in too quickly without knowing if she was trustworthy. I would end up telling her my deepest wound because she had experienced a similar situation in her own life, and that's what made the friendship breakup hurt the most. She had seen the most vulnerable part of me and yet she didn't stay. Then, one day, I twisted my ankle. It was in the middle of the pandemic when non-emergency issues were hard to address, leading to me not being able to walk on it for three weeks. I have always had issues with my ankles because I have surgery scars from when an intern sliced me there for a blood test as a baby (yes, a blood test!). I recalled the last time I'd had an issue, when my now ex-friend had got me to see her family physiotherapist. He'd jumped me to the top of the queue because of her family connections. I called him again, and even though we weren't friends any more I was prioritised in the same way. I would end up having continuous issues with my ankle and he was one of the few physios in the country that had been allowed to stay open because of his medical qualifications. As I walked out of our final appointment, it clicked: I might regret this friendship but I still got something positive out of it, even if it was just a physiotherapist.

INTERACTING WITH HUMANS INVOLVES RISK: THE RISK OF GETTING HURT, OF HEARTBREAK AND YES, THE RISK OF REGRET – BUT MAYBE THERE IS SOMETHING BEAUTIFUL ABOUT THE IDEA THAT WE ARE THE SUM OF ALL THE PEOPLE WE HAVE EVER ENCOUNTERED?

WILL I EVER STOP MISSING THEM?

Closure is an illusion. We grasp on to the hope that if we are able to attain it, the breakup will become easier but that hope for closure can easily become a fixation. We tell ourselves that we will stop missing them as soon as they let us know why the friendship ended/what we did wrong/the answer to all our questions. In reality, sometimes you don't get the answers and you still have to let go and move on anyway. When someone doesn't want to be in your life any more, that is all the closure you need. It's an illusion because even if they gave you all the reasons they don't want to be friends, who says they are right? Let's say they think you are boring; all that means is you are boring *to them*. They do not get to decide that you are boring to everyone. They are not the objective judge on boredom. Who even says they are a more accurate judge than yourself? Most of all, how does that help? You are now more hurt and, without personal development work, will likely carry around an insecurity wondering if you really are boring. Wouldn't it have been so much easier if you had just let it go? Closure is a lofty concept.

WHEN SOMEONE
DOESN'T WANT TO
BE IN YOUR LIFE ANY
MORE, THAT IS ALL THE
CLOSURE YOU NEED.

So is 'forgive and forget'. Instead, I believe in 'let it go and think about them less'. These are measurable. How we really stop missing them is by thinking about them less, letting go of what could have been, if you could have done anything differently, and accepting that the friendship ending is finite. Friendship loss gets easier over time but it's not the time passing that heals, but what you do with that time.

Give grief a home

We often talk about grief in the context of death, but grief is actually an emotion that arises around any loss. You can feel grief around a friendship breakup, a loss of a job or even the loss of a childhood you wish you had. In a study following fifteen women going through friendship breakups, it was found that alongside feelings of liberation and strength, feelings of grief and loss were common.[1] Because we belittle the importance of friendship, the instinct when going through friendship loss is to tell ourselves the way we feel is unimportant, that we are making a big deal about nothing and that we are being silly. Instead, you need to validate your grief. Let it hurt. Kate Leaver writes, 'Several people have told me it's more similar to a death than a break-up, because when you lose someone from your life completely, it's as though they cease to exist.'[2] That's because it *is* a death: a death of a friendship.

In order to process grief, detect where it is sitting in your body and then breathe deeply into it. It will likely get more painful as you breathe it in. Give it a colour and imagine your breath blowing it away. Breathe the coloured air out and picture it leaving your body. I often imagine the in breath as

CLOSURE IS A LOFTY CONCEPT. SO IS 'FORGIVE AND FORGET'. INSTEAD, I BELIEVE IN 'LET IT GO AND THINK ABOUT THEM LESS'.

a white cloud and the out breath as black soot. If you feel the urge to cry, let yourself. If you want to shake, jump up and down or scream, let yourself do that too. This is energy being released. It is moving through your body and because emotions are energy-in-motion and they physically sit in your body, the urge to move or shake or scream is the physical release that accompanies the emotional release. Keep going until it feels like the release is completed or you feel lighter and the emotion feels less intense.

What was told in friendship, stays in friendship

I have been on the receiving end of people sharing my secrets. It is a rubbish feeling and I have vowed never to be that person. I believe that if that information was told to you in confidence out of friendship, even if the friendship ends, that information is kept within the friendship. It is good boundary keeping to keep your word even if the friendship no longer exists. It is not even about the other person; it's more about the person I want to be. I want to be trusted and therefore, no matter what happens between us down the road or what you share about me, I will not engage in a tit-for-tat. I will not lower my standard of behaviour because you have decided to. When making yourself proud becomes one of your main drivers, you no longer act according to what is being done to you. In turn, it also benefits future friendships. Once you have been through a few friendship breakups, you might feel more vulnerable about opening up to the next person but if you behave like this, even in a karmic way, it gives me some reassurance that I should hopefully be treated with the same

IF INFORMATION WAS TOLD TO YOU IN CONFIDENCE OUT OF FRIENDSHIP, EVEN IF THE FRIENDSHIP ENDS, THAT INFORMATION IS KEPT WITHIN THE FRIENDSHIP.

respect. While it might feel satisfying in the moment to share someone's secrets, when you go home that night, you'll be left with a feeling of shame due to not acting in line with your morals and values and you don't want to create more emotions to sort through! Even when a friendship ends in disaster, you want it to be as clean as possible and while you can't control their behaviour, you can decide if you want to contribute to the mess. If you choose not to, you get to hold your head high and that's a win in my book.

Stop poking the wound

Thanks to social media, we have so many tools to make ourselves feel worse during the breakup and if we already miss them and we are feeling bad about ourselves, sometimes we poke the wound that already exists. I believe it's a version of self-harm. You already feel bad and so you stalk their page to make yourself feel worse. We rarely do this when we are happy; we do it when we feel bad because we want to confirm that we deserve to feel this way. This is why I encourage people to remove ex-friends from social media and block their accounts. It may not stop you stalking them but it will add more steps in between and more steps means more time to realise what you are doing and stop yourself. It increases the activation energy. Activation energy is a term that I learned in GCSE physics and refers to the amount of energy needed for an activation to start. In more basic terms, it is all the stuff you have to do before you actually do the thing. It's the commute to work and pulling out your laptop before actually starting work. When we don't want to do something, we want to increase the amount of activation energy and when we want to do something more, we want to decrease the amount of activation energy – for example, putting your clothes out the night before the gym so you have one less step to think about. In terms of stalking ex-friends, having to click the unblock button and actually search their name is more activation energy than them coming up on your feed when you were in the middle of a happy moment. When this happens, it is an intrusion into your day at a time you can't choose and that means that person will have more power over you because they are able to make you think about them, even when you weren't. You aren't blocking them for the happy, confident you who is unbothered by it but for the most vulnerable you, the one who is sad, bored, maybe even drunk and lonely at 2 a.m. See it as the strongest version of you protecting the most vulnerable part of you. By making it harder to stalk them, you have more time to think, *Is this what a person who loves themselves would do?* It doesn't matter if you are a person who loves themselves – behave like one anyway. If you want to become a person who loves themselves then act like it. Someone who loves themselves, or even likes themselves, would not cause themselves more pain. You are already going through enough pain through the loss of the friendship so why are you making it worse for yourself?

There is no end point

Unfortunately, much like a romantic breakup, the grief or sadness around a friendship loss doesn't just stop a few months after it happened. You can be years down the line and suddenly a memory pops into your head, tinged with sadness. It can happen especially around pivotal milestones and while time does make the pain easier and it becomes more bearable to live with, I'm not sure it ever fully goes away. When I turned thirty for example, I had a memory about my ex-best friend. We were in our early twenties at the time and it was on an evening when she was really sad about the guy she was seeing and I was trying to cheer her up. 'When we are thirty, we will both be in our dream relationships and we are going to go on a couple's holiday and make it all bougie because we will be proper adults with money. Business class, five-star hotels, all of it!' I said. She joined in: 'It's going to be a beach holiday and we'll stay in one of those villas in the middle of the sea!' We spent that entire evening planning our thirtieth birthday and when I turned thirty, we were in fact in our dream relationships (at least at the time I was!). We had both been successful in our jobs so could afford a luxury trip, but the one thing we hadn't foreseen was the fact that we would no longer be friends. I felt the pain of that as I was planning my thirtieth birthday, but part of healing a friendship breakup is also accepting where life is at the moment. I didn't want to let our lack of friendship ruin a dream of mine, so I made a plan to go by myself. I had spent years unlearning the idea of waiting for a man to live my dream life and I was certainly not going to let the absence of a friend be the reason I missed out so I booked a solo trip. I didn't stay in one of the villas in the sea, but I did go somewhere with a beach and I stayed in a five-star hotel and flew business class. Sometimes healing is doing the emotional work and sometimes healing looks like doing the practical thing of following through on what you talked about, just without the other person.

CAN YOU EVER GO BACK TO BEING FRIENDS AGAIN?

If Kylie Jenner and Jordyn Woods can reconcile and Paris Hilton and Nicole Richie can reunite, maybe there is hope for reigniting a lost friendship? I have only ever become friends again with one person that I had cut out of my life. She was my best friend when our friendship ended in our final year of university and she is now my best friend again, but our friendship looks very different now. I believe that the fact that we gave each other permission to be different people is the key to making a new friendship out of an old one.

We met on the first day of university. There was a natural comfort in our relationship, an ease where we could climb into each other's bed and watch *The* OC together. Even living together was effortless; she hated cooking, I hated cleaning and so I'd cook every night for us while she was on DJ duty and she would wash up. The worst fight we had was when she would drive me up the wall by playing 'Let Her Go' by Passenger twenty times in a row, never letting the song finish before rewinding it to her favourite part. But everything changed when she became friends with two people who had a mean streak. One of them often made unkind jokes and the other was judgemental under the guise of 'caring for you'. I truly believe that if you get into a toxic friendship group, it will infect even your healthy relationships. While we initially banded together and wouldn't let the other two get between us for most of it, there was a final fight that spelled the end of our friendship. She took their side and I felt abandoned. She texted me later, wanting to talk alone but I didn't trust that it wouldn't be passed back to the other two and I was too hurt to be able to face her. The truth was I was scared and the fear dictated my decisions that day. We wouldn't speak for the next two years until one of our mutual friends invited us both to her birthday party.

We were in the queue for a club when I got a tap on my shoulder with a gentle 'hey'. I was taken off guard and, according to her, I simply nodded back. I don't remember that part but I do remember feeling an overwhelming surge of love and the words 'I miss you' wanting to fly out of my mouth. I resisted it and instead went to the birthday girl and told her instead. 'I just saw Nicole, I miss her, should I tell her that?' She said I should so I walked up to her and did just that. We found a private room with some semblance of quiet, and ended up having a three-hour conversation with us both surfacing to discover the club closing and that all our friends had left. We spoke about every issue we hadn't had the maturity to understand at the time. I told her how I was so hurt that she had taken their side and she spoke about all the times she attempted to be there for me and I'd shut her out. There was hurt on both sides and with that distance, we were able to apologise and forgive each other for our respective parts in the demise of our friendship. After that conversation, it wasn't full steam ahead. We very much baby-stepped into a new relationship. It's now been eight years since that conversation in that club and we are now stronger than we have ever been. I am so grateful we found our way back, and yet it is also true that I know this only works in the minority of cases. Most friendships end for a reason and most doors should stay shut on their friendship.

How do I know if we should try again?

There are a number of factors why this friendship was able to recover. The most important thing is that both people wanted the friendship back. If I had said 'I miss you' and she'd told me to fuck off, it wouldn't have worked and I shouldn't have persevered to convince her. Unrequited love is not romantic and does not work in platonic relationships either. If someone says they don't want you in their life, let them go and respect that. The key to our healing was that conversation in the club. Creating a new friendship out of an old one is not an easy task but if both are willing to do the work, it can be a beautiful thing. You need to have accountability and apologies on both sides. Both people need to be willing to accept responsibility and have resolved to want to be better and do better. A lot of this comes with time, and distance helps too. Trying to bounce back too quickly after a breakup often means falling into the same pattern but the fact it had been two years meant we had both grown up and were capable of

UNREQUITED LOVE
IS NOT ROMANTIC
AND DOES NOT
WORK IN PLATONIC
RELATIONSHIPS EITHER.
IF SOMEONE SAYS THEY
DON'T WANT YOU IN
THEIR LIFE, LET THEM
GO AND RESPECT THAT.

doing things differently. In terms of restarting the friendship, give each other full permission to be different people. Instead of assuming we still knew each other, we recognised that a lot had changed in two years so our new friendship was a discovery of who we were now rather than an attachment to who we used to be. After all, we didn't want our old friendship back, we needed a new friendship where we felt safe and comfortable to voice issues that arise and not bury them until an explosion.

When you are becoming friends again, there will also be moments of awkwardness, whether it's mentioning a guy you were dating when you weren't friends or a significant life event that they had missed while you weren't speaking. Address them with as much care and kindness and do not avoid them. It can be something as simple as, 'Oh you might not know this, but last year, my dad actually got diagnosed with cancer and it was really hard for a bit but I'm managing it better than I was last year.' It doesn't need to be an issue, but if you avoid mentioning the years where you weren't friends, the awkwardness will grow. At times, it is even helpful to have conversations where you check in. This would happen with us naturally where I would say something in passing like, 'I feel like we are much better at communicating now.' In this way, we acknowledge the split and it's being able to marry that with also being able to talk about the pre-split times with as much fondness, like when I texted her to tell her that the guy I dated in my second year at university had just come up on my dating app. Every time one of those moments of awkwardness arises, it's a reminder that we both love each other so much and wanted each other back to such an extent that

IN TERMS OF RESTARTING THE FRIENDSHIP, GIVE EACH OTHER FULL PERMISSION TO BE DIFFERENT PEOPLE.

the conflict was no match for the love we felt for each other. We were both worth the awkwardness!

Sometimes the hurt is too deep and that's OK

Sometimes you can want a friendship back and the other person doesn't feel the same way and sometimes it can happen the other way around. Last year on my birthday, I had an ex-friend reach out. She acknowledged what she had done, apologised for her actions and said that she has regretted our friendship ending every day since and was wondering if there was a chance we could find our way back. It was a lovely message to receive, and while I understand why it came on my birthday, I wished it had come on any other day because as much as I appreciated it, I didn't want to start up a new friendship. One of the biggest signs that a friendship breakup was the right decision is when a person leaves your life and you don't notice their absence at all. In this case, I replied saying:

> Thank you for reaching out, I'm having a lovely birthday. I will always care about you and think about you often. I don't think I am able to rebuild the trust in our relationship but I appreciate the apology and I'm so glad to hear you are doing better! Take care xx

She then ended up reaching out again when she found out about my engagement and with more time having passed, there was a part of me that wanted to reconnect. I was heavily cautious though and I was also wary of leading her on. I wanted to meet up but I didn't want this to imply that

ONE OF THE BIGGEST SIGNS THAT A FRIENDSHIP BREAKUP WAS THE RIGHT DECISION IS WHEN A PERSON LEAVES YOUR LIFE AND YOU DON'T NOTICE THEIR ABSENCE AT ALL.

CAN YOU EVER GO BACK TO BEING FRIENDS AGAIN?

I wanted to go back to being friends, especially not at full force. I wanted to go for lunch without having to commit to anything further and so I made it clear in my reply:

> Hey! Thank you for reaching out. I really appreciate you checking in and I hope you are doing well. I'm not sure I am in the place to be friends again but if you are in London, it would be nice to go for lunch to just catch up?

I truly believe clarity is kindness and by being upfront, I could set expectations. She agreed and said there was no rush or pressure on her end and we ended up going for lunch. Who knows if it will be a one-off but if a friendship is lingering in your mind, feel free to contact them, even more than once. Life changes, people change and the headspace they are in changes too.

It's never too late for clarity

One of the greatest gifts that came from my engagement ending in such a public way is that four ex-friends of mine reached out. They had all seen it in the press and it became my little candle of hope that love always triumphs over hate and anger. Each friend was in a slightly different situation. Some reached out to check I was OK, some reached out saying they didn't want to be friends again but that there was no bad blood and some we were able to clear up any confusion. With one of the friends that reached out, we had had one issue after another and I wasn't even sure our friendship had ended until we were at the same event and we didn't acknowledge each other. She'd reached out to say she thought I was brave for sharing what I did and that it would help so many people. I saw her text as an opening to ask what had happened.

> Hey! Lovely to hear from you! Thank you for reaching out, I really appreciate that. I am not OK but I will be. I just want to say that I don't really know what happened with us but I appreciate the time we were friends and thank you for supporting me through a really tough time in my life, especially with everything I was going through with my family xx

She agreed and apologised for us drifting and that's when I realised that the story in my head probably didn't line up with hers.

> I hope it was drifting? It's OK if it wasn't. I know we disagreed on a few things but on my end, it was never personal. I was always a little unsure if I did something wrong but you were going through so many life changes so I wanted to respect your space. I know none of us were our best selves in the pandemic but I would love to be in a place where we could at least say hi at events. I really appreciate you reaching out, I know that can't have been easy!

She was honest, admitting that she also questioned if she had done something wrong, and said that she would love to be in that place too. Even without being friends again, the clarity was healing. The interaction I will never forget though was with the one that was clear she didn't want to be friends again. I had said I would love to mend and heal and

CAN YOU EVER GO BACK TO BEING FRIENDS AGAIN?

even though she wasn't open to that, she said she knew great things were coming my way. There was something about the enduring quality of love in that interaction that left me with such warmth. Even if some things had been said between us that she didn't think we could come back from, we still cared for each other. I was grateful for that and wanted to convey my thanks.

> I get that. I just want you to know that there is no bad blood. We carried each other through so much and we essentially grew up together so will always be grateful for our friendship and do look back on those memories with fondness and thank you for the time we were in each other's lives. Xx

I have such a deep respect for all the ex-friends who reached out in their own way and communicated with kindness. I know at this moment, I learned from them all. I hoped I would do the same if the situation was reversed but before this happened, I could not say for certain. Now that I've been on the receiving end of it, what I know for sure is that I would do the same for anyone who has ever been in my life.

WHAT IF OUR MUTUAL FRIENDS TAKE SIDES?

Should you break up with a friend because they've done something awful to your other friend? Should you take sides? When you go through a breakup and you have mutual friends, it's understandable to worry about whether this is going to affect your other relationships and if so how. The fear that you are going to be abandoned is real and it feels rubbish to even contemplate all the people you love choosing them over you. For this reason, I am of the belief that you shouldn't put them in that position either. I will never ask my friends to take sides – even if someone has done something horrible to me, it is not within my right to determine what is 'horrible' to another person. When I say this, people will often retort with the concept of loyalty. My mentality has always been that while I might be cautious around a person, I do not make friendship decisions based on what they have done to other people. It's not about loyalty. I believe that everyone must learn their own lessons in their own relationships in their own time, and sometimes a deciding factor for you won't be a deciding factor for someone else. Everyone has different

WHAT IF OUR MUTUAL FRIENDS TAKE SIDES?

boundaries and something that really bothers me might be a non-issue for someone else and we must respect that.

Inevitably though, even if no one takes sides, there will be times you will be left out, like when your ex-friend throws a party. I will always remember the FOMO (fear of missing out) I felt when all my friends attended my ex-friend's party after university and I had to watch it unfold on Snapchat. Worries filled my head about whether I would always be excluded and then I remembered that my ex-friend probably felt the same way. I had just thrown a housewarming party with all the same people and she hadn't been invited so those feelings were likely still raw for her. Being mutual friends with two people who don't get along isn't easy but with some good boundaries, you can toe the line of being impartial and not involving yourself in something that doesn't concern you.

Be secure enough in your decision to not need back-up

Friendship breakups get more complicated when we don't feel valid enough in our decision-making process. We get insecure and so we recruit our friends and their opinions to try to boost what we feel unsure about. This is where it gets messy, because you aren't just asking for an opinion, you are asking with an expectation that they will give you the answer you want to hear and that's when you are putting your mutual friends in a lose–lose situation. Similarly, if the person you are fighting with tries to recruit your mutuals, say to them,

> I'd prefer if we kept it between the two of us.

The moment anyone gets a team behind them, arguments escalate. If it's not one-on-one, it can feel like you are being ganged up on, and that leads to people being more defensive and to unproductive conversations. Even if you don't physically recruit them into the argument, using statements like 'and everyone else thinks so' or 'and Lauren agrees with me' are ways in which we try to bolster our argument. You don't need anyone to agree with you – if you believe it, that's enough. If you are hurt by the words someone says and no one else would be hurt by the same comment, your feelings are still valid and it's still important to communicate them. When we have had a childhood where our feelings were repeatedly undermined by statements like, 'you are making a big deal out of nothing', 'stop overreacting' or 'you are just being dramatic', we learn to use other people to make us not feel crazy and to confirm what we are feeling is actually real. We need to learn that how we feel is important, not because other people say so, but instead because we value ourselves and know that we deserve to be heard.

Let other people make their own friendship mistakes

One of my friendships ended shortly after a Mediterranean holiday with two women, Ren and Molly, who were best friends with each other. They had been best friends for years, and while we all had gone to school together, my friendship with them only came about much later, when I ended up at university with Molly. Within two days of being in Ibiza, Molly and Ren got into the worst fight they had ever had. It started when Molly said that she didn't want to be on medication for her mental health long term. Ren was going through a similar situation and therefore took this as a judgement. I didn't want to take a side, so I let them have it out, hoping it would come to a resolution. When it became obvious there was no end in sight and the blows started getting really low, I decided to step in and suggested they take a break before they said something they regretted. I was shocked that some of their comments were so cruel, especially around such a sensitive topic. I kept my opinions to myself but I would be lying if I said it didn't make me more cautious. There was a part of me that wanted to say to Molly that the way Ren was speaking to her wasn't OK, but then I realised that that was Molly's decision. I personally wouldn't have accepted my best friend speaking to me like that because my belief is that if someone says something out of anger, they were already thinking it. The anger just gave them the confidence to say it. In the moment, I realised that was my own issue, so I didn't say anything more. It took them two days and a few more arguments, but they resolved the fight. To this day, Molly and Ren are still best friends. Molly was OK with being spoken to that way, and I wasn't. It's not to say anyone was wrong or right. I wouldn't end my friendship with Ren over how she spoke to Molly but it was only a matter of time before it was my turn and that's when I set my boundary. Because of my upbringing, I am very sensitive to people being hurtful in conflict and it makes me lose trust and feel unsafe in the friendship. Molly might have greater resilience and the ability to bounce back better than I can. We can't judge other people's choices when we all have a different make-up; the same event will affect us differently.

BAD FRIEND

How to handle mutual events

If you share a friendship group, or even just a friend, there are going to be times when you have to be in the same room as ex-friends. And sometimes, the shoe will be on the other foot and you will be the one navigating ex-friends as the host. In this situation, the best way you can handle this is by inviting both people, letting them know about each other's attendance. I had a friend text me about this recently:

> Hey! I am throwing a birthday thing on Sunday. I would love you to come. Nicky will be there too so I understand if you aren't ready for that and we can do something separate if you prefer!

I was OK to be in the same room and was able to be polite and civil so I replied:

> Thank you for letting me know and really appreciate the thought to arrange separate plans. I'm happy to be in the same room and just to reassure you, there won't be any conflict on my end. Excited to celebrate you! Xx

There are times though when I have been unable to be civil. In these situations, I tell the person without involving them.

> Hey! Are you free on 10th or 11th? I'm back in the country for a week and want to organise a picnic for everyone from school. Would love to see you!

WHAT IF OUR MUTUAL FRIENDS TAKE SIDES?

> Hey love! I would love to see you when you are back! I just want to check, will Evie be coming? I don't want to involve you but we had a falling out. I don't think I'm ready to see her yet and I'm happy to be the one to opt out of the picnic but if you have time, I would love to arrange something just the two of us! Dinner or even a working date if you are busy? Xx

She understood, thanked me for letting her know and we ended up going for coffee separately. If you think there is a chance it won't be civil, it is better to decline. While it can feel frustrating to be the one to have to opt out, I see it as preserving the friendship with the person stuck in the middle. I don't want to put them in an uncomfortable position and they deserve to have a fun party or picnic without your disputes affecting the celebrations. This is what maturity looks like and what differentiates us from being kids in a playground. It's also helpful to remember that this feeling of wanting to avoid them won't last for ever! With some time and distance, being in the same room will get easier.

RULES
FOR BETTER
FRIENDSHIP

WHY YOU SHOULD BE FIGHTING FOR YOUR FRIENDSHIPS

We need to normalise bringing up issues before they become full-blown arguments. We need to learn how to fight fairly. The word 'fight' has a negative connotation because we all have different definitions of what is considered a 'fight', with some differentiating between disagreements, squabbles and bickering. To me, they all fall under the camp of conflict and while it might sound counter-intuitive, conflict can build stronger friendships and bring us a greater understanding of each other. When I look back on my past friendship breakups, I wonder if the friendship would have lasted longer if I'd just brought up my issues earlier instead of letting them accumulate. It can be so tempting to convince yourself that it isn't a big deal and that it doesn't matter but if that issue is still sitting under the surface, before long it will pop back up. It's like trying to push a balloon under water: the more energy you use to keep it submerged, the more intensity it will pop back up with.

The majority of women have been trained to be indirect communicators; we are told to be a 'good woman', we need to keep the peace, not cause a fuss and ideally, not have any needs and wants either. We are told that we should put everyone else first and as a result, when we are upset about something, we tell ourselves that we aren't feeling what we are feeling, that how we are feeling is unimportant and that it's not worth the conversation. None of this is true. It took me a long time to unlearn this messaging and instead learn how to validate how I was feeling. If someone said I was being too emotional, instead of dropping the issue, I learned to say:

> If you don't understand why I am having these emotions, instead of dismissing me, please just ask me and I'll explain.

If someone called me sensitive, I would simply tell them:

> We all have different sensitivities and this is upsetting me.

How you feel is important. Believing that is key to achieving self-esteem, and you will have to learn this if, in childhood, you were dismissed, ignored or simply shut down when your emotions were inconvenient to the people around you. It is your job to see your emotions as legitimate and back yourself when someone is seeking to undermine that.

No more peace-keeping

You deserve friendships where you can simply say 'that upset me' or 'that was unkind'. You know when you are tired and dump one thing on the floor but then you keep doing it through the week and by the weekend, the floor is not visible and you can't walk anywhere – think of your friendship arguments building up that way. When you keep the peace, you are actually just disrupting your own peace. Priya Parker phrases it best in her TedX talk: 'Connection is threatened as much by unhealthy peace as it is by unhealthy conflict.'[1] You might be scared of their response but give them a chance to be a good friend! Trust that they will receive your issues kindly when you voice them. Ignore the fear in your head and instead listen to your past evidence of them being there for you. If your friend was upset about something you did, you would want to know so repay them the favour. It's saying to your friend calmly, 'I'm upset you didn't make it to my birthday.' You can even say it more casually than that, like when a friend said to me, 'You do know that Dalston is as far away from yours as yours is from Dalston?' It doesn't always need to be a serious conversation, but that message was received and I started making an effort to travel to her more. It wasn't malicious or due to the fact I didn't want to see her, it was pure laziness and I appreciated that she called me out on it rather than letting the resentment fester. We create this binary of extremes: either burying it under the carpet and being sworn to silence or ending the friendship. Choose the third option. This dichotomous thinking is false and it prevents us from finding a solution. There is a more moderate middle ground that is easy to ignore. We need to be able to course correct instead of scrapping the whole course. If silence is your go-to when you are annoyed or upset, your next step is to simply say something. It doesn't

**WHEN YOU KEEP
THE PEACE, YOU
ARE ACTUALLY JUST
DISRUPTING YOUR
OWN PEACE.**

need to be phrased perfectly or eloquently, but even if the only word you can say is 'ouch', it's important to move towards a more communicative approach.

Sometimes you have to let things go

New rule: if you aren't willing to communicate it then you have to be willing to let it go. If you can't let it go, you have to communicate it. Historically, I am shit at keeping things in. In life coaching, it's called containment and as a result, I've got a reputation among my friends for wearing every emotion I feel on my face. It took me years to learn that I didn't have to say every single thing that was on my mind. If we brought up every single niggle, we'd be constantly in conflict-resolution mode. We need to be selective. Some issues will just need a small comment like the ones mentioned above, some will need a full-blown conversation and some will just need to be let go. One of the main lessons in friendship is that you cannot be surprised when someone is who they have always been. If you sign up to a friendship with a person who is perpetually late, then why do you act surprised when they turn up late? Absolutely set your boundaries, but if there is a point where they are clearly not changing, then you have a decision to make. Pretending they are not the person they have been all along is not an option. I will choose to let something go if it is really out of character for someone. I will consider it the exception to the rule and I might only bring it up if it happens again. There is no time limit on bringing up an issue. If it is still bugging you, then bring it up, even if it is at a later date. If you are

IF YOU AREN'T WILLING TO COMMUNICATE IT THEN YOU HAVE TO BE WILLING TO LET IT GO.

still thinking about it, you need to talk about it. Here is how you bring up an issue from the past:

> I know I should have told you this earlier but you know last month when you said I was ruthless, it really upset me. I don't know if you meant it as a compliment but it didn't feel like one.

> I know it was a while ago but I still feel quite disappointed by that night in Bristol. From a safety perspective, I believe you never leave a friend in a club alone and the fact you left without telling me and prioritised the guy you were getting with really affected my ability to trust you. Can we talk about it?

Remember that you are not causing a problem, the problem already exists. Marisa G. Franco puts this well: 'You are not creating problems in the friendship by talking about them.'[2]

Learn to tolerate turbulence

When you have known someone for a while, it is normal to have rough patches. Your friends will have less than ideal traits. They might have less patience than you would like but then they outdo you in terms of generosity. It's easy to fight over the things they lack without remembering you lack characteristics that they have likely overlooked too. Your friends are not just your need-satisfying machine, they have their own lives with their own things going on. Sometimes their lack of friendship speaks to their lack of bandwidth or lack of

WE CREATE THIS BINARY OF EXTREMES: EITHER BURYING IT UNDER THE CARPET AND BEING SWORN TO SILENCE OR ENDING THE FRIENDSHIP. CHOOSE THE THIRD OPTION.

time-management skills more than it does your relationship. Adult friendships are hard because we are all tired. In those moments, your friendship won't be as easy as it used to be and that's OK. Thanks to the P!nk song, I have started to view these periods in all relationships as 'turbulence'. When you hit turbulence on a plane, it might feel like you are dying but logically and rationally, planes are built to withstand a lot of turbulence. You will still get to your destination, it will just be a slightly less comfortable ride. The lyrics remind us that it might be scary but it's temporary. Imagine if when you hit a rough patch, you were able to see your friendship from a long-term mindset and understand that this is just a blip in a friendship that will hopefully last years. Recently, this really helped me in one of my friendships when I'd noticed she had been quiet for a while. It took me longer than it probably should have to notice because as mentioned previously, I don't tend to track when a friend doesn't respond. Just after Christmas I realised we hadn't spoken in two months, when we used to speak every day. I spiralled into overthinking and started questioning if I'd done something wrong, if I had why she wouldn't tell me, and whether she didn't care about me any more – then I stopped myself. I was just making up stories, so on New Year's Eve, I sent her a Happy New Year text saying that I missed her and I would love to see her in the New Year. She replied saying she missed me too and when I got back in London, it was like nothing ever happened. It would only be months later I would mention that period and she would share that she dropped off the grid because sometimes she has a bad habit of isolating. When she told me that, I felt guilty that I hadn't noticed but I also felt grateful

ONE OF THE MAIN LESSONS IN FRIENDSHIP IS THAT YOU CANNOT BE SURPRISED WHEN SOMEONE IS WHO THEY HAVE ALWAYS BEEN.

that I hadn't said all the thoughts I'd had in my head. I made a mental note that this is what she does. I told her that I now know to check up on her even more and force myself in if I have to because she doesn't have to do life alone. She said she'd like that and our friendship is stronger for it, just as planes are better designed to withstand greater extents of turbulence than they were in the past.

If you are gonna fight, fight fairly

When it comes to trying to have a productive conversation, there are some basic rules that you can follow in order to minimise the damage and increase the chance of a clear and kind conclusion. There is still no guarantee because you cannot control the other person and a healthy conversation involves two people. You can communicate in the healthiest, most polite way you know how and someone can still think you are toxic. They are allowed to have their narrative. If they avoid taking accountability, that's on them. But you don't need to cause any more pain or hurt than is necessary, and one of the most important ways you do that is by minimising accusations.

- **Emotionally neutral is the aim:** Having this conversation in the heat of the moment is not ideal and yet people are human. That's why I say emotionally neutral is the aim – but even if you can't hit the bullseye, aiming for it will still help. If you are still angry and cannot speak without raising your voice, then you need to ask for space and come back to the conversation when you have processed

ADULT FRIENDSHIPS

ARE HARD BECAUSE

WE ARE ALL TIRED.

more of your emotions. Asking for time and distance is a better solution than powering through in an attempt to finish the conversation.

- **Ground rules for adult communication:** Ground rules are no name-calling, yelling, screaming or saying mean things in anger. This sounds obvious but some of us didn't get taught this growing up and especially if you grew up in turbulent homes, it can be normalised. Arguments are not a competition in who can hurt who more. Marisa G. Franco reframes it by explaining that 'how much you desire to cause pain is proportional to how much you are in pain'.[3] You are only trying to hurt them so that they feel the way you do. If that is the way the fight is going, it is your responsibility to remove yourself from the conversation not only so you don't contribute to it but also because you do not deserve to be on the receiving end of it. We have all had moments when we behave badly and if you have done any of the above, you can still apologise for that behaviour without having to apologise for the whole friendship's demise.

- **Use 'I' statements:** You will notice in the above examples, there is an emphasis on 'I feel' and at no point have I said 'you are'. When you use 'you' statements, they come across as accusations and therefore people become defensive. For example, saying 'you are patronising me' vs. 'I am feeling patronised'. When you start it with a 'you' statement, it will then become a debate because that person might not agree. You cannot debate how you feel though. Another method that is useful in situations like this is called the XYZ approach. When you do X, in situation Y, I feel Z. For example, 'when you make comments about my weight loss in public, I feel self-conscious'.

- **Remove the idea of blame:** Very rarely is an issue down to one person, and even if one person should be taking more accountability, there are always things that both parties could have done better or even differently. When we blame the other person, it's often because we are trying to wash our hands clean of responsibility but in doing so, we are also not learning from the experience. We need to understand our part and that's why in the above examples I showed myself apologising for being distant or not addressing it earlier. The added benefit is that if you apologise for your part, it means the other person is much more likely to apologise for theirs.

When the friendship can't recover from a fight

There will be times when we ask a friend if something is wrong and they will insist there is no issue. It's the cliché of a woman being asked 'what's wrong?' and responding saying 'nothing' until they explode. If you are worried a friend is annoyed at you, we must be courageous and confront it. We have to remember that we have all been taught bad communication and so some people don't feel confident to resurrect old issues because they feel the pressure to let go. We must go back for round two! This can sound like:

WHY YOU SHOULD BE FIGHTING FOR YOUR FRIENDSHIPS

> Hey! I know we had that chat last month and I've noticed that we have been quite distant since. I would love to reconnect so do you have any time this week? Xx

> Hey! I want you to know I love you and I know we have had a few rough months so if there is anything not sitting right with you, I would love to know! I miss how our friendship was and I would love to work through it if there is something bothering you? Xx

It can be really scary because with each conflict, there is a risk of the loss of friendship but we have to remember that we risk that loss anyway by ignoring the issues. Galit Atlas says it best when she says 'the ghosts of the unsaid and unspeakable are there to haunt us' in her book *Emotional Inheritance: A Therapist, Her Patients, and the Legacy of Trauma*.[4] We must stop deluding ourselves into thinking that avoiding the issue stops it existing – it simply delays it.

SAY WHAT YOU MEAN AND MEAN WHAT YOU SAY

Learning to say what I mean and mean what I say changed my life. You might have heard the saying 'your word is your bond' and that's a principle that I believe is important to live by. I take it to such an extreme that I won't even say 'yes, let's go for coffee' unless I have the intention of following through. Not all conversations are meant to be easy, but if you do the hard work of being honest and confronting those difficult moments, then at least the people in your life can trust your word. When you say you are going to do something, then do it. If you aren't going to do it, then don't say you will. Even if it's promising your friend that you won't text your ex, when you know that the moment you have a drink in you, it will be the first thing you do. Know yourself and don't pretend to be anything you are not. As a society that excuses 'white lies', this is the opposite message to what we are usually told. We are told that 'white lies' are polite but they are not. How is it kinder to lie to someone's face?

SAY WHAT YOU MEAN AND MEAN WHAT YOU SAY

Why are we taught to say what people want to hear rather than the truth? And what is the line between a real lie and a white lie? The line is too blurry and that's why I will always pick the side of truth. People get confused because they think honesty means brutal honesty, but the truth never needs to be unkind and it's important to decipher what is unnecessary and better left unsaid.

When you first start 'saying what you mean and meaning what you say', like with any other change, it can be clumsy. There were times when I said something and had to correct myself with, 'actually that's not true, I don't know why I said that', then say what I really meant. I had to learn to start using sentences like 'Would you like the truth?' or 'I'm not sure you want my honest answer', knowing that my friends were likely expecting my past people-pleaser self and, in a way, to prepare them that I was not going to be doing that any more. It was a hard change but one that was worth the work. Since living by this mantra, I've discovered that being direct is often the more vulnerable choice, as when you are open enough to voice your needs, you can open yourself up to rejection, abandonment or accusations that you are too needy. However, there are immense gifts in doing things differently.

The more you are honest, the more they are too?

The first time I asked 'Do you want the truth?' and a friend replied 'no', I was shocked at how amazing it felt. I felt honoured that they felt comfortable enough to say no and trust our friendship enough that I could handle their boundary. I

WE ARE TOLD THAT 'WHITE LIES' ARE POLITE BUT THEY ARE NOT. HOW IS IT KINDER TO LIE TO SOMEONE'S FACE? WHY ARE WE TAUGHT TO SAY WHAT PEOPLE WANT TO HEAR RATHER THAN THE TRUTH? AND WHAT IS THE LINE BETWEEN A REAL LIE AND A WHITE LIE? THE LINE IS TOO BLURRY AND THAT'S WHY I WILL ALWAYS PICK THE SIDE OF TRUTH.

had got so good with boundaries that I saw it as a compliment. She went on: 'I just want to live in my delusion for a little longer but when I'm ready for the truth, I'll let you know.' I replied saying, 'We can do that. I'm so happy for you and I hope you are making the most of your joy!' and I stopped there because that's all I could say that was true. The rest of the sentence was 'and this is going to end in heartbreak and hurt' but she said no to hearing it so I kept that bit to myself. I didn't want to see my friend in pain but if she was choosing that path, then she must also choose the consequence of that decision, and she's allowed to make that decision. When you are clear, you give your friends permission to be clear with you too and the greatest gift is that your relationships become simpler. Once you create a norm for communication, you no longer need to worry if people are secretly angry with you, because they would tell you if they were and if they don't, you can ask. At the end of the day, you want a friendship based on trust. If a friend can't tell you how they are feeling or what has upset them, is the friendship really as strong as you thought it was?

Say it to the person you have a problem with

We have spoken about the negative impact of gossiping but I want to highlight that not gossiping is an extension of 'say what you mean and mean what you say'. When you talk about your friends behind their back, not only are you not saying what you mean to their face but you also don't mean what you say when you tell them there is nothing wrong. Gossiping is a habit and habits don't change by accident, so when you catch yourself gossiping, here are some options. It is very easy to say 'just stop gossiping' but much harder to do, so use one of these baby steps to diminish the hurt you are creating:

- **Change the conversation completely:** This was a technique I learned when people started talking about diets, but I hadn't learned to set a boundary yet. It can be as simple as saying 'let's talk about something else' or even just interrupting with a 'oh, did I tell you about . . . ' and picking the next conversation topic. You do not have to stay in a conversation that makes you uncomfortable. If one person doesn't want to have that conversation, then it is bad boundaries to persevere. They can have that conversation with anyone else!
- **Talk about yourself, not them:** Let's say you are talking about how a mutual friend is drinking more than she would like: instead of contributing to being judgemental, put the focus back on yourself. This could be saying something like, 'I found I had to ban myself from drinking alone' and talking about your experience. You want a friend who doesn't add to the pile-on. If you become concerned about this issue, talk to them about it seriously without judgement.
- **Focus on the behaviour but not the person:** Your friends are talking about how one of your friends never pays for anything and words like 'stingy', 'frugal' and 'selfish' are being thrown around. These are words that label a person and name-calling is unkind. You can empathise about how the behaviour is annoying without

contributing to this by saying 'I can imagine someone owing you money is annoying' or 'it's a shame they are avoiding the conversation'.

- **Acknowledge the gossiping:** If you have done the work to minimise the harm of the gossiping and you've tried to change the conversation but it persists, then you really need to call it what it is. 'Have you noticed that we have been gossiping a lot lately?' is a way to open the conversation in a non-accusatory manner. By entering the conversation as a 'we', you are taking accountability for your contribution and it becomes something you can work on together. You can be more direct than this and say, 'I really want to stop gossiping and it's something I am working on at the moment. Please tell me if you notice me doing it so I can stop.' Bringing your friend in on what you are working on can be a useful way to highlight the fact that you want the dynamic in your friendship to change.

When friends come to you to gossip, it's also your job to end that. Usually I will say 'I can't help you with that, you need to talk to them about it' or 'you should tell them, they probably don't know that it is upsetting you'. Whether they decide to follow through and speak to the other person is their prerogative, but you've sent the message that you don't want to be part of the conversation. If they continue, then I will be more direct and say, 'I don't like talking about people when they are not present' or 'I don't think X would feel great if they heard this conversation right now so we shouldn't be having it'. One thing that I start to notice once gossiping is absent is that some friendships were largely dependent on talking about others and therefore without it, those friendships fell away. But if the only thing you had in common was other people, it is for the best.

GIVE FRIENDSHIPS THE EFFORT THEY DESERVE

Effortless friendships are dead. Imagine for a second that you've been on a few dates with a guy and then he pencils you in for three weeks' time. You'd think he wasn't interested – and yet how many times have you suggested lunch with a friend in three weeks? This is the disparity in effort I am talking about. We must stop treating our friendships like second-tier relationships. Good friendships aren't accidental, they are created, nurtured and, ultimately, invested in. When we are there for our friends, we are investing into a current account. You never know when you'll want to withdraw from that account so you better be sure you keep topping it up. There will be times when the account runs low, and times your friend is putting more money in than you, but overall we want a healthy balance. It's only when we let the account run dry and we keep trying to withdraw but our card gets declined that we notice when a friendship is over; we need to start noticing a lot sooner than that.

Referring to a friendship like a bank account might sound transactional, but it's not; when you know you have a healthy bank balance, you rarely check the numbers. It's only when you are going broke that you check every day. The problem is we are taught that true friendship is one where the other person won't mind if the account is empty. We are told platitudes about how we can disappear and true friendship means picking up where we left off, but why are we normalising neglecting the people that should supposedly matter?

Friendships take work

Nancy Newell found that those who believed making friends was a matter of luck (as opposed to effort) were five times lonelier.[1] This makes sense because if you believe it is effort, you will do the extra work to be approachable at social events and make more plans with new people, which are all contributing factors to actually making new friends. It's not just about making new friends, it's also about the maintenance of old friendships. If we are constantly calculating what we are getting out of our friendships before deciding to give back, then we are doing our friendships an injustice. Very rarely will any human relationship be fifty-fifty. There are times you will have to carry the weight of keeping the friendship afloat and sometimes the other person is going to be doing the heavy lifting. We need to give our friendships more flexibility.

Somewhere in the conversation about boundaries, we have started to communicate like work colleagues in social relationships and I hate it. I believe it's happening because the word 'boundaries' is being thrown around without the education element and you cannot teach maintaining boundaries without teaching good communication skills. The best

VERY RARELY WILL ANY HUMAN RELATIONSHIP BE FIFTY-FIFTY. THERE ARE TIMES YOU WILL HAVE TO CARRY THE WEIGHT OF KEEPING THE FRIENDSHIP AFLOAT AND SOMETIMES THE OTHER PERSON IS GOING TO BE DOING THE HEAVY LIFTING. WE NEED TO GIVE OUR FRIENDSHIPS MORE FLEXIBILITY.

boundaries are firm but flexible and as a culture, we are starting to move towards rigid and immovable boundaries and that makes personal relationships tougher and more fragile. For example, one day when I was writing this book, a friend called. I have a very strict policy of writing two thousand words a day. I do it without fail and I always have tight deadlines for my books so it's needed. The friend who called is the person who I often brainstorm writing ideas with, so picking up the phone in the middle of a writing session is not unusual, but that day I was on a roll. When inspiration hits, you run with it. I am very good at setting boundaries so I could have picked up the phone and said, 'Now is not a good time, can I call you back once I have hit the word target?' or I could have not picked up the phone because as I said in *The Joy of Being Selfish*, 'Just because the phone is ringing doesn't mean you have to pick up.'[2] I could have sent her a text saying I'd call her back when my work was done but for some reason, my intuition told me not to do any of those things. Instead I picked up the phone and said, 'I'm on a writing roll, are you OK though?' 'Are you ok?' is my quick code phrase with all my friends to mean 'Is it something urgent?' and most of the time, they will respond 'all good, call me back'. This time was not the case. 'We just broke up,' she said, and as I looked up to the FaceTime I could see she had been crying. I had been her first call after her relationship had ended, a conversation that she had been working up the courage to have for months. In that second, my work became unimportant. I left the office that I was sharing with my boyfriend at the time and went into another room to take the call. All my friends and partners know when I get a spark of inspiration, I am relentless in not letting it go, but that was unimportant in the face of this. I have all these boundaries in place to keep me productive, but boundaries need to have flexibility.

There are many jokes online about therapy language seeping into the mainstream, with people declaring 'I have no emotional capacity', but it's important you pause long enough to check what the emotional capacity is for. There will be a scale of importance and we cannot have the same boundaries for both ends of the spectrum. We are in danger of trying to sterilise a human experience that is meant to come with mess. There will be times when being a good friend will be the inconvenient choice and yet we should still choose it anyway. There is a fine line of individualism between setting healthy boundaries and never being willing to stretch or extend ourselves unless we benefit. We need to be careful of capitalism's impact on our social life. Capitalism would tell me to forget the call and finish my work because nothing is as important as my job, but relationships are more important to me so that's why I will choose to prioritise them at times. In this instance, I chose the phone call over my work because the phone call was about a breakup. If it had been a chilled catch-up, I would have chosen differently, and that's where we must remember rules have to be adaptable for different contexts. I only found out much later that I had been her first call and my first thought was how glad I was that I decided to ask if she was OK instead of not picking up or texting her to say that I was busy. Heartbreak is raw and vulnerable and it is an honour to be chosen to be the person to receive that. The biggest twist was that I would end up going through a breakup two weeks later and she ended up being my first call when I found out he was cheating.

BAD FRIEND

Give your friends grace

Sometimes it is an effort to not jump to conclusions. As the poet David Whyte once wrote, 'Without tolerance and mercy all friendships die.'³ When someone pisses us off, it is so easy to react without pausing and realising that everyone has something going on in their own life. Recently, an old friend re-entered my life. We had been best friends in the first year of secondary school but we never ended up being in the same classes so we drifted apart until she eventually left the school for sixth form. In my first book, I'd written about our friendship and how much she had helped me survive my surgeries at the time. Five years after the book came out, I got a message from her. She had read it and wanted to apologise that she didn't know more of what I was going through at the time. My response was, 'Did we read the same book? In my mind, the whole first section was a love letter to our friendship.' We ended up living really near each other and started reconnecting. A year into our newfound friendship, she stood me up. We were meant to be going swimming and when I arrived there, I texted her. I called her but she didn't pick up and after thirty minutes, I went back and forth on whether I wanted to swim alone but eventually decided to leave. A few hours later, I got a text saying that she was so sorry, she'd gone for a nap because she felt unwell and her alarm hadn't gone off. I was annoyed but then I remembered a few years before, when I had booked dinner with a friend and just had completely forgotten to put it in my diary; she was sitting at the table waiting and she sent me a text to ask where I was. I felt so guilty but thankfully, she was so kind, forgiving and completely understood. This memory lingered in my mind and I wanted to pass that forward. My anger wanted to have a go at her but my wiser self sent a better text: 'No worries, rest up and feel better soon xx'. I've always believed that if someone already feels bad, you don't need to make them feel worse. It is then their job to make it up to you, organise the next meet-up or put the extra effort in the next time you see each other; if they already feel guilty, berating them will convert that guilt to shame, and shame doesn't help you grow. Most of the time, your friends know when they fuck up, but people are human and mistakes will happen. There is a Hasidic proverb that states, 'One who looks for a friend without faults will find none.' When a friendship has lost all ability to give the other person the benefit of the doubt, I believe it's already over. If you are that quick to assume the worst, then the trust is already lacking.

If you are shit to people, they will be shit to you too

When I was twenty-one, I briefly attempted to stay friends with an ex. It lasted for about a month, long enough for him to come to my birthday party. It was a black-tie event complete with a three-course meal with speeches from my friends. He was originally meant to sit next to me but I moved him to the end of the table, thinking that moving him to another table was too much of a snub. As a result, without meaning to, he had a view of me surrounded by all the people who love me most. He ended up leaving early, saying, 'Any one of the people in that room love you more than any person in my life has ever loved me. All of my friends would throw

WHEN A FRIENDSHIP HAS LOST ALL ABILITY TO GIVE THE OTHER PERSON THE BENEFIT OF THE DOUBT, I BELIEVE IT'S ALREADY OVER.

GIVE FRIENDSHIPS THE EFFORT THEY DESERVE

me under the bus if they were given the chance.' It wasn't the first time he had said something like that but it was the first time it had made sense. It was the same reason I had ended our relationship. He only ever had the ability to take. His motto was 'fuck people over before they fuck you' (he even had a painting of it on his bedroom wall) and so it was no wonder that he had ended up with friends like that. He had ended up with friends just like him. He just lacked the self-awareness to realise that. In order to have a friend, you have to be a friend. I had friends like that because I go above and beyond for my friends. The reason my first boyfriend was like that is because putting effort into friendship is a very vulnerable act. It means you care; it means you are invested. There is no certainty that it will be reciprocated and if we are used to protecting ourselves, that can feel too scary. The problem is if we are constantly walking through the world saying, 'I will only do this for you if you do this for me', it prevents your friendships from growing. Show up, give it a chance and let their response be the determining factor, rather than withdrawing all effort and then deciding it's a them problem. Friendships are what you make of them.

IN ORDER TO HAVE

A FRIEND, YOU HAVE

TO BE A FRIEND.

BE SELECTIVE ABOUT YOUR INNER CIRCLE

Information is power. You have likely heard this phrase before yet we never consider what it means in terms of personal relationships. When you give someone a piece of confidential information about your life, I want you to start seeing it as a key to your house. You want to make sure they aren't going to lose that key, be careless with it or indeed copy it and share it with someone who is dangerous. You can still be friends with someone and have decided not to give them a key to your house and you can also change your mind about how you interact with them in the future and decide you'd like your key back. While we do not want to walk through the world constantly re-evaluating our friends, it is important to check in once in a while and examine whether they are behaving like a person you want in your home. It doesn't mean you'll kick them out of your house, but it might mean that the next time they come over, they are allowed in but they aren't given a key to walk in when they like.

It took me many years to learn that you can control the

access that someone has to not only you and your life but your information. By controlling the information you share with each person, you are also deciding whether they are allowed to have an opinion and whether you want to hear it or not. I am very selective about the information I share with friends when I am dating someone new. I will send some friends a ten-minute voice note debriefing the date; others will get the headlines – 'I went on a date last night with a guy who works in AI' – and some will get even vaguer information: 'Yeah, I've been on a few dates lately.' Access is not an all-or-nothing decision. Instead, decide what extent you want to share and when.

The difference between privacy and honesty

When I introduce the idea of having different boundaries for different friends, people initially feel guilty that their information is no longer a free-for-all. You do not owe people information in order to connect and similarly, other people are allowed to tell you what they want to tell you about their own life on their own timescale. You are not obligated to tell everyone everything. It's important to know the difference between privacy and honesty. This is not you being secretive, it's just you being selective. When you aren't ready to talk about something, this is when boundaries come in. Here are some options:

> I am still processing it but when I'm ready to talk about it, I'll let you know.

IT'S IMPORTANT TO KNOW THE DIFFERENCE BETWEEN PRIVACY AND HONESTY. THIS IS NOT YOU BEING SECRETIVE, IT'S JUST YOU BEING SELECTIVE.

> Thank you so much for asking, I'm not in the mood to talk about it right now but another time?

> It's a lot right now, can we talk about something else?

Determining access is not just about information, it's about access in all forms. When my friend was getting married in Italy, four of our school friends were her bridesmaids. They were all staying with the bride for the weekend and said I was welcome to stay with them too. I really appreciated the offer but I declined. I knew that at the best of times this friendship group had complicated dynamics and I didn't think a cramped Airbnb would lead to the best weekend. When I booked my accommodation, I did so in the town down the road, consciously choosing more distance from them. I did not tell them this was the reason because it felt like unnecessary information. Turns out what I foresaw would happen, did happen, so much so that the bride ended up staying with me the night before her big day to get away from the stress. I had made the right decision and likely saved myself a few friendships by not being in the hotbed that was that flatshare.

You are allowed to have tiers

As Mindy Kaling put it, 'best friend is a tier, not a person'.[1] The amount of access you allow someone to have into your life can change and it doesn't mean that if you don't tell them something now, you never will. In order to build sustainable friendships, it is important that someone earns the right to

BE SELECTIVE ABOUT YOUR INNER CIRCLE

more private information. I once dated a guy who differentiated between acquaintances, mates and friends and similarly, I differentiate between best friends, good friends and just friends, but there is a way to do so without hurting people's feelings. How would you treat a best friend differently from a friend? For me, it looks like how much I am willing to drop for you. I would drop nearly everything for a best friend, but I might only check in on a friend when it works according to my schedule. Sometimes the differences are more practical. A best friend might stay in my bed, a good friend might stay in my guest bed and a friend might not have even been to my house. When it comes to news in my life or things I keep closer to my chest, my friends will likely know later than my best friends. However you measure the difference between best friends, good friends and friends, whether it's the frequency you see them in a year or how well you know the other people in their life, the key is to make sure there is a difference. If you treat all your friends as a monolith, it means you will end up granting people access who haven't earned it, or keeping everyone at arm's length, when some people have shown you that they can be trusted. In adulthood, these tiers are necessary because you cannot make the same amount of effort with everyone – there is simply not enough time and energy, and having tiers means allowing yourself to devote different amounts of energy to each individual.

Different friends for different reasons

No single human can fulfil all your needs, whether that's romantically or platonically. That's why it's good to build a wider support system where you can have different people in your life for different reasons. If you look at friends as a collective group, they should amount to the perfect person for you, but all the traits you look for in a friend don't have to exist within one human. For example, if I want to brainstorm about a new book, I would call a different friend than if I wanted to go and dance on a table in a club. I have friends who are amazing when I am crying and I am looking for comfort and I have other friends who I call when I need a dose of reality. Having different people for different reasons means giving yourself options, and ideally you'll have more than one in each category. I have two FaceTime friends. When I want a long conversation with someone but don't want to leave the house, I have two people I can call. We often leave FaceTime on when we go about our day, catching up while we are cooking or on the toilet. If one doesn't pick up, I can call the other one. I know there are friends who would get annoyed by this. They would either get grossed out that I haven't hung up to go to the toilet or frustrated that I'm not giving them my full attention as I wander through the house, but that's why other people aren't my FaceTime friends. Understanding that different friends give you different things is also understanding that humans are varied and what people look for in friendship can differ immensely too. Another way to phrase it is known as the '2 Beers and a Puppy' test. It was created by Ross McCammon in his book *Works Well With Others* and he suggests evaluating the people in your life by asking yourself two questions:

- Would I have two beers with this person?
- Would I allow this person to look after my puppy over a weekend?

BE SELECTIVE ABOUT YOUR INNER CIRCLE

He writes that if it is a no to both, you should avoid them at all costs. 'Some people are a yes and no. These people are to be cautiously trusted. Some people are no and yes. These people are no fun but they make the world a better place – for puppies especially'.[2] He suggests that what you are looking for are people who are yeses to both but I take a different approach: 'two beers' people have their place. We need 'two beers' people as well!

The importance of acquaintances

I hate small talk and so once I trust someone I like to go deep. As a result, I have been in danger of dismissing superficial relationships in my life as shallow but this is not always true. It's very easy to assume that closeness is always better. In fact, the morning after I lost my virginity, I didn't call the person you might expect. It wasn't a best friend or even one of my good friends but someone I only speak to once or twice a year. She wasn't even someone who I invite to my birthday party, and yet she was my first call in a pivotal point in my life. As women, we are taught that we should always aspire for deeper friendships and that a friendship isn't genuine if you don't share your deepest, darkest secrets. Growing up, I remember being taught that true female friendship was formed over DMCs (deep meaningful conversations) but in my twenties, I learned the importance of acquaintances. When we are time-poor, it is easy to neglect the relationships that are on the periphery of your life and only devote energy to your ride-or-dies, but having acquaintances is often what makes you feel part of a community. The science supports

WHEN WE ARE
TIME-POOR, IT IS
EASY TO NEGLECT THE
RELATIONSHIPS THAT
ARE ON THE PERIPHERY
OF YOUR LIFE AND
ONLY DEVOTE ENERGY
TO YOUR RIDE-OR-DIES
BUT HAVING
ACQUAINTANCES IS
OFTEN WHAT MAKES
YOU FEEL PART OF
A COMMUNITY.

BE SELECTIVE ABOUT YOUR INNER CIRCLE

this and found people who have more 'weak-tie interactions' are happier than those who have fewer.[3] In the last week, I have had a number of moments like that. I went to a publishing party alone, knowing that I'd made enough connections in the publishing industry that I would know someone when I got there. I had a great night. No one I spoke to that evening is someone I would go for dinner with, but they are people I care about. Some I have their number, some I only keep in touch with on social media but I thoroughly enjoy catching up with all of them. Then there is a friend who I only ever see at her birthday once a year. Every year, I stay until the end and it's one of my favourite events, and yet I never see her at any other time. I am not opposed to it and I can't tell you why we don't meet up more often, but you don't have to want more. I don't turn up to her party out of obligation or to show my face; I genuinely love our conversations and our once-a-year interaction, and that's enough! Let's remove the idea that closeness is automatically better and that deeper connections are more important. Every relationship has its place. Can a friendship really be defined by how often you text or how regularly you see each other? Or is it simply the act of kindness and care? Just because we don't get deep with everyone doesn't mean that love and care aren't present in those relationships. When you have an intimate friendship, there is a sense of responsibility. But there is beauty in interactions where even though there is no sense of obligation, they choose to do something for you anyway. Humans caring about other humans is a beautiful thing and we need to get out of the mindset that surface-level friendships are pointless.

BUILD TRUST SLOWLY

Someone rushing to treat me as a best friend when we have just met has become a warning sign for me. Why? Because I used to do it. When you grow up with fewer friends than you would like, it creates a level of urgency of meeting someone new. There is a longing and if I'm honest, it stemmed from a place of insecurity. You feel like you need to cement the bond as quickly as you can otherwise you might lose them and therefore when you make new friends, you do so with a scarcity mindset. Turning a stranger into a friend takes time. Research suggests it takes 30 hours of interaction to make a casual friend, 140 hours to make a good friend and 300 hours to make a best friend. Other studies have indicated it takes more than 200 hours to form a close friendship.[1] No matter where the statistics stand, one thing is for sure, it takes a while, so expecting to be best friends after the first encounter is not only unrealistic but it can actually be dangerous. Building trust slowly is about having the confidence to know that you are not in a rush to make a decision. Forming a friendship is not about securing the bond, it's about assessing whether the connection is right for you and a positive influence in your life. If it is the third time you are hanging out with someone, you are allowed to decide that you are seeing parts of a person that means you don't want to be friends with them. You are allowed to change your mind. Since we have not evolved our conversations about friendship, we tend to believe they follow a natural trajectory without inserting the element of choice. You can choose to be friends with someone and you can also decide that the person you are getting to know is not for you.

Intensity and intimacy are easily confused

When we are scared of intimacy, we will reach for intensity. Harriet Lerner explains this: 'Intense feelings, no matter how consuming, are hardly a measure of true and enduring closeness ... Intensity and intimacy are not the same.'[2] Intensity can look like oversharing or starting a fight with a friend to see if they still care about us. Intimacy takes time, is softer, gentler, and tends to be more boring. We might not have the rapid highs and lows of intense friendships but intimacy builds trustworthy and reliable relationships. Research also shows that when people disclose more, other people see them as anxious and less well adjusted.[3] Oversharing can often be painted as a cute personality quirk, but the truth is it is a protection mechanism. It gives us the illusion that we are safer if they know what they are letting themselves in for, but you do not need to come with a warning or disclaimer. Sharing is a way we form a bond, but when we overshare we are actually trying to push people away by presenting all the information; it reads as 'now is your chance to run'. Brené Brown refers to this as 'floodlighting'. When you lack self-esteem, you

WHEN WE ARE SCARED OF INTIMACY, WE WILL REACH FOR INTENSITY.

bombard people with information as a way to test them. We give ourselves the illusion that if they don't depart at that point, then they are locked in for life. No matter how much you overshare at the outset of a relationship, people can still leave upon the discovery of new information and so this technique doesn't even work. It just leaves you vulnerable to harm as you thrust the most fragile part of yourself into the arms of people you don't know. We do this because we lack self-esteem. We do not believe that we deserve the time to get to know someone and so we overshare in an attempt to secure that 'friend' label. We make these decisions out of a fear of rejection rather than actually believing that we have something valuable to offer in friendship. If we are used to people abandoning us, we befriend people in this way because unconsciously we think we won't have the time to convince the person and so we dump it all in their lap the first chance we get. In order to change this behaviour, you need to believe in who you are as a person. You do not need to overcompensate for who you are with how much you share. People don't want to know you because of how much you do for them, they want to know you because you are worth knowing.

The best analogy I have heard about how to build trust slowly and form friendships on a foundation of intimacy is the story of the marble jar that Brené Brown has shared. She talks about how when someone does something that earns our trust, we put a marble in the jar. Over time, those marbles accumulate but it means that no one in your life can magically have a full jar of marbles. It takes time to fill up the jar.[4] I love this analogy because the marbles are often small things that we rarely notice but should. It could be a friend offering

YOU DO NOT NEED TO OVERCOMPENSATE FOR WHO YOU ARE WITH HOW MUCH YOU SHARE.

to come an hour earlier to your dinner party to help set up, giving you a hand with your move and spending their Sunday lifting boxes, or even something as simple as getting in some regular Coca-Cola because they remembered you prefer it to Diet Coke. We should be noticing these moments because this is how your friends show you who they really are. It is not in the words, it's in showing up and demonstrating what being a friend looks like. The marble-jar analogy also works the other way: there might be times when a friend hurts our feelings or forgets about something that is important to us and in those moments, we might lose a few marbles from the jar, but it doesn't mean the whole jar empties. This analogy is helpful in allowing other people to be human, letting them mess up and being understanding that they have put enough marbles in the jar over the course of your friendship that your friendship can endure blips and moments of human error. It also normalises assessing the state of your friendship. If over the course of your friendship, no marbles are being put in, there will be a point where the jar is empty. If we aren't noticing either the small gestures or the lack of effort, we could be pouring marbles into a jar that has been sitting empty for years.

The faster the friendship, the faster the fallout

As much as friendship loss can truly suck, some things you have to learn the hard way. One of the things I realised is that the faster the rise of the relationship, usually the more disastrous the fall. When you don't allow yourself time to get to know each other and build trust gradually, the bonding often occurs in an unhealthy way. If intensity was used in the creation of the friendship, it is likely that intensity will be used in the destruction of it too. The friendship in which I learned this lesson left such a devastating effect on my life that it led me to declaring 'no more fast friendships' and it even made me wary of befriending anyone. At the time, I was the most cautious I had ever been in friendship, yet I met someone who has since become one of my closest friends. She admits that from the moment we met, she was determined that we were going to be friends – the only issue was that I was still recovering from the fallout of this friendship breakup and reluctant to let anyone in. She was patient and continued to make an effort and despite how resistant I was, I eventually relented and opened up. Looking back, I think that initial scepticism is one of the reasons we have such a strong foundation. It was the first time I had made a friendship slowly and consciously. Let me be clear, I am not encouraging you to be sceptical in all your friendships, but when you are getting to know a stranger, a level of scepticism is needed because you do not know them. You cannot have the same expectations of a new friend as you do for a best friend. When you have an instinct to befriend everyone or a drive to be liked, in order to change that behaviour you need to consciously pull back and keep parts of your life private until a friendship has formed. I believe I am so deeply understood in this friendship because I not only took the time to understand her but she took the time to understand me. In the forming of our friendship, I realised that if you are meant to be friends, you will be. Of course, effort is needed but rushing it achieves nothing other than misaligned friendships. You do not need to rush

YOU CANNOT HAVE THE SAME EXPECTATIONS OF A NEW FRIEND AS YOU DO FOR A BEST FRIEND.

a friendship if it is built on solid ground. I am now wary of people who treat every stranger as a best friend because it demonstrates that they are keen for any friendship, rather than picking me as an individual. If someone is so willing to offer the intimacy and closeness of a best friendship without having earned it, it diminishes the meaning of being their best friend. It also implies that your friendship is replaceable, and there is nothing special about you; you are just a filler of time and space. Instead, we want someone to choose us because they know us, and to be known takes time.

Lowering expectation means lowering disappointment

Friendship often comes with moments of feeling let down and, more often than not, it's a result of an unmet expectation. For me, it often comes on my birthday, when one by one guests start dropping out. Over time, I grew to expect it. It was only when it happened to my partner at the time that I found myself saying the words 'you are allowed to be upset', and so I'll say that to you too. Even if you make peace with it, it can still hurt. Sometimes when our trust is broken, we are placing unrealistic expectations on friendships and in those moments, we have to have enough faith to communicate that we feel let down and readjust our expectations for next time. One of the starting points is to stop expecting people to do things that you are not doing for yourself. We need to be self-aware about whether what we are asking for is realistic. An example of this is that people are shocked when they find out most people in my life haven't read my books. The truth is I don't ask because I don't ask questions

BUILD TRUST SLOWLY

I don't want to know the answer to. I accept everyone has something going on in their own lives and it's not like I read their PowerPoint presentations for work. I would even admit that I don't properly know what some friends do for a living. Taking an interest in my career doesn't have to mean reading my books, it can simply be asking me how my book is going or replying to me when I ask which book cover they prefer. Ultimately, my books are not written for my friends, the same way the content I create on social media is not for my friends. You can love me as a person and not love self-help books. You can want to be my friend and not be interested in the topic of friendship breakups. We have to remember that a lack of interest in an aspect of someone's life is not always personal. Every person is different though. One of my author friends said she cares more about intention. She would hope they have the intention to read the book or at the very least, buy the book and turn up to the book launch. Our friends are not just expectation-meeting devices – they have their own lives too.

HOW TO MAKE NEW FRIENDS

MEETING NEW PEOPLE

It is likely that you won't remember the first time you made friends in your life but if you have ever observed toddlers befriending each other, it seems easy. There is no rhyme or reason to who they befriend; the person who they decide will be their new friend can be as random as the person who shared a cookie with them. They approach each other with no self-consciousness or worry that they might be rejected. This does not happen by accident. The reason they make friends so easily is because they are missing something called theory of mind. Theory of mind is our awareness that not only do we think but others can as well. We become aware at three or four years old that other people can hold different thoughts, beliefs and emotions, and that's when human interaction begins to become more complicated – because if they can think about us, then they can also think badly of us. Instead of doing what we want, whenever we want, we become aware that other people are perceiving us and therefore we might alter our behaviour to come across differently. We change from only thinking about ourselves and what we want, to caring what other people think about us. As we get older, we also begin to form an identity, and with that comes well-rehearsed narratives in our head about what kind of friend we are, what insecurities we have and most of all, what impression we are forming. Making friends stops being as simple as the person you are sitting next to on the first day of school and yet we never stop treating it like this really simple task, even in late childhood. Whenever a child is struggling to make friends in school, at a party or even at an after-school club, we often hear parents say phrases like 'Why don't you go and make some friends?' as if it is a skill we already have when in reality, we are rarely taught how exactly to do this. When an adult is saying they struggle to make friends, they might be saying they don't know how to meet people, but they also could be saying that they struggle to turn an acquaintance into a friend. Some people struggle with initiating a conversation and others struggle with following up and turning a one-off hangout into a continuous relationship. Converting a stranger to a friend involves many stages, and if you are looking to make new friends, we must begin by pinpointing where exactly the problem is in your friend-making process. You can't make new friends if you don't know anyone new and sometimes this first step can be the hardest because you don't know where to begin.

My friend is your friend!

The easiest way to make new friends is to ask your current connections to make introductions. Even if you know just one person, it can work and it did for me! My parents live in Hong Kong and when I was younger and used to visit them in the summer holidays, I would spend all three months alone. I had

MEETING NEW PEOPLE

left for boarding school when I was eleven and while I had a few connections from primary school, over time that number dwindled to just one. That one person unfortunately lived in Australia, so our dates in Hong Kong rarely lined up. One summer, we crossed over by a day and I told her how much I hated coming back to Hong Kong because I didn't know anyone so asked if she could introduce me to someone. She called up one of her friends to join us for a drink. That one friend brought another friend, who introduced me to another, and for the next three months in Hong Kong, I went out every single night with those three people and had the best summer I'd ever had. All three would end up moving to London over the next few years, and these friendships were all because I was vulnerable enough to ask my friend for an introduction.

Over the course of my life, I have met people whom I have started to refer to as 'hubs'. In our university, these were known as BNOCs (big names on campus). One of the best 'hubs' I have known was a guy called Paul. Everyone knew him and he was a brilliant connector of people to the point where I can credit five of my friendships to him. BNOCs weren't necessarily the coolest people, they had just got to know a lot of people in different circles, and by attending one of their events you often made new friendships because they were amazing at introducing people who were likely to get on. Artificially seeking out people who are 'hubs' is hard; it is easier to become a 'hub' yourself by hosting more. Host dinner parties, boardgame nights or even have a scheduled weeknight where your friends can meet you at the pub. Don't know enough people? Host a 'six degrees of separation' party where each person has to invite one person no one else knows and that person has to do the same so that everyone at the party meets five people they don't know. When we have few friends, sometimes we can cling on and be protective of those we do have, but if you share your friends and invite them to get to know each other, it can start to feel more like a community.

We all need a community!

Mutual friends are a great option, but what if you are starting from scratch with zero friends? This is when weekly hobbies, monthly book clubs or local events can be a great option. These sort of events have built-in repetition, and that frequent exposure to each other increases the chance of a friendship forming. Esther Perel, when asked about modern loneliness on the *Pivot* podcast, refers to the art of playing in the street:

> The majority of the people learned to play freely on the street. They learned social negotiation. They learned unscripted, un-choreographed, unmonitored interaction with people. They fought, they made rules, they made peace, they made friends, they broke up, they made friends again. They developed social muscles. And the majority of these very same people's children do not play freely on the street. And I think that an adult needs to play freely on the street as well. For us as adults, that means talking to people in the queue with you, talking to people on the subway, talking to people when you create any kind of group. Book club, movie club, sports club.[1]

MEETING NEW PEOPLE

Whenever I throw book events, people always message me nervously that they are coming alone, but when they arrive, they often discover that the majority of the audience is there by themselves, either because they don't have friends who follow me or simply because they couldn't find someone free on the night. Back in 2018, two of my followers connected when one of them sold the other a ticket for one of my events. Liz and Fay started following each other and messaged back and forth for years. Even without meeting, they considered each other really good friends and then one day Fay needed to have surgery and had no one to pick her up. Liz booked the day off work to be there for her and six years after Liz sold Fay her ticket, they are still really good friends and they speak most days!

Whether it's a weekly fitness class or a monthly book club, finding hobbies where there is a mutual interest often makes it easier to initiate conversation and gives you a talking point when conversation stalls. When you run out of things to say, talk about the book or the exercise you are doing at the moment. It takes the effort out of organising time to meet and you don't need to keep initiating plans if the same group consistently shows up. This is known as the 'propinquity effect', the tendency to form relationships with those who we have more encounters with and have more physical proximity to. This combined with the 'mere exposure effect' – an effect that states the more chances we have to interact with a person, the more we prefer them, as humans prefer familiarity – sets up community-based activities as the most advantageous way to make friends. If you can find one that is local, even better. I recently had a friend move eight minutes away from me. Until then, I didn't realise that having someone in close proximity had such a great impact on feeling part of a community. I found this in the small moments, like her calling me up saying she had cooked too much and asking if I wanted to come over for dinner, or me calling her on the way home from a date wanting to drop in. When adulthood often means making endless plans, I have relished having a person who I can be spontaneous with because she is nearby. Having a weekly or monthly group to gather with also strengthens the feeling of community and allows you to build relationships slowly, without the pressure of having to decide if you are looking for long-term friendships. Activities like a running club or a painting class can also be the perfect way for introverts to meet as it is a way to have human interaction without the need for conversation.

What if you don't have a hobby? I believe that everyone should have a hobby that they are shit at. For me, it started as painting and has now included paddleboarding, squash and kickboxing. It's all about embracing the fun of it as opposed to improving your skill. In school, we are trained to only enjoy things if we are good at them. At my school, this was taught to us by not being allowed to play certain sports past the age of fifteen unless you'd made the school team. You couldn't join the choir unless you were good, and when you were playing a musical instrument, you had to always be taking grades because if you were not consciously trying to get better, what was the point? The point is that these things are fun, and they're the perfect things to bond with your friends over. If you are sporty, there are all kinds of skill levels at Go Mammoth, the social sports club organisation, or if you are looking for something more creative, there are tons of workshops where you can make anything from rugs to pottery. Your options are endless!

We use an app for everything else

Thanks to technology, we have options with apps like Bumble BFF where you can swipe through profiles to find your next friend much like on dating apps. One of my friends started using Bumble BFF during the pandemic. She found that most of her friends lived too far away to go on walks with, so when the lockdown was lifted, she started looking for people who were physically closer to her. The profiles meant that she could look for people who had similar interests. She ended up meeting more than ten people on the app: some were one-time walks and some turned into long-term friendships. There are also apps like Timeleft, which sets groups of strangers up for dinner, and is more of a hybrid between dating and friendship apps: you meet new people but also have the potential of a romantic connection. Some apps are more specific if you are looking to meet people in a certain demographic or at a different life stage, like Peanut for mums who are looking for other mum friends. Most of my friends do not have children and therefore when the first few got pregnant, they went on this app and many found it comforting to spend time with people going through the same things as them.

You might be thinking, *What kind of weirdo has to go on an app to make friends? I don't want to make friends with those kind of people.* Much like dating apps, there is a stigma around friendship apps, and an idea that they suggest a level of desperation, but I implore you to get rid of this outdated way of thinking. You are only judging them because you are judging yourself. Using Bumble BFF myself, most profiles include their reasons for being on the app, which range from having moved to a new location or people's friendship group moving on to the next life stage without them – very normal friendship problems that very normal people go through. Friendship apps are a means to an end. You don't have to love being on them, but you should at least be open to them as they are an incredibly efficient way to get the outcome you would like. Friendship apps give us options; they exist because there is a need for them. We use technology for everything else, from ordering a taxi to getting food, so why not use them to make friends? We have seen copious amounts of evidence that we are living in an age of loneliness like never before, so anyone who takes the vulnerable step of putting themselves on an app and is courageous enough to do something about it is admirable in my books. Being proactive should be encouraged and anyone who judges you for being on a friendship app should just be thankful they have enough friendships that they don't need to put the extra effort into making new relationships.

Creating a friendship profile

With apps that involve profiles, use your profile efficiently. There is no point filling your friendship profiles with platitudes about how you like music and travel. No one has ever decided to stop being friends with someone because they like cats instead of dogs. Profiles include a limited amount of space and

**BEING PROACTIVE
SHOULD BE
ENCOURAGED AND
ANYONE WHO JUDGES
YOU FOR BEING ON
A FRIENDSHIP APP
SHOULD JUST BE
THANKFUL THEY HAVE
ENOUGH FRIENDSHIPS
THAT THEY DON'T NEED
TO PUT THE EXTRA
EFFORT INTO MAKING
NEW RELATIONSHIPS.**

therefore you want yours to communicate important information that not only helps people decide if you would be a good match but that also repels the wrong people. For example, I would list that I'm an opinionated and direct person because I know this isn't to everyone's taste. We want our profiles to list our values, so I would give a vivid example by saying something like 'I'm the kind of friend you don't tell when you get back together with your ex, but the first one you call when it all goes tits up and you need someone to pick up the pieces'. This example works because everyone has a friend like this and therefore it is easier to picture what kind of friend I'll be. Whenever you can, on a profile, 'show don't tell' is the best approach, so instead of saying that you are a reliable friend, it is better to state, 'I'm the kind of friend that will drive you to the airport.' Most people also share the kind of activities they enjoy as well as the kind of friends they are looking for. Some people are newly sober and want more sober friends and some are looking for locals who use the same gym as them. I would avoid listing negative things like 'I hate festivals' or 'no smokers' and instead focus on what you want more of.

When it comes to photos, it is important to include clear photos in which you are visible – so no sunglasses shots or massive group photos where they will have to study the picture to figure out which one you are. Photos in a friendship app is a strange one because I can't say I have ever decided to become friends with someone based on what they look like. But you can use the photos to convey more of your personality. If you are the kind of person who loves being outside, make sure your photos demonstrate that. If you prefer to get all glam and be out all the time, share photos of yourself in restaurants and on nights out. We have very little real estate on a profile, so to not capitalise on this space to show more of yourself is a missed opportunity.

If you are struggling to know what to put on your profile, the best people to ask are those who know you. It's important you only ask friends that you trust, who will be kind and sensitive, but ask questions like 'How would you describe me to a stranger?' or 'If you could summarise me in three words, what would they be?' This will help you decipher what is of importance on your friendship profile.

Any stranger can become an acquaintance

As the saying goes, 'A stranger is just a friend you haven't met yet.' New people come into your life all the time without you noticing. My mum's best friend was the shop attendant at her favourite store and she frequented the store often enough that they eventually became a part of each other's lives; she's my godmother. I've made friends with someone who was sitting next to me at a work conference, I've made friends in a club smoking area and I've even made friends with a guy who I met on a dating app after I discovered he was five years younger than me. I don't know why the app had matched us because my age settings were higher, but he lived around the corner from me and was also an author, so we became writing buddies. I believe one of the keys to turning strangers into friends is having a mindset of being open to making new friends. It means when you meet new people, you make more effort and you never know, you might bump into someone else who is on the lookout to make a new friend.

First date doesn't mean forever

Just like in dating, you can go on a first date and decide you don't want to be friends. Take the pressure off the first date and stop seeing it as a long-term commitment. Making friends is a numbers game, just like dating. If I ask ten people for a coffee, only half will follow through, roughly two I will want to see again and maybe one will flourish into a proper friendship. I have gone on many coffee dates, lunch dates and dinner dates and just let them be a one-off. You don't necessarily even need to have a conversation about it, you just won't follow up with another plan or put in the effort to become friends. I recently had a colleague invite me for lunch. She had been asking for a while and I said I would reach out when I was in her area but every time I was it slipped my mind. As I'm not the kind of person who says they will do something and doesn't follow through, I made a plan and reassured her that I just kept forgetting. We went for lunch and as nice as it was, it was clear we had really different mindsets. A lot of the conversation revolved around dating, and as much as I love dating, many years ago I made a conscious effort not to have my life revolve around the men I am seeing and so this conversation felt like a subject I would have enjoyed in the past. It can be hard to pinpoint why a conversation doesn't flow in the way I would like it to with a friend. That friendship date became a one and done! We still see each other at work events, there is no bad blood and I didn't ever communicate how I felt because I had no intention of becoming friends and she didn't pursue another meet-up. We were on the same page and it doesn't need to be any more than a lunch we had that one time. When we lower the bar for commitment and realise a first date isn't committing to an automatic friendship, it becomes easier to say yes to meeting up. That also means that if you *did* have a good time, you need to make sure they know that and follow up to make plans again!

FACING THE FEAR OF REJECTION

Being liked by our in-group is important to humans as we are tribal creatures; from an evolutionary perspective, we relied on our acceptance as a means of survival. As a result, our body can still interpret being rejected as a threat to life. It hurts; it sucks – but any interaction with another human being involves risk. Are there times you are going to walk up to someone by a buffet table, say hi and have them look at you weird, hesitantly say hi back and wonder why you are talking to them? Probably, but that's not on you. Think about it. If you were at a social gathering and someone approached you and said hi, you would likely be open to engaging in a conversation, right? It's basic human decency and just being kind. If someone does not have that in them, is that someone you want to talk to anyway? I wouldn't. Rather than internalising that rejection and judging yourself, turn it back on them. When we lack self-esteem, we tend to dissect every part of our interaction and decide that we must have done something wrong to elicit that response, but what if that's how they treat everyone? Is it really on you how they responded? Back yourself!

YOU DO NOT HAVE ANY EVIDENCE THAT PEOPLE WILL LIKE YOU AND YOU ALSO DON'T HAVE ANY EVIDENCE THAT THEY WILL NOT. SO PICK THE BELIEF THAT IS MOST USEFUL TO YOU. YOU MIGHT SAY, 'WELL, I HAVE NO REASON TO BELIEVE THEY WILL ACCEPT ME.' YOU DON'T HAVE ANY REASON TO BELIEVE THEY WON'T, BUT YOU'VE RUN AWAY WITH THAT NARRATIVE DESPITE IT NOT BEING USEFUL TO YOU.

Be conscious of your limiting beliefs

Within life coaching, one of the important things we talk about is separating stories from fact. It is so easy to tell ourselves stories, especially when we are missing part of the information, and therefore our brain fills in the gap with the worst-case scenario. If we start telling ourselves stories about how no one is going to like us or accept us, don't be surprised if it turns into a self-fulfilling prophecy. For example, if you walk through the world believing you are ugly and someone stares at you, that stare becomes confirmation that you are ugly. Change the belief, walk through the world thinking that you are beautiful, so when someone stares, you will use that as evidence of your beauty. The beliefs come first and then our brain sorts through the information we get to confirm that. You do not have any evidence that people will like you and you also don't have any evidence that they will not. So pick the belief that is most useful to you. You might say, 'Well, I have no reason to believe they will accept me.' You don't have any reason to believe they won't, but you've run away with that narrative despite it not being useful to you. At least if you assume acceptance, whether it's true or not, it's a helpful belief, and research supports this. Psychology professor Danu Anthony Stinson and his co-authors refer to it as 'the acceptance prophecy' and suggests that when we assume acceptance, we behave more warmly and therefore we get warmth back.[1] In fact, research actually indicates that people tend to systematically underestimate how much their interaction partner liked them, known as the 'liking' gap.[2] When it comes to beliefs, there is no true or false, there is just helpful and unhelpful. We could all do with a little more 'pronoia', a term coined by Fred Goldner to denote the opposite of paranoia.[3] Where paranoia is the belief that people are conspiring against you, pronoia is when you believe everyone is conspiring to do you good. It is not dissimilar to the 'lucky girl' trend on TikTok: by believing you are one of the luckiest people in the world, you tend to reinforce that mindset with the evidence you find. How would a person with pronoia act when someone wants to be friends with them? Of course, why wouldn't they want to be friends!

Being rejected for who you are is better than being accepted for who you are not

If we have been unsuccessful at making friends in the past, it is easy to start thinking that we are the problem. As a defence mechanism, you could develop tricks to assimilate in your peer group that include pretending to be someone you are not and also getting good at saying what people want to hear in order to expedite being accepted. The problem with this is that it is draining to pretend all the time and therefore interactions with this performative mask can be exhausting. It builds a barrier that prevents true intimacy and connection in the long term. If you are unable to maintain that mask it increases the chance of rejection as at some point, people will question why there has been a sudden change in your personality. It is a better approach to be yourself from the outset and let people be repelled by that. If they are not your people, it's better that you know sooner than later.

Turn the focus inwards

Too often when we interact with new people we become preoccupied with how we are coming across, and that can stunt us from being ourselves. When this happens, we are trying to control something that we can't: how we are being perceived. This emphasises the feeling of being out of control and can leave you feeling powerless. The way to flip this perspective is to stop focusing on if the other person likes you and instead ask yourself if you like them. Instead of worrying if you are the kind of person they would want as a friend, start noticing whether they fill your own criteria for friendship. This works at parties too: if you start questioning why no one is talking to you, flip it around. Why are you not talking to anyone? Emphasise the part of human interaction that is within our control and everything else will be what it will be. I love Suzy Kassem's line 'insecurity kills more dreams than failure ever will', and it applies to friendship.[4] Our insecurity around being uncool or looking weird or sounding stupid will kill more potential friendships than rejection will. Ultimately, people are not thinking about you as often as you think they are, and I believe one of the keys to this is to not embarrass easily. So what if you spill your drink when saying hi to a new friend? The only way you learn to not embarrass easily is to embarrass often. The way I see it is you've given someone a laugh that day, even if it's at your expense, and surely making someone smile is a positive. If you've done a particularly incredible job at messing up, you might have even given them a funny story to go home and tell their partner, and then the joy gets passed on! We've all laughed at someone else's expense, so it's only right that you take a turn in taking a hit too.

IF YOU START QUESTIONING WHY NO ONE IS TALKING TO YOU, FLIP IT AROUND. WHY ARE YOU NOT TALKING TO ANYONE?

BAD FRIEND

Put out the energy you want to receive

People rarely wave but they always wave back. People don't like to initiate conversation but once the ice is broken, most will be friendly back; they were just looking for a way in. You just need to break the barrier of strangers who aren't allowed to acknowledge each other. I will never forget when one of my friends from Canada came to visit me in London. On her first day sightseeing, she came home and exclaimed, 'Wow, people in London are so friendly!' I stared at her, confused. 'Are we talking about the same London?' Friendly is one of the last words I would use to describe London, and I'm sure most Londoners would agree. My friend got a different London because *she* was different – she did things I never would have done. We are all guilty of blending into the societal expectations that get put on us and obeying the unspoken rules like not talking to people on the Tube. She had broken that. Every time she got on a train that day, she sat down next to someone and started talking to them. She told me that at one point, the entire carriage was chipping in with advice on where to go and what to visit. In over a decade in London, I have never spoken to a stranger on the Tube, let alone had an entire carriage joining in, so what was the difference? The difference was that she dared to do something different. This taught me a huge lesson: the energy you put out is also the energy you receive.

OUR INSECURITY AROUND BEING UNCOOL OR LOOKING WEIRD OR SOUNDING STUPID WILL KILL MORE POTENTIAL FRIENDSHIPS THAN REJECTION WILL. ULTIMATELY, PEOPLE ARE NOT THINKING ABOUT YOU AS OFTEN AS YOU THINK THEY ARE.

INITIATING CONVERSATIONS WITH STRANGERS

There has been a lot of information put out there about how to be a good conversationalist. It could be the impact a compliment has on a person liking you, and books like *How to Win Friends and Influence People* suggest using someone's name frequently in a conversation.[1] While the research might support this, I am hesitant to fill this chapter with gamified solutions because ultimately, do we want friends who have simply been psychologically predisposed to like us? I don't know about you, but if I started focusing on artificial tricks like that, it would make me be less authentic and that would mean the relationship was less authentic too.

When we don't have the number of friends or the kind of friends we would like in our life, we have to start being more conscious about what part of making new friends we struggle with. I meet new people all the time, I have no issue asking people out for coffee, when I am introduced, I can hold a conversation, and when I like someone, I find it easy to follow up and maintain a relationship. For me, the hard part has always been initiating conversations with strangers. I'm so bad at initiating conversations with strangers that despite having lived in the same building for ten years, and repeatedly saying I want to get to know my neighbours, I know exactly zero neighbours. It gets worse than that though. It was such a running joke with my old agent that he would set me challenges to talk to at least one new person when I went to events, and I had to report back not only their name but their job title. He used to ask me what the point of going to all these events was if I met no one, because I might as well be sitting at home. So I'm going to say the same thing to you: there is no point in meeting new people, being in rooms with new people but talking to none of them and then going home to complain that you have no new friends. Yes, it's scary. Yes, it's hard. But if it's some comfort, the fact I find it hard too means my advice works, because I was my first guinea pig.

Be bold enough to go alone

My first piece of advice is a very practical one. Force yourself out of your comfort zone and go to events alone. The fact is, if I go to a house party and I know someone who is going, I will rarely leave their side. Humans will always take the easy way out and therefore I do not give myself that as an option. Sometimes I purposely decline plus-ones to force myself to socialise. The next obstacle is the phone in your hand. What is the first thing people do when they are standing in a room alone, thinking everyone is judging them for being a loner? They look at their phone. Your phone makes you look like you are busy, but that is a problem too. If you look busy, no one will approach you. You have to be able to risk that moment of vulnerability, of looking like you want to talk to someone, in order to look approachable. Otherwise, people won't approach you because they will think they are interrupting you. Leave your phone in your bag or your pocket, and even if you just go five minutes without reaching for it, that is plenty of time to meet someone new. The next time you are at an event alone, challenge yourself to talk to one new person. Turn it into a game or an experiment!

Be approachable

Keeping your phone out of sight is not the only way to make yourself more approachable. Being alone makes you inherently more approachable because interrupting a group is intimidating. Where you stand at an event also affects your approachability because if someone has to walk across the room to engage with you and then you reject them, there is an awkward walk back. Positioning yourself either by the bar or by the food is often a good way to break the ice. It also means you can initiate a conversation about the food or drink. Another tip is to smile when someone looks in your direction to indicate that you welcome a conversation. When you are talking to someone else, leave the circle open to allow new people to enter too. I will even start being approachable before I have entered the venue. Usually, if I am going to a smarter event, it is quite obvious when someone is going in the same direction by how they are dressed. I recently overheard someone asking for directions to the ballroom I was on my way to, and so I initiated conversation by asking, 'Do you know what direction we need to be going in?' None of these conversation-starters are revolutionary, but it's about breaking the ice and altering your position from stranger to someone people can talk to. To carry on the conversation, I only need to add, 'Oh, by the way, I'm Michelle,' and then we'll both enter the room knowing someone. Of course, some people will exchange names and then the moment you go inside, walk off in the opposite direction in search of someone they know, but more times than not they'll end up at your table, or the host might introduce you as you walk in together.

What to talk about

Learning to hold a conversation is an art form and it takes practice. We have a fixed idea that we are either born an extroverted person or we aren't, and while there is an element of truth in that, I think it is a very different skill to be able to hold a conversation with someone you know and someone that you don't. Until I had to do it often in my job, I was rubbish at it, and I'm an outgoing person. If people are good at it, they appear natural, but we aren't all born with it, some of us are just good at hiding it. Since we live in a culture that tends to label everyone and our social skills are judged very early on in school by how we interact with peers and how outgoing and liked we are in our class, it is no wonder we are reluctant to admit when we have had to learn how to converse with others. How many children in school were labelled 'shy' as a coded way to say awkward just because they didn't warm up as quickly as others? I have never been shy but I have no

SINCE WE LIVE IN A CULTURE THAT TENDS TO LABEL EVERYONE AND OUR SOCIAL SKILLS ARE JUDGED VERY EARLY ON IN SCHOOL BY HOW WE INTERACT WITH PEERS AND HOW OUTGOING AND LIKED WE ARE IN OUR CLASS, IT IS NO WONDER WE ARE RELUCTANT TO ADMIT WHEN WE HAVE HAD TO LEARN HOW TO CONVERSE WITH OTHERS.

shame in admitting that, even to this day, I have to keep a framework in my head when I am talking to new people because it is so far out of my comfort zone. Whenever someone says something, you have three options – comment, question, opinion. If someone says they just came back from a holiday in Turkey, you can then respond with:

COMMENT: I heard the food is good there.
QUESTION: How long were you there for?
OPINION: Turkey is one of my favourite places I have visited!

It might seem silly that I have to keep this framework in my head, but I've personally always found it frustrating that people expect you to know how to socialise without actually teaching you. Sometimes it's not even a lack of social skills; sometimes I'm just exhausted, and interacting with someone new does consume more energy. Having this framework to fall back on makes me feel less scared to initiate conversation.

The art of a good conversation

Research demonstrates that conversations with strangers tend to be less awkward, more enjoyable and more connecting than people expect.[2] If you have read my book *The Selfish Romantic*, you will also know that I never respond to 'How are you?' directly. I learned this in my job because I am interviewed a lot and found that I often got bored of being asked the same question over and over. Instead of answering the question directly, I would answer with what I want to talk about.

'How are you?' is a rubbish question and answering 'yeah, good' will lead to a dead response. Instead mention a book you are reading, talk about your plans at the weekend or even something you've been thinking about. It can feel clumsy to respond to 'How are you?' with 'Yeah, good, I've just been reading a book on friendship breakups and I was thinking, do you think they are more painful than romantic breakups?' but the other person is likely going to be grateful to have a more interesting conversation than the bog-standard 'Yeah, good, you?' Research also found that even with strangers, people tend to prefer to have deep conversations than shallow ones, so if you are having a rubbish day, feel free to answer 'How are you?' honestly, rather than with the ordinary superficial response.[3] Becoming a good conversationalist is a skill, so here is where to get started:

- **Be Curious**: Curiosity is an excellent emotion to nurture when forming new connections because it takes the focus off yourself. It might just be because I'm a psychology nerd, but humans are fascinating and if you can tap into that interest to discover more about a person, you will be focused on them instead of focusing on whether you are standing weirdly.
- **Learn One New Thing:** I believe you can learn something new from everyone. When we first talk to strangers, if we don't have a goal, the default can be trying to impress them; changing the objective means you are less likely to change yourself.
- **Actively Listen:** It's so tempting only to listen in order to respond, especially if we are nervous or anxious. We

worry that the moment they stop speaking, we have to say something new, funny and interesting, which means that we are in our own heads when they are talking to us. You are allowed to pause in order to reply. Let the space exist.

Paying it forward

My friend Samantha is the kind of friend who always looks out for the one person standing alone in a room. It doesn't happen by accident; she does it on purpose. I often say she has 'host-like behaviour' even when she isn't a host. You know how a good host will not only greet you but ask if you know anyone and then be sure to introduce you to someone else before greeting their next guest? Samantha does that and I've seen her do it even when she knows no one in the room. She always makes a concerted effort to make sure everyone feels welcome, and if she notices someone on their own, she will be the first to go over and say hi. I've always admired this quality and then one day it occurred to me that I could do the same thing. Since I know the discomfort of being alone in a room and I know how much I hate initiating a conversation, if I see someone standing on their own at a party (especially if I know loads of people in the room), I will often bring them into the group of people I know. I did this recently at a dating event. I had gone with one friend and we were both talking to a guy we had met there when I spotted a woman standing alone in the corner. I invited her to join us. It's tempting when you are in a room full of people you know to get wrapped up in your own conversations, but I always try to remember that I might not be the person standing alone in this room but I could be in the next one. I am always grateful when someone approaches me, so I believe it is good karma to be that welcoming person when you can be.

I MIGHT NOT BE THE PERSON STANDING ALONE IN THIS ROOM BUT I COULD BE IN THE NEXT ONE. I AM ALWAYS GRATEFUL WHEN SOMEONE APPROACHES ME, SO I BELIEVE IT IS GOOD KARMA TO BE THAT WELCOMING PERSON WHEN YOU CAN BE.

FOLLOWING UP AND MAINTAINING FRIENDSHIPS

One of the biggest reasons I shout about prioritising female friendship is because if you have good friendships in your life, you don't want them to dwindle simply because you have neglected them. Whether it's following up after a first date or putting in the work to turn it into a fully-fledged friendship, the art of keeping friends as an adult is a skill when everyone is so time-poor. One of the most common frustrations I hear from women is that when we want to see our friends, it often means arranging plans two to three months in advance. Gone are the spontaneous nights outs and unfortunately there isn't a solution to this unless we all individually take responsibility for saying no to the events we don't want to attend in order to leave space for the people we actually want to see! Of course, we all go through busy periods in life, but anytime I am scheduling friends that far in advance, I start to actually look at all the plans in my life and make room for more balance, because friends deserve your time!

FOLLOWING UP AND MAINTAINING FRIENDSHIPS

Improve your current friendships

It's important to recognise that wanting better friendships doesn't necessarily mean getting new friends. It can also mean investing more in the friendships we currently have to improve the quality of the friendship. We have this idea that the perfect friendship comes in the perfect person, but the best friendships are not just born, they are developed. Who initiates first and how much each person does can become a real sore point in friendship when it doesn't need to be. Assume the responsibility initially and then you can ask them to reciprocate if you note there is a disparity in effort. Carve out time. Make plans. Show up. A common piece of advice I hear from new mums is that they wish people would stop asking them how they can help and just do *anything* to help, from cooking food to dropping off groceries. I took that ethos and applied it to a friend going through a breakup. I kept asking her if she wanted to talk but she never wanted to so instead I booked us a rage room so she could smash up things and release any anger she was feeling.

Improving your friendships could mean injecting more affection into them. When is the last time you hugged a friend properly? Research conducted at the University of North Carolina found that women who are frequently hugged have lower blood pressure.[1] When did you last send a friend a thank you card or even take the time to write a birthday card properly, not scribbling in it at the Tube station on your way to the party? Give your friends compliments, and bonus points if they aren't about their appearance. Limit your screen time when you actually hang out with your friends.

WANTING BETTER FRIENDSHIPS DOESN'T NECESSARILY MEAN GETTING NEW FRIENDS. IT CAN ALSO MEAN INVESTING MORE IN THE FRIENDSHIPS WE CURRENTLY HAVE TO IMPROVE THE QUALITY OF THE FRIENDSHIP. WE HAVE THIS IDEA THAT THE PERFECT FRIENDSHIP COMES IN THE PERFECT PERSON, BUT THE BEST FRIENDSHIPS ARE NOT JUST BORN, THEY ARE DEVELOPED.

FOLLOWING UP AND MAINTAINING FRIENDSHIPS

You know that there is no way in hell you will have a quality interaction with your friend if you are keeping one eye on your phone to see if your crush has replied. Make a memory box for your friendship. I have kept cards, little titbits from concerts or even Post-its, along with photo-booth photos and small keepsakes that you would treasure if it was a romantic relationship.

Make time for play. We underestimate the power of play as adults and when we are exhausted, we often think we need more rest. You can be tired because you need more sleep, but you can also be tired because you need more fun. One of my favourite ways to play is a dance class called 5Rhythms, which is the embodiment of the phrase 'dance like no one is watching'. It is a judgement-free space to move your body to music in the weirdest and most wonderful way that feels most natural to you.

End the never-ending catch-up

In my mid-twenties I found myself getting frustrated with how my diary looked. Being single, my weekends were always empty since my friends would be with their partners and then my weekday evenings would be filled with one-to-one dinners catching up with friends. It started feeling like a never-ending hamster wheel – once I'd seen the final friend on the list, it would have been a few months since I saw the first friend and I would start all over again. I obviously liked hearing about my friends' lives, but sometimes I would get bored of repeating the same stories over and over again. I was increasingly feeling like I was no longer a part of their life, just the receiver of the story of their life. In school and university, we lived life together so this was never an issue, but as we go further into adulthood, without a course correction, the natural route is for your time together to just be a series of updates on what has happened since you last saw each other. The first way I changed this was to stop doing dinners. I love the intimacy and connection they can provide, but if I wanted us to be experiencing life together more, we needed to book in more experiences. I booked squash dates, we went axe throwing, and I even found a place where you can book a hot tub in Canary Wharf. I would normally go around and check if anyone is free and then get frustrated when the only available date that everyone can do is next year, so I just booked it. Whoever was free was invited: five said yes, two cancelled and it ended up being me and three friends! I forced my friends to go paddleboarding with me on my birthday, and while that meant enduring complaints about how their hair would be ruined or that it was cold, I was insistent that this was better than the standard daytime chill in a pub over some drinks. I found a local shop that lets you rent rollerblades, and while I didn't have the natural ability I did when I used to play roller hockey as a child, my friends and I giggled as we fell over and eventually gave up. Making more space for experiences meant I also made more room for play with my friends. That joy not only breathes life into your friendships but also into your week! I know a lot of these activities require financial investment, but even if it's going for a walk instead of a dinner, mix it up! Even if you are busy, you could plan more sleepovers and working dates. Both give more time so you don't feel like you have to rush and squeeze in every titbit of information. As more and more of us work from home, working dates allow for company and when it comes to sleepovers, there is something so much more relaxing about not having to race home to be in bed for work the next day.

By becoming the friend who is up for anything you become the go-to for others. When a friend suddenly had a spare ticket to a white-collar boxing match, I was the first person they called to fill in. I asked her why she thought I would be into white-collar boxing, she said she didn't think I would be but I'm her 'up for anything' friend and she was right. It was way too violent for me – never again! – but I'll try anything once and was so grateful to get the call. I felt the same when my friend needed someone to kayak twelve kilometres from Greenwich to Battersea on the Thames with them and no one else would do it. I said yes even though I had never been in a kayak before. I couldn't squeeze my shampoo bottle for a week after that, but it made for an incredible experience! It's why when someone I had worked with had a spare space to go dance with Nicole Scherzinger and the Pussycat Dolls, she asked me despite my lack of dance knowledge or experience. Getting a reputation as the friend who is up for anything means anything can land in your lap, and that makes life very fun!

Don't let perfect be the enemy of good

Every so often you find a low-maintenance friendship, and that can be so precious but more and more, I've started thinking that they can't be created, they just happen. I personally only have one in my life. We have transitioned from good friends to best friends for five years, to friends and then back to good friends without so much as a conversation about it. I called her up to ask why that was and she was equally as unsure. Neither of us understands why with each other we never take our space or silence personally. We are able to fluctuate in closeness without an issue whereas in other friendships, the increased distance often leads to hurt feelings and ultimately a dispute. I have tried to reverse engineer it to get clues as to how to replicate it. We guessed it might be down to low expectations while still having the solid knowledge that we have always been there for each other. Since she's the only person who I have been travelling with for a whole month alone, we each have an intrinsic unspoken understanding of the other. Ultimately, I concluded that maybe it's not helpful to try to make your friendships like each other. Maybe each friendship is its own unique dynamic that can't be replicated and, for whatever reason, we should just be glad we work so effortlessly.

Every other friendship has needed maintenance to keep it healthy, and when I worried about being a bad friend, I would put a lot of pressure on myself to always be there, often to the detriment of myself. Then, one day, a friend called me on his drive home. It was a four-hour drive and there would have been a time in my life where I would have questioned if he was just using me for entertainment or because he was bored, but as you grow up and become more mature, you realise that doesn't matter. We had an interesting conversation where we bonded and connected and it doesn't mean anything that he had my full attention when I didn't have his. In the past, I used to stress myself out trying to find a time to call a friend back, then I realised my attempt to block out an hour where I was doing nothing else was actually preventing me from making the call sooner than I would. It's ironic that in trying to be a better friend, waiting for a moment where they could have my full attention, it often made me a worse friend because I would take longer to return their call. Now I will call friends when I'm cooking or folding laundry. I will often tell them I am doing that and yes there are moments of inconvenience when the kettle is boiling a little too loudly but realising that imperfect catch-ups are better than no catch-ups at all improved my ability to maintain friendships dramatically. It is not that my friends never deserve my full attention. Sometimes I call when I am doing nothing other than listening to them – the point is I now don't delay a call because it's not the ideal time and situation. Don't underestimate the small touchpoints of connection. Have you ever thought about a friend and then stopped yourself from sending a 'thinking of you' text because you were too drained to have a full conversation? Sending the 'I miss you' text is better than nothing! This works for more than phone calls. Have you ever said no to hanging out because you can't stay the whole evening? Or cancelled plans because you aren't 100 per cent on form? You are worth hanging out with even if you aren't your best self, and most of your friends would rather see the imperfect you than not see you at all.

YOU ARE WORTH HANGING OUT WITH EVEN IF YOU AREN'T YOUR BEST SELF AND MOST OF YOUR FRIENDS WOULD RATHER SEE THE IMPERFECT YOU THAN NOT SEE YOU AT ALL.

FOLLOWING UP AND MAINTAINING FRIENDSHIPS

Be interested in the mundane

If you do life right, the majority of it is actually boring. There is a section of life that has high highs and a section that has low lows, but the bulk of it is in the middle of the road. When we have had a lot of trauma in our life, we can crave the rollercoaster ride of the ups and downs but if we actually want a healthy life and healthy friendships, we have to be OK in the safe and calm ... and the safe and calm can be boring. It might not be the most riveting friendships in your life that you call to ask how to phrase a work email but you'll be so grateful when someone picks up the phone and helps you through those moments of adulting. Calling your friend and asking how to unruin your favourite top that shrank in the wash doesn't sound hugely romantic but it's in those small mundane moments that I actually believe those friendships shine, and when you add a few marbles to the friendship jar!

EPILOGUE

There was a really big part of me that was hoping that by the time I finished this book, I would be in the place in my friendships to provide you the 'happy ending' that perfectly closes off the book in a neat and tidy way, but that is neither true nor realistic. Friendships are complicated and messy and we have to be willing to get in the mud together to be able to work through it. I still get jealous when I hear about childhood best friends who last for decades. I sometimes long for that forever best friend or get sad when I have an event to go to and all my friends are busy. I have moments when I question whether I should have stuck it out with some of my ex-friends and other moments, when I know I need to end a friendship but don't want to have the conversation. I am not a bad friend but I am an imperfect friend, as we all are, and I have let go of the idea that perfect friendship is what we should aspire to.

When I first started writing this book, one thing after another kept going wrong. Between my first editor going on maternity leave, my publisher being bought by another publisher, my agent leaving my agency, it was like I was being sent signs to wait. I kept feeling like I wasn't ready, like I didn't have all the answers. It was like the universe didn't want me to write it yet.

The whole time I thought all these signs were clues I was going to be in a better place in my own friendships to write with more hopefulness and joy, and then halfway through writing it, a friendship breakup happened unexpectedly. Upon the realisation that the friendship was over, I found the words 'I thought I was done with this' come out of my mouth. I am very cautious around ending friendships now; I have lived long enough to know how much people can change and that some friendships can come back around. Life is hard enough and sometimes burning the bridge is not necessary. I'd learned over the years that you never know which friends are going to move down the road from you, come back into your life or be going through the same life stage as you and, most importantly, I had learned the importance of people, community and letting humans be flawed. I had moved on from friendship breakups – I hadn't had one in years. I thought I was writing this book in hindsight with the learnings of the past and instead I got to write it in the midst of a fresh one. It's only now, upon finishing writing that I realised this perfect place of friendship doesn't exist. I had kept waiting in the hope that I would have all the answers, but I've come to understand that we don't need answers as much as we need reassurance that we aren't alone.

I am a better friend than I give myself credit for and I believe that is true for a lot of women. Whether we do friendship right or wrong, the majority avoid conflict, steer clear of the hard conversations and even ghost with the best of intentions. They do these missteps out of kindness more often than not and hopefully with more tools, that kindness can be communicated more clearly and directly.

I have become a better friend through writing this book. The day before I submitted the first draft, I got into my first issue with my closest friend. Months earlier, we had made plans to go back to the place where my ex-fiancé proposed as a way of reclaiming it and she had forgotten and made other plans. I was hurt but it was also the night before a big presentation she had at work, a presentation I was meant to be attending out of support. I thought about the sentence I'd written about how sometimes friendship is about you and sometimes it's about them, and chose to say nothing out of respect for her nervousness around her talk. The next day, her talk went brilliantly, with me cheering her on in the front row, and the moment she was done she turned to me and apologised. She knew I was upset. I acknowledged that she had been the person who had supported me through my breakup the most but told her that I was hurt because those plans had meant a lot to me. I said that since writing the book, I'm trying to get better at just saying when it's a small issue – I was attempting to do friendship differently. In the past, I wouldn't have bothered saying anything because she couldn't change her plans – so what was the point of mentioning it? But if I don't voice it, it will turn into disappointment or resentment. I didn't need her to change her plans, I just needed her to acknowledge how I was feeling. We even made space for our imperfect feelings; she said she was annoyed the night before because she had been there for me throughout everything else but then realised I was also allowed to be upset about this. I voiced my 'bad' thoughts of wanting to cancel on her presentation because if she wasn't going to show up, why should I bother, and she laughed and said she'd worried about that and that's why she had texted to see if I was still coming.

One of the main things I have learned is if you are worried about something, you should say it. She thanked me for still coming and showing up. I thanked her for the apology and understanding where I was coming from. We told each other that we still loved each other and that we were all good and then we high-fived because we had realised we had survived our first fight (if you can call it that!) and not a single person at the table of this work event was aware because it had been a cool, calm, collected and adult conversation. And that's all we can want from our friends. We want to be seen, understood and to have friends where we feel safe enough to voice when feelings come up.

Writing the chapter on marriage and children both from the perspective of a person who was trying for a baby and then suddenly as the single friend taught me that life changes quickly. On reflection, I didn't just sympathise for the friends on both ends of the spectrum, I *was* the friend on both ends of the spectrum, and I still am unsure of the solution. People I have encountered over the last year have told me about hen parties that are out of their budget, how they get left out of double dates as the single friend and how their best friend went crazy the moment they became a bride. And on the other side, I've heard from brides who look back at their wedding party photo and feel sad that they no longer speak to some of their bridesmaids, or who struggled to let a friend know that they are not the maid of honour because they don't

EPILOGUE

want to hurt their feelings. Hearing the complexity and intricacies of each situation has made me realise that everyone is doing their best and it's time we all gave each other a little more room to mess up. There are people in the world who feel so lost and lonely without friends, people who've moved to a new city and don't know how to start all over again, people wanting to be part of a friendship group who don't fully accept them and people who won't turn their back on frenemies because they believe it's better to have someone than no one. Some women are still struggling to believe their friends like them and others fear that if they set boundaries, their friends will abandon them. My heart is with all of you.

My intention with this book has always been to give the conversation of friendship the validity that it deserves and in turn, the pain of a friendship breakup the importance it so needs. In devoting ninety thousand words to it, I hope it shows you that it's not only worth the conversation, it's a long and complex conversation that is still largely absent from society. We have been so quick to throw away friendship, to judge harshly rather than being a little bit more lenient. We are so conflict avoidant that the conflict eventually gets worse because so much gets stuffed down that when it surfaces, it overflows. I want better for us all.

It's time we welcome in a new wave of friendship. Gone are the days where we take our friends for granted. Let's give our friendships the time and respect they deserve. Friendships are truly the bedrock of having the best life and we can only have those kind of friendships in our lives if we persevere through the hard conversations and acknowledge there will be difficulties in every friendship, much like every other relationship, and that they are worth facing. Maybe the goal isn't to save every friendship that ends in a breakup but instead to value the friendship for as long as it lasts. If it ends in a breakup, then you are equipped to handle that too. The heartbreak that arises is born out of love and, as painful as it is, refuse to let it turn you inwards. Your time is too important to spend with people who treat you less than you are worth and it's your job to decide how you deserve to be treated. Your friendships shape you, for better or worse, and if you want better, it all starts with communicating better. Be brave enough to let them in. Stop avoiding the messy part of friendship. And bother to tell them how you feel. Most of all, please always remember that you are worthy of good friendship. It's a privilege for anyone to get to be in your life. And to get to call you a friend? Well, they should be so lucky!

ACKNOWLEDGEMENTS

> 'Take your broken heart and turn it into art.'
>
> *Carrie Fisher*

This book came at a very interesting time in my life. I wrote half of it as a woman who was on the precipice of being engaged, trying for a baby in a long-term relationship, and the other half as a newly single woman in the midst of romantic heartbreak and, in many ways, this book became my tether through it all. It was my one constant while everything was changing, and on the days I struggled to get out of bed, I would tell myself that all I needed to do that day was write two thousand words. It was a way I could work without having to face the world, especially when it all became so public, and it gave me the escape I so needed from my life, the public eye and the scrutiny that came with it. It helped remind me that I am still an intelligent woman and a successful author and it made me so damn grateful for my friendships. When my engagement ended in infidelity, the future I imagined shattered but my world did not fall apart. I had done enough personal development work to know never to make a man your whole life and in the middle of that crisis, I was so proud that I'd had that wisdom because I had a whole life outside of him and that was the life I could return to without him. A life full of love, family, friends and success that carried me through the worst days.

Writing the acknowledgements section of my books has always been my favourite part and with this book, it feels even more so – I had an entire team of people holding me together with tape and glue to make sure not only that I was OK but also that this book would still be the best it could be. It sounds silly to say I still cared about this book in the eye of the storm, but I did and my team understood that because they know me. I understand the standard psychology advice would be to worry about your mental health more than your job, but anyone who knows me well knows that my career has always been more than a job. What I do in my books and in my work is very much a part of who I am; it gives me a purpose and a lot of that stems from a little girl in a hospital bed who was never listened to. She buried how she felt because she thought she wasn't important, so now that I have a voice, I'll be damned if I let anyone take it away from me! This book gave me so much drive and strength to keep going and I am immensely proud to be writing this, having finished the book I always dreamed of writing.

If I'm being honest, the only way I've been able to write this book truthfully is by pretending my friends will never read it. This book is a testament to all of them though because they taught me friendship. Ultimately, I wrote this book because I believe in the power of friendship, and this phase in my

ACKNOWLEDGEMENTS

life has never echoed that more. To my friends, I adore you all deeply. Thanking you for being there for me feels like an understatement but to every one of you who showed up, held my hand, checked in on me, replied to my texts, stayed over when my apartment felt too lonely, picked up my FaceTimes, kept me company and hugged me while I cried through the pain, I couldn't have kept standing without you. It was in the small moments of you turning up with painting supplies that made me feel so understood or calling to check that I had eaten that made me feel so cared for. Honey, Bex, Grace, Jordann, Megan, Terri, Abi, Amy, Sofie, Theo and Helen, you all taught me what being a good friend means.

Thank you to Michelle Zelli; you taught me to open my heart so I could be a good friend back. You showed me that being a good friend didn't mean having no boundaries. You demonstrated how I could look after myself while still being there for the people in my life and taught me self-worth so when people told me they wanted to be my friend, I could believe them. You were the perfect example of allowing space for honest, compassionate and communicative friendships and always encouraged me only to keep people around if they treated me with kindness and respect. Most of all though, you stayed solid while my faith wavered through each friendship breakup. Thank you for continuing to remind me that it was simply making space for something new.

Christina, you were the dream I was waiting for! When I pitched this book, I kept saying I wanted to find someone who believed in me and my words as much as I believed in myself, and when you popped into my inbox, it felt too good to be true. I truly believe we were meant to meet and it felt like the universe just knew we had to work together! It has meant more than I can say to work with someone who not only believes in my writing but has been such a supporter of my work over the years. Having an editor who just gets me has been the most heartwarming experience, and I am so grateful for all your support through this. I think our first meeting will go down as the most iconic work meeting I have ever had, but let's keep that as a story for another day (or another book). Thank you also to the whole Renegade team for making this book a reality and giving me the space to shine a spotlight on a topic that has been overdue for some attention. I'm so thrilled that you also believe the topic of female friendships had been overlooked and that it was time to create even more room for the heartbreak and hurt that all too often has been dismissed and diminished.

Charlotte, Steph and the whole Belle PR team, where do I even start? Thank you for having my back at a time when I felt so lost. You stood up for me, you advocated for me and you were the reason I survived the eye of the storm. Thank you for handling everything so I didn't have to – that gave me space to be the mess I needed to be. You have not just been there through the lows, you are also always the first to shout from the rooftops about the highs and you can take a lot of credit for whatever sanity I managed to maintain through this phase of my life!

To Megan, thank you so much for keeping everything afloat amid the chaos and being a listening ear every time I ranted about how much female friendship is undervalued. You made my writing the best it needed to be to give this book the best shot and helped me turn my idea into a fully-fledged plan. It's

ACKNOWLEDGEMENTS

not how you are spoken about when you are in the room that matters, it's how people speak about you when you are not there, so my greatest thanks is for shouting about me in rooms that I was not in, because none of this would be happening if you hadn't mentioned me at a party!

And finally, an extra thanks must go to Honey Ross and Abigail Mann, who got me across the finish line when I wasn't sure I would make it. Being an author can be quite a lonely job and you two were always there when I needed to flesh out an idea, spitball a thought that hadn't fully formed or try to land on a fitting subtitle. Thank you for helping me get words on the page – this book wouldn't exist without you!

ENDNOTES

Introduction
1. Healy, Melissa, 'Our innate need for friendship', *Los Angeles Times*, 9 May 2005, https://www.latimes.com/archives/la-xpm-2005-may-09-he-friends9-story.html.
2. The Newsroom, 'Only six friends will last a lifetime for Britons', *Scotsman*, 15 September 2014, https://www.scotsman.com/news/uk-news/only-six-friends-will-last-a-lifetime-for-britons-1526251.

Why Are Friendships Important?
1. Law, Courtney, 'When friendships fall apart', Dalhousie News, 25 February 2019, https://www.dal.ca/news/2019/02/25/when-friendships-fall-apart.html.
2. Ficino, Marsilio, *Commentary on Plato's Symposium*, trans. by S. Jayne (Columbia, MO: University of Missouri Studies, 1944), p. 140.
3. Fowler, James and Christakis, Nicholas, 'Dynamic spread of happiness in a large social network: Longitudinal analysis over 20 years in the Framingham Heart Study', *BMJ (Clinical Research Ed.)*, 337 (2008), pp. 1–7.
4. Waldinger, Robert and Schulz, Marc, *The Good Life: Lessons from the World's Longest Study on Happiness* (London: Rider, 2023).
5. Holt-Lunstad, Julianne, Smith, Timothy B. and Layton, J. Bradley, 'Social relationships and mortality risk: A meta-analytic review', *PLOS Medicine*, 7:7 (2010), https://doi.org/10.1371/journal.pmed.1000316.
6. Kent, Robert, Uchino, Bert, Cribbet, Matthew, Bowen, Kimberly and Smith, Timothy, 'Social relationships and sleep

quality', *Annals of Behavioral Medicine*, 49:6 (2015), pp. 912–7, https://doi.org/10.1007/s12160-015-9711-6.
7. Gouin, Jean-Philippe and Kiecolt-Glaser, Janice K., 'The impact of psychological stress on wound healing: Methods and mechanisms', *Immunology and Allergy Clinics of North America*, 31:1 (2011), pp. 81–93.
8. Holt-Lunstad, Smith and Layton, 'Social relationships and mortality risk: A meta-analytic review'.
9. Choi, Kristen R., Heilemann, MarySue V., Fauer, Alex and Mead, Meredith, 'A second pandemic: Mental health spillover from the novel coronavirus (COVID-19)', *Journal of the American Psychiatric Nurses Association*, 26:4 (2020), pp. 340–3.
10. Masten, Ann S. and Motti-Stefanidi, Frosso, 'Multisystem resilience for children and youth in disaster: Reflections in the context of COVID-19', *Adversity and Resilience Science*, 1 (2020), pp. 95–106.
11. Myers, D. G., 'The funds, friends, and faith of happy people', *American Psychologist*, 55:1 (2000), pp. 56–67, https://doi.org/10.1037/0003-066X.55.1.56.
12. Halpern, D. F., 'How time-flexible work policies can reduce stress, improve health, and save money', *Stress and Health: Journal of the International Society for the Investigation of Stress*, 21:3 (2005), pp. 157–68.
13. Holt-Lunstad, Smith and Layton, 'Social relationships and mortality risk: A meta-analytic review'.
14. Chopik, William, 'Associations among relational values, support, health, and well-being across the adult lifespan', *Personal Relationships*, 24 (2017), pp. 408–22.
15. Keneski, Elizabeth, Neff, Lisa and Loving, Timothy, 'The importance of a few good friends: Perceived network support moderates the association between daily marital conflict and diurnal cortisol', *Social Psychological and Personality Science*, 9 (2017), https://www.doi.org/10.1177/1948550617731499.
16. Abbas, J., Aqeel, M., Abbas, J., Shaher, B., A., J., Sundas, J. and Zhang, W., 'The moderating role of social support for marital adjustment, depression, anxiety, and stress: Evidence from Pakistani working and nonworking women', *Journal of Affective Disorders*, 244 (2019), pp. 231–38.
17. Fiori, Katherine L., Rauer, Amy J., Birditt, Kira S., Marini, Christina M., Jager, Justin, Brown, Edna and Orbuch, Terri L., '"I love you, not your friends": Links between partners' early

disapproval of friends and divorce across 16 years', *Journal of Social and Personal Relationships*, 35:9 (2017), https://doi.org/10.1177/026540751770706.

The Myths About Friendship

1. Chalker, Brian A. 'Drew', 'Reason, Season and Lifetime', unpublished (2002).
2. Simpkins, Sandra D. and Parke, Ross D., 'The relations between parental friendships and children's friendships: Self-report and observational analysis', *Child Development*, 72:2 (2001), pp. 569–82.

In Defence of Friendship Breakups

1. Rankin Saltwire, Andrew, 'Profs say ditching troublesome friend can be risky', *Guardian*, 6 June 2024, https://www.pressreader.com/canada/the-guardian-charlottetown/20240606/281754159467053.
2. Franco, Marisa G., *Platonic* (London: Bluebird, 2022), p. 190.
3. *The Mash Up American Podcast*, 'Alua Arthur on demystifying death', 17 April 2019, https://podcasts.apple.com/lb/podcast/alua-arthur-on-demystifying-death/id1055903427?i=1000435127914.
4. Mollenhorst, G., Völker, B. and Flap, H., 'Changes in personal relationships: How social contexts affect the emergence and discontinuation of relationships', *Social Networks*, 37:1 (2014), pp. 65–80, https://doi.org/10.1016/j.socnet.2013.12.003.
5. Mroz, Jacqueline, *Girl Talk: What Science Can Tell Us About Female Friendship* (London: Seal Press, 2018).
6. Leaver, Kate, *The Friendship Cure* (London: Duckworth Books, 2018), p. 231.
7. Ibid., p. 178.
8. Day, Elizabeth, *Friendaholic* (London: Fourth Estate, 2023), p. 29.

Am I the Problem?

1. Gilbert, Elizabeth, 'Learn to be lonely', Elizabeth Gilbert, 2 July 2014, https://www.elizabethgilbert.com/learn-to-be-lonely-dear-ones-a-friend-of-this-page-asked-me-today-if-i-wo/.

Are Male And Female Friendships Different?

1. Greif, Geoffrey, *Buddy System* (Oxford: Oxford University Press, 2008).
2. Klavan, Spencer A., 'Games boys play', *Atlantic*, September 2019, https://www.theatlantic.com/magazine/archive/2019/09/video-games-masculinity/594712/.
3. Williams, Keelah E. G., Krems, Jaimie Arona, Ayers, Jessica D. and Rankin, Ashley M., 'Sex differences in friendship preferences', *Evolution and Human Behavior*, 43:1 (2022), pp. 44–52.
4. Mroz, *Girl Talk: What Science Can Tell Us About Female Friendship* (London: Seal Press, 2018).
5. Robertson, Duncan, 'Men "are fickle when it comes to friendship"', *Daily Mail*, 8 March 2007, https://www.dailymail.co.uk/news/article-440871/Men-fickle-comes-friendship.html.
6. Morrow Lindbergh, Anne, *Locked Rooms and Open Doors* (Boston, MA: G. K. Hall, 1974), p. 7.
7. Bingham, John, '2.5 million men "have no close friends"', *Telegraph*, 14 November 2015, https://www.telegraph.co.uk/men/active/mens-health/11996473/2.5-million-men-have-no-close-friends.html.
8. Vigil, Jacob M., 'Asymmetries in the friendship preferences and social styles of men and women', *Human Nature*, 18 (2007), pp. 143–61.
9. Sapadin, Linda A., 'Gender and friendships: Hers and his, same-sex and cross-sex', Annual Meeting of the American Psychological Association, Atlanta, GA, 12–16 August 1988, https://files.eric.ed.gov/fulltext/ED303707.pdf.
10. Rodgers, Erin (@ErinMRodgers), 'I want the term "gold digger" to include dudes who look for a woman who will do tons of emotional labour for them', X, 2 June 2016, https://x.com/ErinMRodgers/status/738195765030313985.
11. Way, Niobe, *Deep Secrets: Boys' Friendships and the Crisis of Connection* (Cambridge, MA: Harvard University Press, 2011).
12. Brittain, Vera, *Testament of Friendship: The Story of Winifred Holtby* (London: Macmillan, 1942), p. 2.

What Are You Looking for in Friendship?

1. Mroz, *Girl Talk: What Science Can Tell Us About Female Friendship* (London: Seal Press, 2018).

ENDNOTES

2. Dwyer, M. J., 'Friendship values: A cross-cultural study', *Journal of Social and Personal Relationships*, 29:2 (2012), pp. 129–46.
3. *We Can Do Hard Things*, 'Are your friendships draining or charging you? with Luvvie Ajayi Jones', 13 January 2022.
4. Argyle, Michael and Henderson, Monika, 'The rules of friendship', *Journal of Social and Personal Relationships*, 1:2 (1984), pp. 211–37, https://doi.org/10.1177/0265407584012005.

Why Do I Have So Few Friends?

1. Eisenberger, Naomi I., 'The neural bases of social pain: Evidence for shared representations with physical pain', *Psychosomatic Medicine*, 74:2 (2012), pp. 126–35, https://www.doi.org/10.1097/PSY.0b013e3182464dd1.
2. French Gates, Melinda, 'Moments That Make Us: How friendship helped Oprah Winfrey & Gayle King navigate life's big changes', YouTube, 24 June 2024, https://www.youtube.com/watch?v=XBKa7PDnoVA.
3. Anon., 'Facts and statistics about loneliness', Campaign to End Loneliness, https://www.campaigntoendloneliness.org/facts-and-statistics/.
4. Cox, Daniel A., 'The decline of friendship and social connectivity', American Enterprise Institute, 8 June 2021, https://www.americansurveycenter.org/research/the-state-of-american-friendship-change-challenges-and-loss/.
5. Putnam, Robert, *Bowling Alone* (New York: Simon & Schuster, 2000).
6. Campaign to End Loneliness, 'Loneliness beyond COVID-19', Campaign to End Loneliness, July 2021, pp. 1–30, https://www.campaigntoendloneliness.org/wp-content/uploads/Loneliness-beyond-COVID-19-July-2021.pdf.
7. Brooks, Arthur C., 'How we learned to be lonely', *Atlantic*, 5 January 2003, https://www.theatlantic.com/family/archive/2023/01/loneliness-solitude-pandemic-habit/672631/.
8. Brown, Brené, *Dare to Lead* (London: Random House, 2018), p. 160.
9. Leaver, Kate, *The Friendship Cure* (London: Duckworth Books, 2018), p. 211.

Does Everyone Have a Friendship Group Apart From Me?

1. Fink, Elian and Hughes, Claire, 'Children's friendships', *Psychologist*, 5 February 2019, https://www.bps.org.uk/psychologist/childrens-friendships.
2. French Gates, Melinda, 'Moments That Make Us: How friendship helped Oprah Winfrey & Gayle King navigate life's big changes', YouTube, 24 June 2024, https:// www.youtube.com/ watch?v=XBKa7PDnoVA.

What Does It Mean if My Friend Doesn't Like My Instagram Posts?

1. Drago, Emily, 'The effect of technology on face-to-face communication', *Elon Journal of Undergraduate Research in Communications*, 6:1 (2015), http://www.inquiriesjournal.com/a?id=1137.
2. Misra, Shalini, Cheng, Lulu, Genevie, Jamie and Yuan, Miao, 'The iPhone effect: The quality of in-person social interactions in the presence of mobile devices', *Environment and Behavior*, 48:1 (2014), pp. 1–22.
3. *Pivot*, 'Israel-Hamas War, Search for a Speaker, and Guest Esther Perel', October 2023, https://open.spotify.com/episode/6YOPdZzZrl8OujI4B3P3TL.
4. Wirtz, Derrick, Tucker, Amanda, Briggs, Chloe and Schoemann, Alexander, 'How and why social media affect subjective well-being: Multi-site use and social comparison as predictors of change across time', *Journal of Happiness Studies*, 22:1 (2021), pp. 1–20.

What Do I Do If I Hate Who They Are Dating?

1. 'Where The Wild Things Are', *Grey's Anatomy*, Disney+, 24 April 2008.
2. Rose, Amanda J., Carlson, Wendy and Waller, Erika M., 'Prospective associations of co-rumination with friendship and emotional adjustment: Considering the socioemotional trade-offs of co-rumination', *Developmental Psychology*, 43:4 (2007), pp. 1019–31.

Are We Really Friends or Just Colleagues?

1. Eramian, Laura and Mallory, Peter, 'Unclear endings: Difficult friendship and the limits of the therapeutic

ethic', *Families, Relationships, and Societies*, 10:2 (2021), pp. 359–73.
2. Anon., 'Anatomy of work: Burnout', Asana, 2022, https://resources.asana.com/americas-anatomy-of-work-burnout-ebook.html.
3. Grayson, Kent, 'Friendship versus business in marketing relationships', *Journal of Marketing*, 71:4 (2007), pp. 121–39.
4. Ibid.

Why Do Weddings Complicate Friendships?
1. *Lifestyle* Co-Editor, 'Weddings revealed as the most stressful life event for over 1 in 4 brides', *Lifestyle Daily*, 1 March 2024, https://www.lifestyledaily.co.uk/article/2024/03/01/weddings-revealed-most-stressful-life-event-over-1-4-brides.
2. Ibid.
3. Burke, Zoe, 'How much does a wedding cost? The 2024 UK average revealed', *Hitched*, 29 January 2024, https://www.hitched.co.uk/wedding-planning/organising-and-planning/the-average-wedding-cost-in-the-uk-revealed.

Can Our Friendship Adjust Through Families, Children and Fertility Issues?
1. Klein, Joanna, 'What old monkeys and old humans have in common', *New York Times*, 23 June 2016, https://www.nytimes.com/2016/06/24/science/old-monkeys-picky-behavior.html.
2. Bhattacharya, Kunal, Ghosh, Asim, Monsivais, Daniel, Dunbar, Robin I. M. and Kaski, Kimmo, 'Sex differences in social focus across the life cycle in humans', *Royal Society Open Science*, 3:4 (2016), https://doi.org/10.1098/rsos.160097.
3. Beck, Julie, 'How friendships change in adulthood', *Atlantic*, 22 October 2015, https://www.theatlantic.com/health/archive/2015/10/how-friendships-change-over-time-in-adulthood/411466/.
4. Heti, Sheila, *How Should a Person Be?* (London: Vintage, 2014).
5. Giles, Lynne C., Glonek, Gary F. V., Luszcz, Mary A. and Andrews, Gary R., 'Effect of social networks on 10 year survival in very old Australians: The Australian longitudinal study of aging', *Journal of Epidemiology and Community Health*, 59:7 (2005), pp. 574–9, https://doi.org/10.1136/jech.2004.025429.

6. Mroz, Jacqueline, *Girl Talk: What Science Can Tell Us About Female Friendship* (London: Seal Press, 2018), p. 227.

How Do I Support My Friend Through Mental Health Difficulties?

1. *Late Night with Seth Meyers*, NBC, 4 November 2022.

Is Living Together Going To End The Friendship?

1. Ross, Michael and Sicoly, Fiore, 'Egocentric biases in availability and attribution', *Journal of Personality and Social Psychology*, 37 (1979), pp. 322–36.
2. Grant, Adam, *Give and Take* (London: W&N, 2014).
3. 'The One with Five Steaks and an Eggplant', *Friends*, NBC, 19 October 1995.

Why are Female Friendships Full of Competition, Jealousy and Gossip?

1. Briles, Judith, *Woman to Woman: From Sabotage to Support* (Far Hills, NJ: New Horizon, 1989).
2. 'Out of The Shadows', *Bridgerton*, Netflix, 16 May 2024.
3. Wheeler, Ladd and Miyake, Kunitate, 'Social comparison in everyday life', *Journal of Personality and Social Psychology*, 62:5, pp. 760–73, https://doi.org/10.1037/0022-3514.62.5.760.
4. French Gates, Melinda, 'Moments That Make Us: How friendship helped Oprah Winfrey & Gayle King navigate life's big changes', YouTube, 24 June 2024, https://www.youtube.com/watch?v=XBKa7PDnoVA.
5. Jones, Deborah, 'Gossip: Notes on women's oral culture', *Women's Studies International Quarterly*, 3:2–3 (1980), pp. 193–98.
6. Sow, Aminatou and Friedman, Ann, *Big Friendship* (London: Virago, 2020), p. 70.
7. Ibid., p. 71.
8. Ibid., p. 74.
9. Ibid., p. 73.

Can I Still Fix the Friendship?

1. Beyond Blue, 'Toxic friends: An interview with Susan Shapiro Barash', Beliefnet, January 2010, https://www.beliefnet.com/columnists/beyondblue/2010/01/toxic-friends-an-interview-wit.html.

ENDNOTES

2. Lahad, Kinneret and van Hooff, Jenny, 'Is my best friend toxic? A textual analysis of online advice on difficult relationships', *Families, Relationships and Societies*, 12:4, pp. 572–87.
3. Yip, Sarah, 'Couples therapy: A supplement, not a medication', A Space Between, 8 October 2021, https://aspacebetween.com.sg/blog/couples-therapy-supplement.
4. Law, Courtney, 'When friendships fall apart', Dalhousie News, 25 February 2019, https://www.dal.ca/news/2019/02/25/when-friendships-fall-apart.html.

Is It Ever Acceptable To Ghost A Friend?
1. *The Light We Carry: Michelle Obama and Oprah Winfrey*, Netflix, 25 April 2023.
2. Pryor, Liz, *What Did I Do Wrong?* (New York: Free Press, 2011), p. 27.

How Do I Tell Them It Is Over?
1. Leaver, Kate, *The Friendship Cure* (London: Duckworth Books, 2018), pp. 180–181.
2. Gilbert, Elizabeth (@GilbertLiz), 'Your fear should always be allowed to have a voice, and a seat in the vehicle of your life. But whatever you do — don't let your fear DRIVE.', Facebook, 11 March 2016, https://www.facebook.com/GilbertLiz/posts/pfbid02BsVJBcmyocq7HLu9bEnfw7caCHtEf8AeYTLkuMn6PZjg4qriW3w2sMhA7JoDaCZvl/.

Why Do I Feel So Guilty?
1. *Swagger* Staff, 'Think twice before ditching imperfect friendships: They can be valuable too, first-of-its-kind study shows', *Swagger*, 7 June 2024, https://www.swaggermagazine.com/features/think-twice-before-ditching-imperfect-friendships-they-can-be-valuable-too-first-of-its-kind-study-shows/.

How Do I Stop Regretting We Ever Met?
1. Franco, Marisa G., *Platonic* (London: Bluebird, 2022), p. 196.

Will I Ever Stop Missing Them?
1. Jalma, Katie S., 'Women's friendship dissolution: A qualitative study', doctoral thesis (Minneapolis, MN: University of Minnesota, 2008).

2. Leaver, Kate, *The Friendship Cure* (London: Duckworth Books, 2018), p. 174.

Why You Should Be Fighting For Your Friendships

1. Parker, Priya, '3 steps to turn everyday get-togethers into transformative gatherings', TEDx, 15 July 2019, https://www.ted.com/talks/priya_parker_3_steps_to_turn_everyday_get_togethers_into_transformative_gatherings?subtitle=en.
2. Franco, Marisa G., *Platonic* (London: Bluebird, 2022), p. 184.
3. Ibid., p. 186.
4. Atlas, Galit, *Emotional Inheritance: A Therapist, Her Patients, and the Legacy of Trauma* (London: Short Books, 2022), p. 11.

Give Friendships The Effort They Deserve

1. Newall, Nancy, Chipperfield, Judith G., Clifton, Rodney A., Perry, Raymond P., Swift, Audrey U. and Ruthig, Joelle C., 'Causal beliefs, social participation, and loneliness among older adults: A longitudinal study', *Journal of Social and Personal Relationships*, 26:2–3 (2009), pp. 273–90, https://doi.org/10.1177/0265407509106718.
2. Elman, Michelle, *The Joy of Being Selfish* (London: Welbeck, 2021), p. 118.
3. Whyte, David, *Consolations* (n.p.: Many Rivers Press, 2015), p. 55.

Be Selective About Your Inner Circle

1. 'Harry & Sally', *The Mindy Project*, Fox, 29 January 2013.
2. McCammon, Ross, *Works Well with Others* (London: Penguin, 2016).
3. Sandstrom, Gillian M. and Dunn, Elizabeth, 'Social interactions and well-being: The surprising power of weak ties', *Personality and Social Psychology Bulletin*, 40:7 (2014), pp. 910–22, https://doi.org/10.1177/0146167214529799.

Build Trust Slowly

1. Hall, Jeffrey A., 'How many hours does it take to make a friend?', *Journal of Social and Personal Relationships*, 36:4 (2019), pp. 1278–96, https://doi.org/10.1177/0265407518761225.
2. Lerner, Harriet, *The Dance of Intimacy: A Woman's Guide to Courageous Acts of Change in Key Relationships* (New York: HarperCollins, 1997).
3. Miller, John G. and Steinberg, L. E., 'Between people: A new

analysis of interpersonal communication', *Psychological Review*, 82:1 (1975), pp. 1–18.
4. OWN, 'Brené Brown on Vulnerability and Courage', YouTube, 6 November 2015, https://www.youtube.com/watch?v=6442YcvEUH8.

Meeting New People

1. *Pivot*, 'Israel-Hamas War, Search for a Speaker and Guest Esther Perel', 13 October 2023, https://open.spotify.com/episode/6YOPdZzZrl8OujI4B3P3TL.

Facing The Fear of Rejection

1. Stinson, Danu Anthony, Cameron, Jessica J., Wood, Joanne V., Gaucher, Danielle and Holmes, John G., 'Deconstructing the "reign of error": Interpersonal warmth explains the self-fulfilling prophecy of anticipated acceptance', *Personality & Social Psychology Bulletin*, 35:9 (2009), pp. 1165–78, https://doi.org/10.1177/0146167209338629.
2. Boothby, Erica J., Cooney, Gus, Sandstrom, Gillian M. and Clark, Margaret S., 'The liking gap in conversations: Do people like us more than we think?', *Psychological Science*, 29:11 (2018), pp. 1742–56.
3. Goldner, Fred H., 'Pronoia', *Social Problems*, 30:1 (1982), pp. 82–91, https://doi.org/10.2307/800186.
4. Kassem, Suzy, *Rise Up and Salute the Sun: The Writings of Suzy Kassem* (n.p.: self-published, 2010).

Initiating Conversations with Strangers

1. Carnegie, Dale, *How to Win Friends and Influence People* (London: Vermillion, 2006).
2. Epley, Nicholas and Schroeder, Juliana, 'The surprising power of talking to strangers', *Psychological Science*, 25:10 (2014), pp. 2009–18, https://www.doi.org/10.1177/0956797614545132.
3. Ibid.

Following Up and Maintaining Friendships

1. Taylor, S. E., Klein, L. C., Lewis, B. P., Gruenewald, T. L., Gurung, R. A. R. and Updegraff, J. A., 'Biobehavioral responses to stress in females: Tend-and-befriend, not fight-or-flight', *Psychological Review*, 107:3 (2000), pp. 411–29, https://psycnet.apa.org/record/2000-08671-001.

FURTHER READING

So Thrilled For You – Holly Bourne

Friendaholic: Confessions of a Friendship Addict – Elizabeth Day

Platonic: How Understanding Your Attachment Style Can Help You Make and Keep Friends – Marisa G. Franco

Big Friendship: How We Keep Each Other Close – Ann Friedman and Aminatou Sow

The Friendship Cure: Reconnecting in the Modern World – Kate Leaver

Idol – Louise O'Neill

Bringing a book from manuscript to what you are reading is a team effort.

Renegade Books would like to thank everyone who helped to publish *Bad Friend* in the UK.

Editorial
Christina Demosthenous
Eleanor Gaffney

Contracts
Stephanie Evans
Sasha Duszynska Lewis
Isabel Camara

Sales
Megan Schaffer
Kyla Dean
Dominic Smith
Sinead White
Georgina Cutler-Ross
Kerri Hood
Jess Harvey
Natasha Weninger Kong

Design
Charlotte Stroomer
Sara Mahon
Sasha Egonu

Production
Narges Nojoumi
Amanda Jones

Marketing
Mia Oakley

Operations
Rosie Stevens

Finance
Chris Vale
Jonathan Gant

Audio
Dominic Gribben

Copy-Editor
David Bamford

Proofreader
Jon Appleton